Minitel

Platform Studies
Nick Montfort and Ian Bogost, editors

Minitel

Welcome to the Internet

Julien Mailland and Kevin Driscoll

The MIT Press   Cambridge, Massachusetts   London, England

This book was set in ITC Stone Serif Std by Toppan Best-set Premedia Limited.

Library of Congress Cataloging-in-Publication Data

Names: Mailland, Julien, author. | Driscoll, Kevin, author.
Title: Minitel : welcome to the Internet / Julien Mailland and Kevin Driscoll.
Description: Cambridge, MA : The MIT Press, 2017. | Series: Platform studies
  | Includes bibliographical references and index.
Identifiers: LCCN 2016042225 | ISBN 9780262036221 (hardcover : alk. paper), 9780262537759 (pb)
Subjects: LCSH: Minitel (Videotex system) | Technology and
   state--France--History--20th century. | Technology and
   state--France--History--21st century.
Classification: LCC QA76.57.M55 M35 2017 | DDC 384.3/3--dc23 LC record available at https://lccn.loc.gov/2016042225

Contents

Series Foreword

How can someone create a breakthrough game for a mobile phone or a compelling work of art for an immersive 3D environment without understanding that the mobile phone and the 3D environment are different sorts of computing platforms? The best artists, writers, programmers, and designers are well aware of how certain platforms facilitate certain types of computational expression and innovation. Likewise, computer science and engineering have long considered how underlying computing systems can be analyzed and improved. As important as scientific and engineering approaches are, and as significant as work by creative artists has been, there is also much to be learned from the sustained, intensive, humanistic study of digital media. We believe it is time for humanists to seriously consider the lowest level of computing systems and their relationship to culture and creativity.

The Platform Studies series has been established to promote the investigation of underlying computing systems and of how they enable, constrain, shape, and support the creative work that is done on them. The series investigates the foundations of digital media—the computing systems, both hardware and software, that developers and users depend upon for artistic, literary, and gaming development. Books in the series will certainly vary in their approaches, but they will all share certain features:

- a focus on a single platform or a closely related family of platforms
- technical rigor and in-depth investigation of how computing technologies work
- an awareness of and a discussion of how computing platforms exist in a context of culture and society, being developed on the basis of cultural concepts and then contributing to culture in a variety of ways—for instance, by affecting how people perceive computing.

Acknowledgments

Minitel was brought to life through the ingenuity of countless engineers, entrepreneurs, administrators, and enthusiasts. While Internet folklore tends to celebrate small groups of computer wizards hacking away in basements and garages, Minitel thrived at the forefront of French popular culture. During the 1980s and 1990s, Minitel was on the street, in the cinema, on the radio, and in the news. People from all over France experimented with the new medium—men and women, young and old, urbanites and country dwellers, rich and poor, gay and straight. That Minitel continues to provoke our thinking about technology, policy, and culture is a tribute to the creativity and curiosity of its diverse users.

Just as Minitel was produced by a multitude, many different people assisted in the preparation of this book. We would like to thank the staff at Orange/Direction de la Gestion et de la Conservation de l'Information, the Conseil d'État, and the Archives Nationales whose help in locating and scanning materials was crucial—in particular, Emmanuelle Flament-Guelfucci, Pierre Philippi, and Irmine Vieira as well as the community of researchers and Orange employees and former employees in Brittany, Paris, and San Francisco who provided us with access, support, feedback, and unbridled enthusiasm about the ongoing relevance of Minitel: Isabelle Astic, Patrice Battiston, Yochai Benkler, Jean-Luc Beraudo De Pralormo, John Coate, Daniel Hannaby, Bernard Louvel, Jean-Paul Maury, Georges Nahon, Camille Paloque-Berges, Bernard Peuto, Monroe Price, Valérie Schafer, Gérard Théry, Benjamin Thierry, and Marc Weber. In addition to archival research, this book depends on several firsthand accounts, and we are grateful to those individuals who agreed to sit for interviews: Michel Baujard, Jean-Luc Beraudo De Pralormo, Laurent Chemla, John Coate, Daniel Hannaby, Jean-Baptiste Ingold, Michel Landaret, Bernard Louvel, Allan Lundell, Jean-Marc Manach, Bernard Marti, Jean-Paul Maury, Georges Nahon, Dusty Parks, Jean-Eudes Queffélec, Christian Quest, Gérard Théry, and LaRoy Tymes.

A big shout-out goes to today's Minitel enthusiasts whose hacks, pranks, and tributes provided us with inspiration and insight during the preparation of this book. We are especially grateful to those *minitelistes* who document their explorations for other to follow. Special thanks are due to Frédéric Cambus, whose archives of Minitel and French bulletin board systems materials were invaluable during the research process.

We would like to thank Ian Bogost and Nick Montfort, editors of the Platform Studies series, for their early enthusiasm and ongoing support for the project, and Doug Sery, acquisitions editor at the MIT Press, Virginia Crossman, assistant editor at the MIT Press, and Susan Clark, catalog manager at the MIT Press, for their stewardship. Finally, we would like to thank the anonymous reviewers for their thoughtful feedback.

Julien would like to thank his colleagues at Indiana University, especially Barb Cherry, Annie Lang, Matt Pierce, Harmeet Sawhney, and David Waterman for always lending a keen Minitel ear, Vicki Nash and the participants in the 2011 Oxford Internet Institute Summer Doctoral Program, and his committee members at the University of Southern California Annenberg School for Communication and Journalism: Jonathan Aronson, François Bar, Steve Lamy, Daniel Lynch, and Philip Seib.

Kevin wishes to thank his colleagues at Microsoft Research New England for their guidance and support, particularly Andrea Alarcon, Nancy Baym, Christian Borgs, Sarah Brayne, Jennifer Chayes, Tarleton Gillespie, Sharon Gillett, Mary Gray, Rebecca Hoffman, Jessa Lingel, Lana Swartz, and all of the wonderful interns and visitors who passed through the Social Media Collective. He is also indebted to Henry Jenkins for many years of mentorship and inspiration. Finally, Kevin is grateful to his family, Ed, Katie, Mark, and Mary, and especially his spouse, Lana Swartz, for her wisdom, humor, and grace.

Lastly, Julien and Kevin would like to acknowledge the invaluable contributions of Cooper, the Minitel dog.

Le Minitel est mort, vive le Net!

June 29, 2012. A large crowd is gathered in a covered passage outside a digital start-up incubator in the up-and-coming Silicon Sentier neighborhood of Paris, grabbing bottles of the city's newly revived ancestral microbrew, Gallia, from milk crates. It doesn't get much more hipster than this. It's the third half of a Minitel "wake," and Minitel enthusiasts—mostly entrepreneurs both old and young—are gathered here to celebrate and bid adieu to a time where France was the most wired country in the world. The 1980s: when anyone in France could easily jump online to order groceries for same-day delivery, preorder movie tickets before a night on the town, play video games with strangers, register for school and check their grades, and of course, frolic in a sexy chat room—all using the same convenient little Minitel box. While in the United States, access to the online world was the privilege of a geeky few until the privatization of the Internet backbone in 1995, all of France had been online for more than a decade, discovering and enjoying the new electronic frontier in the form of a mass consumer service.

The June 29 alley party followed a roundtable discussion and animated question-and-answer session with the lively audience. The men sitting on stage were stewards and champions of the online world: Louis Pouzin, the engineer credited for inventing the datagram concept that evolved into the Transmission Control Protocol (TCP)/Internet Protocol (IP), and Laurent Chemla, cofounder of France's largest Internet registrar and the first person in the country to have been indicted for hacking into a computer system ... using a Minitel terminal.[1] One notorious figure is missing in action. Xavier Niel, the telecom entrepreneur who instigated a price war that made France one of the most competitive markets for Internet access in the world, declined the organizer's invitation. His apology e-mail—"sorry, not my thing"—is projected on a large screen. Maybe the fact that Niel made his first fortune—one that enabled him to open a free computer science school—running cybersex services on Minitel plays a role in his absence. Michel Landaret, however, is in the room. Landaret is often said to have invented *les messageries*, the online chat rooms that propelled the popular adoption and commercial success of Minitel.[2] While claims to invention and "firsts" are often dubious, Landaret's 1981 system captivated early users, observers, and journalists from the US and abroad, heralding the arrival of thousands of chat rooms, message boards, and social games on Minitel.[3]

This Minitel wake is wild. The attendees represent the wide range of stakeholders in the Minitel industries—from former lobbyists and trade journalists to subversive countercultural figures. All are joyfully putting to rest an old friend, the platform that brought the whole of France online years ahead of the rest of the world. The current media is here, too. Earlier that day, *Le Monde* featured the efforts of two researchers in the United States working to document Minitel for a US audience.[4] International newspapers and websites—*WIRED*, the *New York Times*, the *Guardian*, Ars Technica, and *Fox Business News*—have been covering the end of *le Minitel* for weeks. AP reporters at the party are taking people aside for video interviews.[5] Meanwhile, hackers are providing entertainment: one old-timer turned a Minitel terminal into a Twitter client and is streaming tweets from the #minitel hashtag; a group of younger enthusiasts is showing off Minitel-based videotex art. As the sun goes down and less legal substances come out, the sustained energy of the crowded party reflects the goodwill felt by so many hackers and entrepreneurs for the deceased. For these creative minds, Minitel was a platform that empowered them to distribute their creations widely, cheaply, with few constraints, and often to great personal profit, long before the commercialization of the World Wide Web and the dot-com boom.

There is a strong irony in the history of the Internet that the great hope of cyberlibertarianism was a network funded by the US government and justified by its military applications (note that when we say "Internet," we refer to the specific IP-based family of networks that grew out of the ARPANET family of experimental networks).[6] In France, likewise, it was the government, through the Post, Telegraph, and Telephone (PTT) administration, that supported Minitel. But while both the Internet and Minitel were born out of a combination of public and private investment, the two networks are frequently depicted in opposition to one another. In the typical comparison, the Internet is said to represent massive private investment, decentralized control, and a lack of regulation, while Minitel is presumed to be a failed state project, beset with slow-moving bureaucracy and centralized authority. Perhaps this historiography fits a familiar frame in the US imagination pitting free market capitalism against authoritarian socialism, but it does not hold up to historical scrutiny. Indeed, strategic French interventionism is precisely what enabled a vibrant and innovative private market to form around Minitel in the 1980s, just as the decision of the US government to privatize the Internet backbone enabled a commercial Internet boom during the 1990s.[7] Neither system could have succeeded without the combination of public and private support.

The French State was indeed a key player in the domestic success of Minitel, albeit not exactly as it is commonly remembered by champions of the US-centric Internet story, but State administrators were absent from the raucous Minitel wake.[8] So, the day after the rogue entrepreneurs' party, we traveled to the historic heart of French telecommunications, the Brittany region, to see how the brainchild of State planning would be laid to rest.

June 30, 2012, Cesson-Sévigné, France. The sky is crying over a grey industrial development in Brittany, France's west coast region. Fifty years earlier, the State had earmarked the area for redevelopment. It would become the Silicon Valley of France, the epicenter of domestic telecommunications excellence and international prestige. While start-ups tend to congregate in Paris these days, large historical players such as Orange (formerly France Telecom, which itself is formerly the PTT administration), Alcatel, Thomson, Matra, and SAGEM, as well as many specialized schools, gathered in Brittany.[9] The legacy is strong, but the area, populated with run-down, Stalinist buildings, aches with a brutalist gloom—a fitting decor for the official wake of a high-modernist State project: a data network for the people, Minitel.

Just as the networking experiments that produced the Internet had roots in the Cold War politics of the 1960s, Minitel was developed in response to the unstable politics of the period. Convinced that France needed a domestic military-industrial complex to gain independence from US and UK network standards and manufacturers, French policy makers endeavored to stimulate local development in information and communication technology—a vision of the future known as *telematics*. This was a period in which France pulled out of the North Atlantic Treaty Organization, kicked US troops out of the country, built its first radar dome, and launched its first satellite. A decade later, with information being increasingly digitized, commodified, and distributed internationally, some began to see a threat to French independence in the design and implementation of communication infrastructure. In this battle for information sovereignty, France's enemies were IBM and the British PTT—outsider organizations promoting their own standards for building online systems.

In 1974, the State's joint television and telephony research center, le Centre commun d'études de télévision et télécommunications (CCETT), began developing Antiope, its own standard for the display of information on video screens. Antiope was infrastructure neutral. It could be transmitted through any channel, from over-the-air radio broadcast to fiber-optic cables. At the time, the French telephone network was one of the worst in the industrial world and in dire need of improvement. Saddled with flagging technology and feeling the pressure of foreign competition, the executive branch committed to a series of ambitious upgrades. After working to improve residential service in 1974, it decided in 1978 to create a new information service pairing Antiope with analog modems. The ambitious telematics project would drive the investment needed to replace the analog telephone network with a fully digital system while providing private entrepreneurs with an open platform for innovation. It was part of a broader array of related projects, such as developing widespread fax and videoconferencing systems. Supporters hoped that this aggressive strategy might jump-start a new French industry to rival their US opponent, IBM, in both the domestic and international markets for information technologies.[10]

To realize its dream of nationwide telematics, however, the State had to take charge of the overall ecosystem, absorbing the massive sunk costs of building out new infrastructure as well as artificially creating demand for telematics products and services. The growth of information and communication systems like Minitel depends on an economic phenomenon known as *network effects*. The term refers to the relationship between the value of a network to any individual user and the total number of connected users. A canonical example is the telephone: a telephone is only useful if there are other people to call. Two-sided platforms such as social networking sites exhibit network effects on both sides of the market: no user will go online if there is no content, and no content will be produced if there are no users. Conversely, as more users come online, the network's content and services grows, thereby attracting yet more users in a positive feedback loop. The chief problem for a new network is to attract enough participants on at least one side of the market early on to get this virtuous cycle started before running out of money.[11]

In the early 1980s, growing a platform like Minitel was especially difficult because the general public did not yet see the point of going online. To wit, the failure of early commercial online services like the Source, Viewtron, Covidea, Trintex, or Keycom in the United States. One strategy for attracting a critical mass of users and service providers to a new network is to "prime the pump"—that is, to create a temporary stimulus that will attract demand on one or more sides of the market and kick-start the positive feedback loop. This is exactly what happened in France. The State ordered millions of terminals from private manufacturers (which prompted the creation of new manufacturing lines) and gave away the equipment, free of cost, to every French telephone subscriber—free computers for everyone! The State further incited this fresh user base to actually connect to the network by creating a free, online phone book, *l'annuaire électronique*. Finally, it substantially lowered the barrier to entry for end users by not implementing an up-front subscription model but rather charging users based on their connection time and adding the resulting fees onto users' monthly phone bills—play now, pay later. To support the creation of new services, the telephone company rebated about two-thirds of the connection fees to the service providers. The billing and rebate system was named Kiosk (*le kiosque*), a reference to the role of traditional newspaper kiosks as intermediaries between publishers and readers. With an artificially created user base and built-in business model, content creators flocked to the platform, eager to deploy experimental new services. In short order, this positive feedback loop resulted in a lively Minitel ecosystem with a growing variety of activities and increasingly diverse population of users.

In retrospect, one can see that Minitel was also hindered by some of the decisions that enabled its explosive early growth. The terminal technology was frozen in time, the administrative bureaucracy created chilling effects on innovation, and the centralized accounting system based on virtual circuit routing protocols limited the adoption of interoperable "end-to-end" protocols characteristic of the Internet. But it is also these centralized aspects that made Minitel viable at a time when privately run gated communities in the United States resulted in fragmentation and commercial failure.

Whereas the Minitel wake at Orange in Brittany was a somber affair, the entrepreneurs' wake in Paris had been a rave-up, infused with a belief that the energy, wonder, and possibility that had animated the earliest days of Minitel are still with us, and that tremendous online futures are

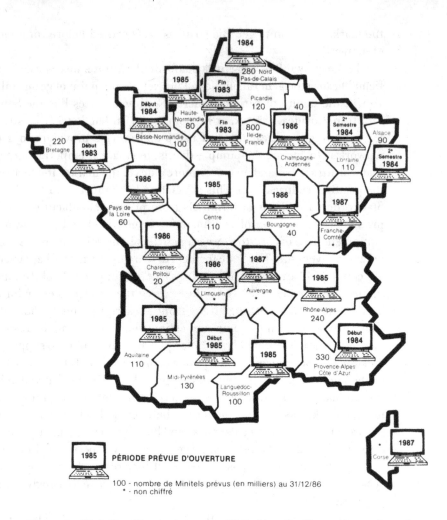

Figure 1.1 Minitel implementation map published in 1984. The numbers refer to the number of terminals (in thousands) requested by local authorities—a projection into the future. In the following years, terminals were distributed in even greater numbers to many of these regions. *Source*: Orange/DGCI référence photo Foo8571.

yet to come. We took a similar forward-looking approach in writing this book and posit that there is much to learn from the Minitel experience that will help us apprehend and devise better policies for the future. The official wake, in contrast, offered a vision of the past that has no future. "General, Mister Mayor," started the speaker at the military transmissions museum set in the middle of the industrial zone. The only real excitement came from the crowd of cadets with the local telecommunications military squadron, glad to get out of the barracks, if only for an afternoon. And then there were the Orange public relations officers, happy to see that the local television station was covering the event for a two-minute segment on the evening news, and a few engineers from the 1970s, some still wearing their bell-bottom suits, bright eyed from what they'd accomplished. There were trays of lavish petits fours. But even the endless supply of champagne could not relax the stiff atmosphere. By 9:00 p.m., the party had wrapped up. We were offered a to-go tray of food so it wouldn't go to waste. For all that the attendees had accomplished, the event was blanketed by a glum administrative nostalgia for the 1970s.

The third category of Minitel constituents, the users, said adieu without a party of their own, though many certainly attended some of the other events that took place that week. As a wave of nostalgia swept the country, numerous conferences, dance parties, faux wakes, and art exhibits were held to commemorate, venerate, and poke fun at the system. By 2012, most (but not all) users had abandoned their Minitel terminals and messageries for laptops and web browsers, smartphones and apps.[12] As a result, a new collector's market for Minitel artifacts blossomed in online auction sites, and hackers playfully adapted the millions of remaining devices, connecting them to the modern-day Internet and demonstrating their surprising durability. Minitel was finally put to rest with an outpouring of affection.

Minitel was a technical marvel, commercial success, and ambitious social experiment. By providing terminal equipment free of charge and supporting risk-taking entrepreneurs, Minitel propelled France into the information age. Other networks may have introduced protocols and software standards that continue to be used today, but Minitel presaged the social, political, economic, and regulatory issues pertaining to widespread telecomputing. By the end of the 1980s, Minitel mirrored the patterns of everyday life, as a platform for curiosity, play, commerce, politics, work, sex, and love.

For contemporary readers, Minitel offers a unique model for thinking about the design and regulation of platforms, and their resulting place in society. The massive public investment in information and communication technologies—what the French called la télématique (a combination of the words telecommunications and informatics)—represents a natural experiment in the use of computer networks as infrastructures for public culture. Unsurprising, yet seldom explored, the challenges and controversies that arose during the Minitel period reflect many of the same tensions that animate the "platformization" of the Internet today.[13] In particular, the history of Minitel invites us to revisit three of the conventional dialectics used to analyze media systems. Minitel was, at once, open and closed, public and private, centralized and decentralized, pushing us to think with greater nuance about how we characterize online systems. Instead of attempting to position Minitel as either/or, we examine the shades of difference between these extremes, and draw observations that others can use in the future to better design information services and network policies to foster innovation and civic participation.

What Do We Mean When We Say Minitel?

From its public debut in the early 1980s to its retirement in 2012, the term *Minitel* has been used colloquially to refer to the public videotex system in France (*videotex* itself refers to a family of two-way interactive media systems that bridge the telephone and television). From services, software, and protocols, to networks, switches, and computers, it's all *le Minitel*. Initially, however, the word *Minitel* referred only to the videotex terminal equipment deployed in the homes and offices of end users. Tracing the etymology of the term reveals a technical name for a generic input/output (I/O) device: *le médium interactif par numérisation d'information téléphonique*.[14] In the beginning, Minitel was just a terminal.

The transition from Minitel as a technical term with a specific meaning to Minitel as a metonym for the whole system reflects the way that everyday users encountered the platform. For the overwhelming majority, the terminal, monthly phone bill, and advertisements on the street provided their only points of contact with the system. The vast network that carried data to and from their terminals and calculated the cost of their time online was, like so much infrastructure, invisible. This invisibility is not unique to Minitel, of course, and many previous scholars and writers have pursued networks underground, across oceans, and into outer space. Computer historian Paul Ceruzzi found himself tromping through empty parking garages and construction sites in search of "the granddaddy of all switches" somewhere beneath Tysons Corner, Virginia.[15] Silicon Valley chronicler Po Bronson encountered "three gigabit switches, each the size of a microwave" during a tour of the main Bay Area switching office, leading him to conclude that "[t]he great Internet hub of hubs in the heart of Silicon Valley is composed of less high-tech equipment than most people have in their living rooms."[16] And artist Ingrid Burrington described New York City as an environment laden with "markings and remnants" of infrastructure that only become visible "once you know how to look for them."[17] Our task is similar: to invert the invisibility of infrastructure, crawling into the network through the video terminal and beyond the telephone jack to understand how the various technical components, economic models, and regulatory bodies came together to produce the system we call Minitel.[18]

An important characteristic of the colloquial use of *Minitel* is that it refers to the entire system in the singular. Although there were many different terminals, services, and peripherals, there was only ever one Minitel. In this respect, Minitel is more like the midcentury US telephone network than the Internet. Consider a term like *the Bell System*, used by AT&T to refer to the entire Bell assemblage—from the handset to the switching board to the interstate long-distance lines—as a single system with many components. But whereas the Bell System came to be known colloquially as *the phone*, Minitel was never replaced by a generic term. There were many videotex systems in Europe but only France had Minitel. Speaking about Minitel in the singular calls attention to the invisible, infrastructural components of the platform. In this respect, each individual Minitel terminal was not a stand-alone device but rather the end point or leaf node of a massive, *singular* telematics network blanketing the nation. Just as there is only one France, there was only one Minitel.

The singular meaning of Minitel also facilitates a convenient comparison between Minitel and the present-day Internet. In spite of its singular name, the Internet is fundamentally multiple. It is, by design and definition, a dynamic composition of independent systems—a network of networks—joined by gateways that translate local networking protocols into the widely understood Internet Protocol. As a result, it is difficult to think or write about *the Internet* without providing some context—temporal, geographic, technological, or economic. Minitel, by contrast, is a singular, stable object of study.

Exploring the differences between the singular Minitel and multiple Internet draws out the political, ontological, and technical characteristics of the two systems. Whereas the particular networks, protocols, and regulatory regimes that make up the Internet are constantly changing, the component parts of Minitel remained largely unchanged for more than thirty years. Unlike the Internet, Minitel has clear edges and boundaries, as well as a beginning and end. The system was brought to life by State edict in 1978 and shut down with the push of a button in 2012.

How Did Minitel Grow over Time?

Minitel was a public service, accessible to anyone in France. Terminals were distributed incrementally by geographic region between 1983 and 1987.[19] Minitel use was voluntary and expensive, however, so while everyone in France was aware of Minitel, not everyone chose to participate.

France Telecom gathered and published a variety of statistics regarding the size and growth of Minitel, including the diffusion of hardware, amount of time people spent online, and growth of commercial videotex services. The simplest measure was to estimate Minitel penetration by dividing the number of installed terminals by the total number of active telephone lines. In 1991, this method indicated that approximately one-fifth of all telephone subscribers in France owned a Minitel terminal. Although this approach produced a seemingly easy to interpret percentage, it offers a limited account of Minitel as it was actually used by the population. Minitel connection fees could be quite costly, and many people never brought a terminal into their homes. The lack of home use did not mean that they were nonusers, though. Minitel access was also available from public kiosks and terminals installed in the workplace. The distribution of Minitel terminal equipment described just a slice of the overall number of active users on the system.

A second limitation of measuring penetration by system-wide proportion is that it masks the unequal geographic distribution of Minitel. In 1991, for example, near the system's historical peak, France Telecom issued a map showing the penetration of Minitel across twenty-two cities. Major metropoles consistently ranked higher than their rural counterparts. Penetration rates ranged from 23.9 percent in Paris and 22.4 percent in Lille to 16.2 percent in Clermont-Ferrand and 15.3 percent in Ajaccio on the island of Corsica. Furthermore, socioeconomic status could have qualitative effects on the experience of using Minitel. A typical Parisian would be more likely than a farmer in Brittany to engage in casual chat over Minitel, due to the high connection cost. Conversely, a Parisian would have little interest in using Minitel to check the latest swine trade rates or regional news. Although every effort was made to deploy Minitel as a universally accessible system, it could not entirely overcome the existing differences between city and country life.

Instead of counting terminals, another approach to measuring the growth of Minitel was to examine the aggregate number of hours that people spent connected to the platform. This is also the most comprehensive quantitative data available because France Telecom reported the number of connection hours annually from 1985 to 2007 (except for 1995 and 2004), whereas data regarding sites, terminals, average call length, and penetration rate were not systematically nor comprehensively made available after 1994. Time spent online reflects a few different aspects of platform growth. First, it is an indication of both population and utility. We can reasonably assume that growth in the amount of time people spend online reflects a growing recognition of the value of online services across

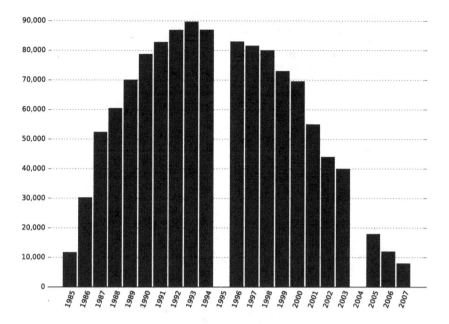

Figure 1.2 Connection hours (in thousands), 1985–2007. *Source:* Data published by France Telecom and available at Orange/DGCI.

the population of potential users. Second, the number of connection hours per year offers a general impression of economic growth because the revenue of most Minitel services came directly from the connection hours billed by France Telecom.

During the early years of the platform, approximately 1983–1993, when Minitel was booming, France Telecom published a number of additional statistics that provide a sense of how the various components of the system grew in relation to each other. These include the number of registered third-party services, number of installed terminals, and estimated proportion of the population with access to the platform. To facilitate comparison between these statistics, we constructed an index for each one by calculating their growth relative to a base year of 1985, when a majority of the country was connected (figure 1.3). While all the measures rose from year to year during this period, their patterns of growth differed in interesting ways.

In the early years of Minitel, between 1983 and 1987, the number of services used and hours that people spent connected to the network grew much faster than the diffusion of terminals and user population. Indeed, the number of services grew approximately 36.75 percent per year, on average, compared to 19.12 percent annual growth for the user population.

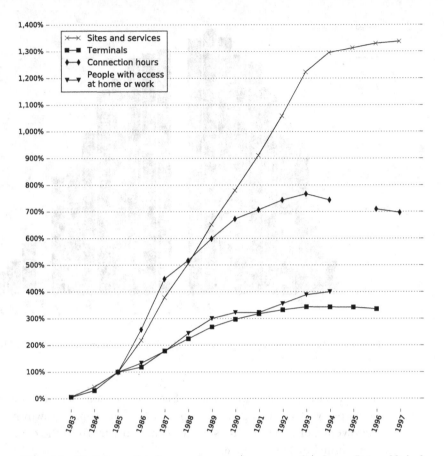

Figure 1.3 Minitel growth indexes, 1983–1997 (base year: 1985). *Source*: Data published by France Telecom and available at Orange/DGCI.

This rapid and steady growth reflected the low barriers to entry for entrepreneurs, value of hosting a service, and commercial promise of the Kiosk billing system. Building a Minitel service was a low-risk investment with a relatively strong potential for a good return. Furthermore, as Minitel became a part of popular culture, French organizations may have felt compelled to hang a shingle out in cyberspace, much in the same way that US companies later felt compelled to advertise a website.

The population of Minitel users grew steadily from 1983 to 1993, but the growth in annual connection hours began to slow down after an initial boom. This leveling off reflects the different practices of early and late adopters. Indeed, these data suggest that early adopters were eager to get online and explore. They had the money and interest to spend an unusual amount of time on the system, experimenting with new applications and returning to their favorite services night after night. As the system continued to grow, however, Minitel started to spread to a less enthusiastic population. These folks might use the system occasionally for utilitarian tasks like booking a train ticket but they were less likely to have the resources and inclination to become dedicated *minitelistes*. This gap between casual and hard-core users was especially pronounced after 1991. The overall number of people with access continued to rise steadily, but the growth of connection hours actually began to fall; new users were accessing the system less often than earlier groups. Crucially, while Minitel is frequently remembered for ostentatious advertising and ribald messageries, the typical connection lasted just five minutes. Nearly everyone in France had access to Minitel, and everyone was required to use it at least once in their life since certain public institutions such as universities required online registration, but a much smaller proportion became devoted minitelistes.

Table 1.1   Statistics published by France Telecom, 1983–1995

	Sites and services	Terminals	Connections hours per year	Proportion of population with access at home or work
1983	142	120,000		
1984	844	581,000		
1985	1,899	1,887,000	11,700,000	9%
1986	4,152	2,237,000	30,266,000	12%
1987	7,196	3,373,000	52,395,000	16%
1988	9,578	4,228,000	60,487,000	22%
1989	12,377	5,062,000	70,090,000	27%
1990	14,800	5,607,000	78,710,000	29%
1991	17,297	6,001,000	82,735,000	29%
1992	20,112	6,272,000	86,943,000	32%
1993	23,227	6,485,000	89,688,000	35%
1994	24,599	6,473,000	87,000,000	36%
1995	24,940	6,461,000		
1996	25,263	6,341,000	83,000,000	
1997	25,405		81,500,000	

Note: Empty cells were not reported in the applicable year.
Source: Orange/DGCI.

In discussions of telecommunications policy and technology development in the United States, Minitel is occasionally cited as the prototypical "wrong way" to build a mass-scale information system. It is decried as the quintessential public works project gone awry: centrally planned, controlled, censored, and laden with bureaucracy. Economist Eli Noam called it a "technologically backward system," and as media historian Fred Turner observed, Minitel is considered a "joke" in Silicon Valley, and an example of "what not to do."[20]

The historical record does not support the myth that Minitel was a radically closed system. Yet the stereotype persists, in part through firsthand histories of the Internet written by researchers and engineers. These accounts tend to frame the late twentieth century as a period of competition among protocol standards and networking technologies, each with their own values and ideological commitments. From this perspective, the emergence of the Internet Protocol, domain name system, and World Wide Web as de facto standards in the 1990s is seen as a victory of horizontal, engineer-driven development over more administrative approaches à la Minitel.

The notion that Minitel represents strict State control reflects a general misunderstanding outside France of how the platform functioned in practice. In the absence of firsthand experience, US technologists might reasonably have assumed that the Minitel was a walled garden sponsored by the State—a publicly funded CompuServe. In a popular history published in 2003, former Stanford Research Institute researcher and current Silicon Valley venture capitalist Jacques Vallée described Minitel as the "exact opposite" of the Internet: "a closed system with no ability to grow organically."[21] While the growth of Minitel as a technical infrastructure was limited by its commitment to the videotex standards of the late 1970s, it nevertheless *did* grow, tremendously, as a platform for experimentation and entrepreneurship in the application of computer networks in everyday life. These dimensions of growth were simply beyond the scope of Vallée's analysis.

To reduce the history of Minitel—the first mass-scale telecomputing system—to a competition among arcane networking protocols, or between a backward state-centric economic system and forward-looking free market economy is an odd historiographical choice. Odd, that is, if one's goal is to provide a holistic account of early computer-mediated communication. The focus on technical development in histories such as Vallée's is not malicious. Rather, the lack of attention to the applications, politics, and culture of Minitel is the result of a generation of engineers being called on, by circumstance, to explain the social changes that seemed to follow from the diffusion of computer networks into everyday life.

Dismantling the Minitel myth also unsettles widely accepted beliefs about the development of the Internet. Indeed, significant components of the global information infrastructure themselves are controlled, censored, and centralized to an extent unimaginable in the 1980s. As the ongoing controversy regarding "net neutrality" reveals, the Internet of the 2010s is a complex tangle of national and institutional gateways, policies, and protocols. Furthermore, its commercial growth post-1995 was made possible by tremendous previous public investments and subsidies. Historical analyses of early systems like Minitel offer important context to the study of institutional and infrastructural power in the present. In particular, the balance of public and private interests in Minitel provides us with an alternative schema for understanding the enclosure of today's Internet by private institutions like Apple, Facebook, Google, or Comcast.

What Are We Talking about When We Talk about "Platforms"?

Admittedly, talking about Minitel as a platform is a mild anachronism. There is no evidence that the term *platform* was used to describe communication networks of the 1980s. Indeed, the use of *platform* in the context of computing emerged only at the end of the 1990s, prompted by the impact of Microsoft Windows on the software industry.[22] During the antitrust case against Microsoft, expert testimony from economist Richard Schmalensee gestured toward a more inclusive meaning of the term. Schmalensee argued that Java, America Online, and Netscape Navigator should all be considered competitors to Windows because each provided a "platform" for the development of new software.[23] Microsoft Windows may have seemed dominant in the narrow market for operating systems, but it faced real competition in the dynamic market for software development platforms.

Amid a cross-examination dense with technical detail, the court pushed Schmalensee to clarify his definition of *platform*.[24] Sitting judge Justice Thomas Penfield Jackson asked if a program for porting Windows applications to Unix would be considered a "platform" in competition with Microsoft since it strengthened the appeal of Unix. No, replied Schmalensee, such a program would be a "link between" platforms, but it was not a platform in itself. "I'm having difficulty at this point," admitted Justice Jackson. "Is [Java] a platform?" Schmalensee agreed that, yes, "pure" Java was a platform because new software could be built directly on top of it. In fact, he continued, any computing system with an interface "to which [software] applications can be written" is potentially a platform. By this definition, the typical personal computer of the period represented a matryoshka doll of recursive platforms: an Intel x86 microprocessor, Microsoft Windows operating system, the Java Virtual Machine, and the Netscape Navigator web browser.

Although the court was not convinced by Microsoft's argument, the tussle over the meaning of *platform* presaged a bloom of academic interest in the technical, economic, regulatory, and rhetorical implications of platforms.[25] Schmalensee's testimony gestured to an emerging area of economic theory that drew together questions regarding information products, standardization, and network effects.[26] Beginning in 2003, the term *platform* was routinely used to refer to firms operating as intermediaries in a multisided market.[27] Recurring examples in this literature included a variety of information and communication technologies such as payment cards, video game consoles, broadcast media, and online services.[28] In this context, *platform* refers to a metaphorical space enabling two or more groups of economic agents to interact. Platform providers such as American Express or Nintendo strategically "court" each side of their platform through competitive pricing while maximizing their own overall profit.[29]

Meanwhile, Silicon Valley was struggling to recover from the dot-com crash. Amid the wreckage of countless failed websites, platform economics suggested an alternative way of thinking about the World Wide Web. Beginning in 2004, rather than continue to approach the web as a hypertext publishing system, adherents of Tim O'Reilly's "Web 2.0" doctrine started to use commonplace web technologies such as HTTP, HTML, CSS, and JavaScript to create stand-alone programs, or "web apps."[30] By 2006, Google was offering a suite of office productivity software that ran in a standard web browser—an almost pitch-perfect realization of the future envisioned by Microsoft and others a decade before. As users and developers alike began to accept the concept of the web as a platform, web applications grew in complexity, becoming programmable platforms in their own right. In the course of everyday use, the architecture of the web started to fade from view, becoming a commodity infrastructure for new platforms.[31]

The technical transition from web "sites" to web "platforms" after 2004, described by media scholar Anne Helmond as "platformization," was accompanied by wide-ranging changes in the social, political, and economic character of the web.[32] On the one hand, the borders of the ideal

Web 2.0 platform are designed to be porous, with user-generated data flowing in and out through publicly accessible programming interfaces, while on the other hand, enterprising platform providers must necessarily limit interoperability to prevent users from leaving for a competitor. Facebook, the canonical example of platformization, transformed itself from being a network of user profiles to a programmable platform by supplying third-party developers with convenient "plug-ins" and "widgets."[33] As third parties added "Like" and "Login with Facebook" buttons to their sites, Facebook shifted from being one of many social network sites on the web to a de facto standard infrastructure for sharing media with friends and verifying one's identity. Facebook's functionality seemed to explode outward onto the web while at the same time the entire web felt increasingly enclosed by Facebook.[34]

The platformization of the web by firms like Facebook was not a quiet transformation. Beginning around 2006, countless firms—from dot-com survivors like PayPal to newcomers like YouTube—started describing themselves as platforms. In 2010, communication scholar Tarleton Gillespie examined the use of *platform* in Silicon Valley discourse and found that firms routinely exploited the polysemy of the term to distract from their growing role as private mediators of public culture.[35] By portraying themselves as platforms rather than, say, intermediaries, social media providers hoped to position themselves as neutral channels, open to anyone. Of course, as Gillespie's analysis reveals, this populist appeal was not borne out in practice. The administrator of a social media platform always retains the power to determine who can participate and on what terms. These platforms not only host public discourse, they actively shape it.

Minitel was a platform in all these senses: computational, economic, and cultural. It was a platform for technical creativity, a platform for entrepreneurship, and a platform for the citizens of France to meet, chat, trade, and play.

How Do We Know What We Know about the Minitel Platform?

Most of the activity on Minitel was ephemeral. We have few records of the endless chats that took place on messageries, nor of the countless conferences, databases, and videotex pages that were published on the network. There is no surviving system to explore, no vestigial messageries to log on to. Minitel ended with finality in 2012, but the liveliest social systems had already faded away many years before. There is no way to emulate or simulate the experience of hanging out at home alone, dialing 3615, and flirting with strangers all night on a messagerie as we might have done back in 1987.

Fortunately (or unfortunately, depending on one's perspective), this problem is not unique to Minitel. Media historian Megan Sapnar Ankerson notes that historians of radio and television have long struggled with the problems of ephemerality and incomplete archives.[36] Early broadcast programming was performed live, and even when a performance was recorded, the resulting tapes were not thought of as archival documents. Tapes were routinely recorded over, mislabeled, or destroyed. Preservation is the exercise of power to shape our knowledge of the past. Careful record keeping tends to reflect the cultural preferences of elites as opposed to providing a holistic snapshot of a medium. As a result, early entertainment—such as the daytime dramas aimed at women—were less often preserved than other sorts of programming.

Multiuser systems like Minitel introduce a second set of complications. Not only is the infrastructure and most of the content gone, but so are the users. Even if we were to build a replica Minitel network, complete with replica messageries, who would be there to chat with? Games scholars face this problem in the preservation of multiplayer games—particularly massively multiplayer online games and virtual worlds.[37] "Game worlds aren't games," writes researcher Richard Bartle, "they're *places*."[38] A depopulated World of Warcraft hardly represents the game as it was played. Faced with such an empty world, researchers rely on the firsthand accounts of former players as they are recorded in oral histories and paratexts such as blog posts, message board threads, screenshots, and gameplay videos.[39]

This book offers a history of Minitel as both a technical system and cultural phenomenon. The key analytic challenge in this approach is to synthesize these two aspects of the Minitel story in an effort to understand the social, economic, and political tenets of its technical design. Toward this end, we draw from a variety of primary and secondary sources, found in both official and informal collections. Whereas contemporaneous networks like the National Science Foundation Network (NSFNET) or Cyclades were developed largely outside the public eye, Minitel was deeply woven into the fabric of everyday life, as commonplace in French homes as the telephone and television, and omnipresent in the media.

Our study began with the mass-produced terminal devices that sojourned in domestic and professional spaces across France. Before the flurry of nostalgia that accompanied the end of the system in 2012, disused Minitels were shoved into closets and abandoned to the trash. During several years of trips back and forth to Paris and Brittany between 2008 and 2012, we assembled a collection of terminal equipment, peripherals, software, and related ephemera. Through hands-on experimentation, we came to know these devices as working technologies, material objects with dimension and weight, sounds and smells.[40] The design and function of Minitel terminal equipment was revealed to us through both hobbyist forums on the web and the documentation produced by France Telecom (known as the Direction générale des télécommunications [DGT] until 1988, and Orange after 2013—note that we use France Telecom and DGT interchangeably throughout the book).

As a publicly funded infrastructure project, the development of Minitel was the subject of public policy, and the Bibliothèque Nationale de France, Archives Nationales, and France Telecom archives formally collected Minitel-related materials. As part of the State's effort to encourage entrepreneurship and third-party innovation, the technical components of Minitel were unusually well documented in technical manuals and user guides, all carefully edited and attractively designed. In addition, France Telecom was compelled to document the economic development of Minitel. Annual reports and periodic newsletters provide a source of quantitative data regarding the diffusion, adoption, and habitual use of Minitel services during the 1980s and 1990s. Unfortunately, these data are of limited use for serious statistical analysis. Published as part of the Minitel public relations strategy, the annual reports tend to paint a rosy picture, documenting the rise but not the decline of the platform. Similarly, some of the reports were simultaneously published in French and English in an effort to appeal to international investors. As a result, they offered a sanitized portrayal of Minitel. For this reason and also because of domestic political pressures, the vast market of sexually explicit services known as *Minitel rose* was largely absent, for example, despite its massive commercial success. Due to these biases, it was necessary to complement the official documentation of Minitel with secondary sources and first-person accounts.

Beyond the official output of France Telecom, Parliament, and the various government ministries and agencies involved, we turned to a large volume of paratextual Minitel materials such as periodicals, trade books, and ephemeral literature. Unofficial directories such as *Listel* and *Le Guide du Minitel* served as a kind of yellow pages for videotex services. Published seasonally and jammed with advertising for messageries and other adult services, these fat paperback tomes provide a view of Minitel from the ground up. A small number of how-to books were written for new users and would-be entrepreneurs. News and opinion writing about Minitel services, peripherals, industry, and culture were routinely featured in hobbyist and trade magazines, such as *Science et Vie Micro, La Revue du Minitel,*

Vidéotex, and *Minitel Magazine* as well as in magazines aimed at general interest readers. As a public utility, Minitel was often discussed in the editorial pages of newspapers and on television. Likewise, news reporters frequently asked politicians to comment on various features of the system. With all this discourse, it can be difficult to know when to stop searching. As Ankerson notes about web history, there is both "too much and too little."[41]

Whereas France Telecom, the National Archives, and the National Library (from which we also acquired most of the news reports we cite throughout the book) collected most of the official documentation of Minitel, there is no single, authoritative source for Minitel ephemera.

Beyond formal collecting institutions, we turned to online auction sites and used book dealers to find Minitel materials circulating in the collector market. During our search, we benefited significantly from the voluntary labor of Minitel enthusiasts, especially the online collections maintained by Frédéric Cambus at Minitel.org and GOTO10.fr. Cambus's collection features an idiosyncratic index of Minitel media on the public web including scanned documentation, advertisements, news clippings, documentary video, and related software. Without the efforts of enthusiasts like Cambus, much of the popular culture of Minitel would be lost.

In addition to documentary sources, we conducted over thirty interviews with engineers and administrators within France Telecom along with other administrative agencies, private entrepreneurs building services to run on the platform, hackers, industry lobbyists, and journalists. These interviews took place in Paris, Brittany, and the San Francisco Bay Area, where Orange maintains a research lab. In particular, on the administration's side, we met with Gérard Théry, former head of the DGT; Jean-Paul Maury, former head of the Minitel project, and two of his young engineers, Jean-Luc Beraudo de Pralormo and Bernard Louvel; Bernard Marti, the CCETT lead engineer for the Antiope video standard; and Georges Nahon, former head of France Telecom's Minitel export arm, Intelmatique. On the private sector and users side, we met in particular with Daniel Hannaby and Michel Landaret, pioneers of Minitel rose; other entrepreneurs such as Jean-Eudes Queffélec, Christian Quest, and Laurent Chemla, a notable hacker; and Michel Baujard, an industry lobbyist. These interviews served multiple purposes. They helped to triangulate data and explain gaps in the official documentation, provided background for well-documented events, drew our attention to conflicts and tensions that animated the development of the system, and most important, supplied a qualitative account of some people's firsthand experience of working with Minitel.

There were many possible avenues into this uneven archive of devices, documents, paratexts, and interview transcripts. Our chosen point of entry is the idea of the *platform*.[42] At the micro scale, platforms represent a set of creative constraints for users and developers, while at the macro scale, platforms shape the interactions among individuals, firms, governments, and other institutions.[43] Understanding the mechanics of a computational platform like Minitel enables us to make inferences about the governing role of the platform in society at a particular time and in a particular place. In spite of its singular name, the Minitel platform is constituted by several subsystems—terminals, networks, and servers—each with its own architectures, protocols, institutions, and histories. To make sense of Minitel as a platform with both technical and social characteristics, we perform a historical *disaggregation*, exploring the various components and their relationships.[44]

Platform studies offers an unusual perspective for analyzing the place of Minitel in French society during the 1980s and 1990s. As we delve into the architectural details of Minitel, we will regularly return to questions about the social and cultural consequences of this admittedly arcane technology. As a platform for computation, communication, and commerce, we wish to know how Minitel allocated power and authority among millions of users. What functions were exposed to whom? Who decided which programs could run and what they could do? Who could make money on Minitel? How did they set their prices and get paid? What were the barriers to entry? Who could speak on Minitel? What could they say? Who set the rules? What happened if a rule was broken?

Learning from Minitel

One purpose of this book is to bring Minitel to the attention of readers outside France, many of whom have never heard of the system before. As the first computer network to reach mass-scale participation, Minitel presaged the near-universal adoption of Internet access in many major metropolitan regions today. For critics and policy makers, Minitel provides an empirical case study of a system that was actually implemented and used by a diverse French public. Many of the matters of public concern and political scrutiny that arise from ubiquitous Internet use, from the regulation of speech by state institutions and private actors, including the issue of net neutrality, to the conditions of anonymity and privacy protections, first emerged on Minitel. Similarly, Minitel supplies an example of a platform built and maintained with an explicit mandate to serve the public interest. As more and more critics in the United States and Europe regard Internet access as a matter of public safety and prosperity, the study of Minitel grows even more vital. Through comparisons with the Internet and private platforms such as the Apple and Facebook ecosystems, the exceptional Minitel story enables us to grasp subtle shades on the openness spectrum as well as shed new light on the entangled roles of the state and private sector in fostering digital innovation in ways that defy conventional Internet policy wisdom.

The rest of this book is divided into six chapters. Each chapter addresses a different aspect of the relationship between Minitel and society, and may be read independently from the rest. Chapter 2 maps out the key technical components of Minitel, including its physical infrastructure, routing protocols, addressing scheme, video standard, software interface, and unusual accounting and billing apparatuses. Together, these elements sustained a generative platform for the creation of novel online services and the emergence of thriving virtual communities. Chapter 3 explains how the unique French culture got embedded in the protocols, and how state policy and national identity were woven deeply into the design and implementation of the system. In particular, we discuss the relationship between specific features of the Minitel platform and the French political tradition of centralization. The PTT at the center of all networked activity plays as a leitmotiv on a backdrop of economic and infrastructure development. Most Minitel stories, especially on the US side of the Atlantic, stop there.

In chapter 4, we show another side of the story: the fact that the Minitel architecture was actually a novel hybrid model, with innovation decentralized to the edges of the network. This marked an ideological shift in French policy—one that enhanced spontaneity, mobility, and imagination, and marked a transition from traditional dirigisme to state venture capitalism *à la française*. In chapter 5, we detail the results of this public–private partnership on content creation, with a particular focus on Minitel rose and other private-sector digital innovations that the United States would not see appear until after 1995. In chapter 6, we return to a consideration of the radical potential of the Minitel system in the hands of a creative populace, and show that the seemingly tight grip of the State over Minitel did not prevent fringe uses of the network. The life of the Minitel platform involves complex interactions between technology, policy, law, business, and culture. Finally, in the conclusion, we revisit the overarching question of the book: What do we learn from the Minitel experience that we can use to better design information networks in the future to foster innovation and civic participation? The alternative example of yesterday's Minitel provokes us to think differently about the Internet we will inhabit tomorrow.

A typical Tuesday night in Paris, February 1987. The weather outside is raw, and you're propped up on the couch, idly watching reruns of *Médecins de nuit*, bored. It's too late to make plans for the evening, and anyway, it's hard enough to wake up for work without the hangover. Leaning forward, you pick up a dog-eared book from the side table. Above a photo of a Minitel terminal, in a font reminiscent of *Star Trek*, the cover reads, *Listel: REPERTOIRE DES SERVICES TELETEL*. At 650 pages, this is a substantial tome.

Thumbing through, the book falls open naturally on a handful of full-color advertisements sprinkled among the cheap, two-color newsprint. All the major newspapers in France are represented here, their ads carefully crafted to mirror their editorial personalities. *Le Monde* invites you, the discriminating Parisian intellectual, to chat about politics, food, and travel: *"Le Monde* by Minitel, it's you. It's your state of mind."[1] The left-leaning *Libération* offers a new, "unbeatable" database of law complete with online games and quizzes to test your legal knowledge. Not exactly the kind of entertainment you had in mind.

A pair of ads for the recently renamed daily *Le Parisien* are a bit more intriguing. Toward the front of the book, a saturated blue foldout promises a "non-stop happening" with "more news, more information, more sports, more games, more conferences, more tenderness, and more laughter." Near the back, however, a second ad stands out. Against a field of bright pink, two lines of text state mysteriously: *"La vie en rose. Du nouveau."* Turning the pages, you encounter a set of smiling faces arranged in a grid. Young and old, all fair skinned, with curly hair and straight, the copy explains that this team of "twenty-two seducers" tested the romantic chat rooms, or *les messageries du coeur*, and found them fun, friendly, and more than a bit steamy. On the last page, the ad cajoles, "Now, it's your turn."[2]

Sufficiently seduced, you lift your Minitel off the floor by its handle and place it on the coffee table in front of you. The wires connecting the terminal to the wall upset the contents of your ashtray, but you'll deal with that later. Releasing a latch on the top of the brown plastic case, the side hinges forward, revealing a dark glass screen and keyboard. You press the power button, and wait for the screen to brighten and the system to boot, which takes less than a couple seconds. Taking your phone off the hook, you dial "3615," and stare out the window until the familiar carrier tone buzzes in your ear. You tap a green button on the Minitel, replace the phone's handset on its cradle, and watch the menu of your local gateway fill the screen. "P ... L ... NUIT," you narrate to no one in particular, as you type in the mnemonic code for one of the newspaper's more mysterious messageries. As the gateway menu is replaced by a grayscale carnival masque, you reach over and snap off the television set. It's not long until you notice sunlight over your neighbor's roof. So much for that hangover, I guess. And another hangover is looming: the one that will come with the next phone bill accounting for your night of digital masquerade.

At its peak, Minitel provided an electronic platform for popular expression and public culture. The thousands of surviving advertisements, pop songs, magazine articles, and how-to books attest to its pervasive influence on the lives of everyday French citizens. Beginning with the iconic terminal equipment, this chapter maps out the key technical components of Minitel, including its terminal equipment, servers, and network infrastructure. Together, these elements sustained a generative platform for the creation of novel online services and the emergence of thriving virtual communities.

Disaggregating the Minitel Platform

Colloquially, *Minitel* referred to an assemblage of networks, servers, and terminals. As part of a government project to modernize the nation's telecommunications infrastructure and stimulate a domestic informatics industry, the Minitel platform brought together new and old technologies. Officially, the term *Minitel* referred only to the terminal equipment: the ubiquitous brown box with a keyboard that flips down along with a black-and-white screen. Each Minitel was equipped with a modem that could translate between sequences of digital bits and waves of sound. The Minitel fit right alongside one's existing telecommunications apparatus; the telephone plugged into the Minitel, and the Minitel plugged into the telephone jack on the wall (see figure 2.1).

By default, Minitel terminals were designed to decode and display pages of data in videotex format. In the late 1970s, *videotex* referred to an emerging family of media technologies intended to bridge the twin pillars of midcentury telecommunications: the telephone and television. The simplest implementations of videotex broadcast a revolving set of static "pages" including a mix of text and images to be displayed on a home television. One can imagine such a system being used to circulate announcements about weather, civic matters, or a calendar of local events. This was called *teletext*. Minitel was more ambitious; Minitel was interactive.

Figure 2.1   The Minitel 1B video terminal produced by Telic-Alcatel. *Source*: Authors' collection.

Comment installer votre Minitel

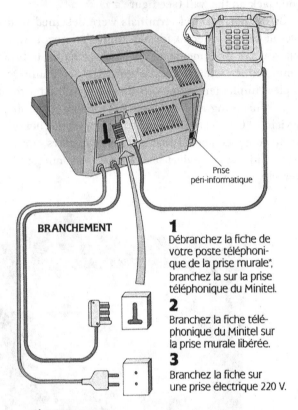

BRANCHEMENT

1
Débranchez la fiche de votre poste téléphonique de la prise murale*, branchez la sur la prise téléphonique du Minitel.

2
Branchez la fiche téléphonique du Minitel sur la prise murale libérée.

3
Branchez la fiche sur une prise électrique 220 V.

VÉRIFICATIONS
Branchement téléphonique : en décrochant le combiné vous devez obtenir la tonalité. Sinon vérifiez le bon branchement des fiches.
Branchement électrique : vous mettez sous tension l'écran en appuyant sur l'interrupteur marche-arrêt. La lettre F s'affiche en haut à droite.

*Si vous utilisez le Minitel sur une installation privée fournie par un installateur agréé, l'entretien de la prise téléphonique murale sera assuré par celui-ci et non par l'Administration. Pour toute modification, adressez-vous à ce même installateur.

Figure 2.2   How to install your Minitel: a terminal, a telephone, three wires, et voilà! France Telecom, *Minitel 1: Mode d'emploi, modèle TELIC*, n.d. *Source*: Authors' collection.

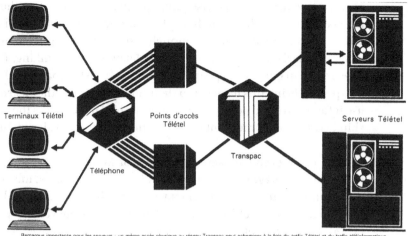

Remarque importante pour les serveurs : un même accès physique au réseau Transpac peut acheminer à la fois du trafic Télétel et du trafic téléinformatique.

Figure 2.3 Diagram of the Télétel platform showing the interconnection between the analog, circuit-switched telephone network and digital, packet-switched Transpac network. Direction générale des télécommunications, comment mettre en oeuvre un service Télétel, n.d. *Source*: Orange/DGCI.

Télétel was the official brand name of the overall ecosystem that connected Minitel terminals to videotex services. Télétel was itself composed of a variety of technologies for managing the traffic that flowed through the system, addressing, routing, billing, and accounting for each byte as it moved across the country. Crucially, it created a gateway between the pre-existing, switched telephone network and newly built public data network, Transpac. Transpac was a packet-switched network using the (then cutting-edge) virtual circuit X.25 protocol.[3] Télétel placed specialized computers, called *points d'accès vidéotex* (videotex access points), in regional switching stations throughout the country. These machines were on-the-ground traffic coordinators, modulating and demodulating, translating among a variety of data communication protocols—the unsung heroes of Minitel.

To understand how these disparate parts gave rise to the popular understanding of Minitel as a single, coherent system, we need to disaggregate the platform and examine each component in turn.[4]

Discovering Minitel

Let us return to that hypothetical late night on 3615 PLNUIT. Such a casual exploration of an online community was simply not possible for the vast majority of people across the world in 1987. Beyond the obvious barriers of infrastructure and expertise, most people would not have thought of telematics as a medium for fun, play, entertainment, and exploration. While microcomputers were routinely used for gaming, modems were generally marketed as tools for serious business—telebanking, database research, managing travel plans, and working from the road. So why would a layperson bring this device into their home? How did they learn how to use it for leisure and popular communication? And what was the relationship between this process of domestication and the broader institutional goals of Télétel?

For many eventual users, awareness of Minitel began around 1980 with media coverage of several public videotex experiments, including the distribution of terminal equipment to more than two thousand households in the suburbs of Paris that was later known as the Vélizy experiment or T3V.[5] The concept of an interactive information service, connecting directly to the home, and combining telephony and television, generated considerable curiosity across France, and the T3V experiment was widely covered in the press.[6] Another key experiment was the creation of an online directory of phone numbers, *un annuaire électronique*, in the region of Ille-et-Vilaine on the west coast of France. At once familiar and futuristic, the electronic phone book project was extremely effective, rhetorically and technically, for introducing people to Minitel. It helped citizens, politicians, and entrepreneurs alike imagine how an interactive information service might be used in the course of everyday life. The computerization of a familiar analog technology like the phone book offered a quite-different vision of computing from the large-scale mainframes that were otherwise dominant in television and film. As a reporter from *Le Monde* enthused after hearing the plans for Télétel in 1979: user-friendly telematics were no longer just a dream.[7]

The electronic phone book provided an accessible point of entry into the practice of telematics, but crafting a system for novices was no easy task. Rather than a mere database, the electronic phone book was shaped by the needs of its diverse user population into an early artificial intelligence system. For many users connecting to the phone book, Minitel was their only direct experience with interactive computing. The back-and-forth, turn-taking structure of the phone book's text mode interface suggested a conversational type of interaction more comparable to calling the switchboard operator for directory assistance than looking up information in a printed book. As a result, the developers of the electronic phone book strove to create a flexible, adaptive system that could accommodate misspellings and other errors.[8] As one early report described it, the system aimed to be an "intelligent interlocutor" instead of a "stupid machine."[9]

The electronic phone book—later known as *Le 11*, its dial-in number—became an engine driving the diffusion of Minitel. The computerized directory was operated locally in ten regions, and as each region came online, it opened up a new segment of the population to Minitel. Late in 1982, the Direction générale des télécommunications (DGT) announced that the electronic phone book would soon arrive in Île-de-France, home to the city of Paris and more than 10,000,000 residents.[10] Just as the print phone book was distributed free of charge, the DGT promised to provide a basic terminal, the Minitel 1, for free to anyone living in the region. Beginning in 1983, curious Parisians could pick up a brand-new terminal, free of charge, from their local post office. At the end of the year, more than 120,000 videotex terminals were installed in France, and the DGT had already put in orders for nearly 500,000 more.[11]

With the mass adoption of the electronic phone book, the DGT had "primed the pump" and created a potential customer base for new, privately run videotex services. The challenge for service providers was to convince these new Minitel owners to venture out beyond the familiar (and mostly free) electronic phone book. The concept of an electronic phone book was simple enough for the novice to understand, but it scarcely hinted at the potential uses of videotex for communication and community building.[12] By fall 1984, several new publications, public and private, were available to facilitate discovery and exploration of the new system. An official directory of private digital services, organized by the DGT, was occasionally published in print and searchable via Télétel, and exciting innovations were circulated in newly founded magazines such as *Minitel Magazine*, *La Revue du Minitel*, and *Vidéotex*.[13]

As the number of services running on the platform grew from a few dozen to a few thousand in 1986, discovery became an even greater challenge.[14] *Listel*, published quarterly starting in December 1985, provided a comprehensive account of this growth. With no editorial content, *Listel* was strictly a directory of Télétel services. In each issue, the thousands of active services were divided into two categories—services for the general public and services aimed at professionals—and organized according to more than twenty themes from agriculture and finance, to sports and leisure. Each listing included a brief description of the features of the service, its hours of operation, and the regions it served. The listings were hardly the most compelling feature of *Listel*, though. Like the yellow pages in the United States, more than half of *Listel* was taken up by advertising. And whereas the listings covered a broad array of services, most of which seemed to fall into a practical category such as tax consultation, the advertisements overwhelmingly featured social computing services: chat rooms, message boards, classified ads, and multiplayer games.

One online community, *La Voix du Parano* (Voice of the Paranoid), explicitly hailed the novice reader with its advertising. A self-described destination for "non-conformists," *La Voix* was advertised with a sleek new-wave illustration reminiscent of Max Headroom and claimed to serve "7,000 plugged-in users daily." The ad copy began with a familiar narrative: "When you got your Minitel, they explained the practical operation of the device and, of course, your first act as a '*miniteliste*' was to search the electronic phonebook." But, it continues, "have you heard of the *messageries*? The mailboxes? Or the confessions?" Interpellating the reader as overwhelmed, the copy concludes: "You'll encounter even more new '*miniteliste*' terminology [but] do not panic, *La Voix du Parano* will explain."[15]

The appeal of *La Voix du Parano* brings us back to our hypothetical evening in 1987. A Minitel is sitting on your side table because you picked it up when the electronic phone book came to your region. The services advertised in *Listel* are specifically targeting you, the neophyte—inviting you to participate in the emerging online communities being assembled on the Minitel platform. In spite of the abundance of how-to information in *Listel* and elsewhere, Minitel remained a black box system for most users. For the rest of this chapter, we will walk step-by-step through the process of a typical Minitel session, exploring the components of the platform as we go.

Les terminaux

At its core, the Minitel terminal was defined simply as "a keyboard + a screen + a modem."[16] The basic terminal, distributed for free beginning in 1983, was called the Minitel 1. Over the years, the Minitel 1 was produced by a number of different manufacturers including Telic-Alcatel, Matra, Philips, and La Radiotechnique Industrielle et Commerciale. While each manufacturer introduced variations in the design and feature set, the core functionality was constant. Over the years, many new terminals were designed and manufactured, but the Minitel 1 remained the iconic mascot of the network.[17] Indeed, the success of the platform depended on the reliability of its end user devices. If Minitel was to reach mass adoption, it was essential that all the terminals, from the simplest to the most complex, were interoperable, regardless of which assembly line they rolled off of. The present analysis focuses specifically on the Minitel 1B, a terminal produced by Telic-Alcatel and released shortly after the original

Minitel 1. In addition to the standard videotex mode, the Minitel 1B offered a second mode for interacting with microcomputers and timesharing systems.[18] In spite of its technical differences, the label on the exterior of Minitel 1B still read "Minitel 1" and the "bistandard" model became one of the most prevalent variations of the original terminal.

The Minitel 1B is a self-contained data terminal. All the hardware fits into a molded plastic case approximately eight inches tall, ten inches wide, and ten inches deep. The front of the Minitel 1B is dark brown, and the rear of the case is a lighter beige color. The keyboard is attached to the bottom edge of the front of the case by a hinge. When not in use, the keyboard folds up and is held in place by a latch at the top of the case. In the rear, the case bumps out to accommodate the electron guns of the built-in cathode-ray tube. A large knob embedded in the case controls the brightness of the display. On one side of the rear of the case, a small plastic window lifts up to reveal a serial port with a five-pin DIN connection. On the other side, two long black cables lead out. One cable ends with a standard "Type-C Europlug" AC power plug, and the other ends with a standard T-plug for connecting to the French telephone network. Unlatching the keyboard reveals a small glass screen, or *l'écran*, approximately eight inches across. A square power button and small red LED are below the screen.

The keyboard, or *le clavier*, includes sixty-four keys. The keys are "chiclet" style, similar to the Sinclair ZX-80 or IBM PCjr, with a few millimeters of space between each. In addition to twenty-six letters, ten numerals, nine punctuation keys, and a space bar, the keyboard includes both a shift key and unlabeled modifier key. The effect of the shift and modifier keys is indicated by a set of color-coded alternate characters printed on the surface of the keyboard. Ten keys at the top of the keyboard correspond to Télétel commands, such as *sommaire* (table of contents) and *envoi* (send). Although most Minitel keyboards are laid out in the same AZERTY style found on French typewriters, some early models featured an alphabetic layout (ABCDE ...).[19] It was believed that this layout would be easier for novice typists with no prior experience of either typewriters or microcomputers.

The Minitel 1 was delivered with a small pamphlet explaining how to install and start using the device (see figure 2.2).[20] The terminal was designed to complement rather than replace the existing telephonic appliances already at work in the home. Step one was to unplug the existing telephone from the wall and replace it with the Minitel. Step two was to plug the telephone into the Minitel. Finally, step three was to connect the terminal to a 220-volt main power source. To test the installation, one first lifted the handset to be sure that the dial tone was audible. Next, one pressed the power button, listened for a beep, and waited for a capital *F* to appear on the screen. The Minitel was now happily in its "local" state, or *état local*, awaiting an incoming data connection.[21]

As the ads for *la Voix* suggested, a typical first foray into the world of Minitel was to query the electronic phone book. Calls to the phone book were free of charge for the first three minutes, which provided a low-risk opportunity for experimentation. With the Minitel 1 properly installed and powered on, one initiated a connection by lifting the handset, dialing "11," and waiting for an answer. As the phone rang, the call was being routed to a regional office where a computerized switch, the CIT-Alcatel E-10, provided a gateway between the standard telephone network and the electronic phone book's data network. On successful routing, a high-pitched tone (*la tonalité aiguë*) would sound in the earpiece.[22] By pressing the button marked *Connexion/Fin* on the keyboard, the Minitel would enter "remote" mode, join the call, and handshake with the remote service. At this point, one returned the telephone handset to its cradle and watched as the menu of the electronic phone book appeared on the screen at 1,200 bits per second. At the conclusion of the session, pressing the Connexion/ Fin button caused the Minitel to "hang up" and return to local mode.

The example of the electronic phone book demonstrates the core capacity of the Minitel 1. A true "dumb terminal," the Minitel supplied a reliable interface to remote information services while performing minimal computing of its own. It is often said that the Minitel did not have a CPU or memory, but this is not strictly true. While the Minitel 1 was not a generally programmable computer, a microprocessor was necessary to operate the modem, serial port, keyboard, and screen. Similarly, the Minitel 1 did not have an operating system or BIOS but rather a small set of software burned into ROM that implemented decoders for the keyboard and display as well as protocols for serial communication and error correction.[23] Additional volatile memory was used to store the current state of the screen and provide a buffer for user input. More expensive models such as the Minitel 10 included additional hardware and software features, including a built-in tone generator and automatic telephone dialer.[24]

Le modem

The modem module is the key technical feature differentiating the Minitel from other I/O devices. It was purposely built for communicating with data services over noisy telephone lines. The electronic interface between the modem and incoming telephone line was designed to adapt to voltage irregularities that might occur on infrastructures not originally intended to carry data.[25] Anticipating future network scenarios, the Minitel modem also did not require a live telephone line and could be used to directly connect two telematics devices "*modem à modem.*"[26]

The word modem is a contraction of "modulator–demodulator." The job of the modem is to provide a gateway between the interior world of a digital device and the external analog world by translating digital information into sound. This is accomplished by following a prearranged set of rules to slightly alter, or "modulate," a continuous tone. These variations can then be detected and translated back into digital information by a second device. The Minitel modem was an asymmetrical duplex modem—a communication standard that had been continuously negotiated and refined by the International Telecommunication Union (ITU) since 1964.[27] In practice, this meant that the Minitel could receive (demodulate) data at 1,200 baud while simultaneously sending (modulating) at 75 baud.[28]

The communication standard adopted by Minitel, ITU-T V.23, defined specifically how the modem should convert digital information into sound. By conforming to the ITU standard, the Minitel modem could communicate with a variety of telecommunications equipment. In the default mode, the Minitel modem generated a carrier signal of 420 Hz, easily audible to the human ear. To transmit a 0 or 1, the frequency of this tone was raised or lowered by 30 Hz, respectively. To ensure that incoming and outgoing data were not confused, incoming data were sent 1,700 Hz and modulated by +/- 400 Hz. This type of data communication is known as audio frequency-shift keying (AFSK), and was widely used by professional and amateur telecommunications. Teletype, packet radio, and caller ID are all examples of AFSK applications.

One unusual feature of the Minitel 1B was the option to "flip" the transmission rates (*retournement du modem*). The default asymmetry (1,200 receiving, and 75 sending) was appropriate for typical menu-driven videotex applications in which most of the transmission was made up of visual information to be displayed on the terminal. In such a case, 75 baud would be sufficient to send infrequent keyboard commands. The engineers imagined rare cases, however, where it would be desirable to transmit large amounts of information over a network. One example provided by the DGT technical documentation involved transmitting the contents of a data storage medium like a memory card via Minitel.[29] Either the user or a remote service sending special commands could engage the flip mode, which could also be used to rapidly transmit data between two Minitels.

Although the official documentation only hinted at this use, the Minitel could act as an external modem for a standard PC.[30] This was an enormous opportunity for microcomputer hobbyists in France. Whereas a comparable PC modem might cost fifteen hundred francs, the Minitel was free. The process of connecting the Minitel to a PC was not simple—both soldering and programming were required—but the cost-saving hack was documented in widely circulated magazines for the microcomputer enthusiast. By the late 1980s, Minitel–PC interface cables were commercially available for PCs such as the Atari ST and Amstrad series.

Whereas modems were relatively uncommon among microcomputer owners in the United States, the prevalence of Minitel meant that nearly all PC owners in France could potentially participate in telecomputing. Taking advantage of this unusually high modem ownership, software makers and service providers occasionally sold boxed software with interface cables included. For example, 3614 Gestcomptes 2 was a personal finance application, not unlike many packages sold elsewhere in Europe and North America. But as the dial-up short code—3614—in its name indicated, Gestcomptes 2 included telebanking features. For users with accounts in compatible banks, the program would use Minitel as a peripheral to synchronize with the remote accounts—no PC modem required. Similarly, 3615 Amstrad, a for-profit archive of software for the Amstrad family of

Figure 2.4 Typical use of semigraphic characters to display images on Minitel. A videotex page about the French Open tennis tournament from 1984. *Source*: Orange/ DGCI référence photo F013262.

personal computers sold a small "download kit" (*kit de téléchargement*) that included a cassette and interface cable. The packaging promised that the "Minitel–Micro" interface would offer access to a wide variety of software programs for no more than the cost of standard Télétel connection fees.

L'écran

As with many early computing systems, the visual apparatus of Minitel is often anachronistically described as "primitive" or "crude," but at the time of its debut, videotex was undoubtedly received as both an informational and *visual* innovation. In 1983, after receiving a grant from the National Endowment for the Arts to start a videotex workshop for artists in the US, marketing researcher Martin Nisenholtz enthused, "The paint is an electron beam, and the canvas is a luminescent bubble of glass."[31]

The Minitel 1B supplied two display modes: *Télétel* mode was for the display of videotex, and *téléinformatique* mode provided an ASCII-compatible text display. Implementing two standards offered advantages to both the end user and potential service providers. For the burgeoning population of informatics entrepreneurs, the twin modes gave them greater flexibility in the design of their services and peripherals. For the user, it meant that their terminal could interface with the majority of information and communication networks in operation: local network and time-sharing systems as well as videotex services. Beyond conforming to the 7-bit ASCII standard, a Minitel in téléinformatique mode could display eighty columns of crisp alphanumeric text—a density of information that would not have been legible on the typical television screen. Téléinformatique mode enabled the Minitel to be used for typical knowledge work such as processing text, manipulating spreadsheets, and programming a database. Although the alternate display mode might have positioned the Minitel as a potential replacement for much more expensive video terminal equipment, it was minimally documented and rarely used in practice. Indeed, videotex is the default setting for the Minitel 1B. Switching modes requires typing an unintuitive combination of keys (Fnct + F, A). Nothing printed on the keyboard or in the terminal's user manual advertised the alternate mode. Remote services could automatically change modes to display a large amount of text, but it is possible that most users never once consciously placed their terminals in téléinformatique mode.

In the early 1980s, although there were several videotex systems in operation, there was not yet an agreed-on standard videotex protocol.[32] The Télétel specification, Antiope, was designed under the leadership of Bernard Marti at the CCETT.[33] The development of Antiope played out against a backdrop of rivalry with the British Broadcasting Corporation (BBC) and British Post Office administrations, which had already developed a functioning teletext standard, Ceefax (literally, a system to "see facts"), and videotex standard (Viewdata, later integrated into the Prestel product).[34]

With the Antiope display system, the images appearing on the screen of the Minitel 1B were produced by a video controller (*un processeur de visualisation*). The video controller includes a character generator with a set of 256 characters—half alphanumeric and half semigraphic characters—represented by pairs of binary octets.[35] Like most European videotex platforms, the display of a Minitel 1B in Télétel mode was divided into a logical grid of forty columns and twenty-four rows.[36] As the Minitel receives characters from the network, serial port, or keyboard, a continuously running program stores them in an area of volatile memory dubbed *la mémoire de page*. Fifty times per second, the display data stored in this area of memory is queried by the video controller and used to update the on-screen display.

Unlike more expensive videotex terminal equipment, including television interfaces, the Minitel 1B could not display color. To accommodate videotex services that were designed for color displays, the video controller behaved as though it were producing a color display. Each time that the controller read the screen status from memory, the data was combined with the character generator to produce an RGB video signal. Before directing the electron ray, however, the color signal was converted into a luminance signal corresponding to a grayscale palette of eight shades against a black ground—for example, blue was rendered at 40 percent luminance, magenta at 60 percent, and yellow at 90 percent. Service providers needed to be aware that many—and perhaps most—of their users would see their interfaces in grayscale.

The character generator was preprogrammed to render both text and graphics on the screen. A preprogrammed ROM chip proscribed the characters available to the generator. Each character in memory was expressed as a "mosaic" 8 *points* wide and 10 *lignes* tall (although most characters occupied only a five-by-seven subset in the top left of the grid). Each ligne corresponded to a horizontal sweep of the electron beam through the cathode tube, and each point corresponded to an opportunity for the beam to change luminance.[37] The default ROM of a video terminal like the DEC VT100 typically included only the fifty-two upper- and lowercase alphabetic characters defined in the 7-bit ASCII standard.[38] For a French-speaking country, of course, this was unacceptable. The Minitel ROM therefore included a superset of the ASCII alphabetic characters including the ligature œ as well as the accented characters à, è, ù, é, â, ê, î, ô, û, and ç. The CCETT research center also aimed at imposing its standard as a European one (again in the context of the competition with the British). For this reason, and based on research by the linguistics department of the nearby University of Rennes, it developed a 334-character set that took into account the needs of thirty-nine European languages, with characters such as ß, ä, ë, ï, ö, and ü, used in Germanic and Nordic languages, and Cyrillic characters in order to demonstrate the system at a 1976 trade show in Moscow.[39] Beyond the alphanumeric characters, the ROM included a set of "semigraphic" characters, defined by painting different regions of the eight-by-ten mosaic (see figure 2.5). When a character is displayed, it is assigned a foreground color, background color, position, and whether it should flash or not. To create all the graphics displayed on the Minitel screen, the characters had to be dynamically arranged and updated on a forty-by-twenty-four grid.

Le clavier

The keyboard was designed under the leadership of Jean-Paul Maury, then head of the digital phone book project at the DGT, in collaboration with the research teams of the Centre national d'études des télécommunications (CNET) and the CCETT.[40] The keyboard of the Minitel 1B is made up of six groups of keys. The familiar alphabetic keys are made of the same material and color as the base of the keyboard, and are labeled with white letters, numbers, and punctuation. Pressing one of these keys causes a numerical code to be sent to the microprocessor. Combining these keys with the "Ctrl," "Fnct," or unmarked "special key" (la touche spéciale) caused a different code to be emitted. Depending on the state of the terminal, the processor will handle these codes differently. For example, in "local" mode, the keyboard code is passed along to the video controller and added to the display. In other modes, the code may be sent out of the serial port or modem to be added to the outgoing data stream.

A group of Télétel-specific "function keys" (les touches de fonction) were colored and shaped differently from the rest of the keyboard. The titles and functions of these keys reflected an arbitrage between different visions of what the keyboard interface should achieve—namely, helping inexperienced users to navigate the system versus improving the speed of interaction for more experienced users.[41] Several keys were intended to facilitate the navigation of form input fields: Suite and Retour moved the cursor from one field to the next, and Envoi submitted the data. The DGT published a set of recommendations for the standard meaning of these keys—for example, Guide should lead to a remote help system—but the

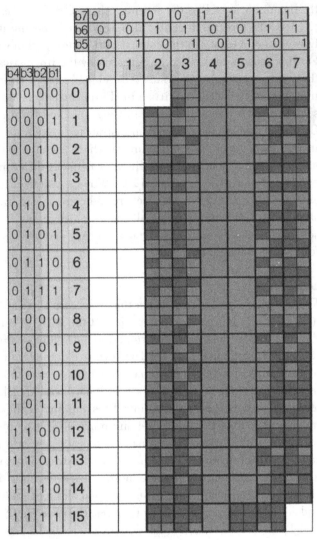

JEU G1
Schéma 2.6

Figure 2.5 Mapping of the semigraphic characters displayed by Minitel terminals to the corresponding numerical codes transmitted along the network. Direction générale des télécommunications, *Télétel, Minitel 1B: Spécifications techniques d'utilisation* (Paris: Ministère des Postes et des Télécommunications, 1986), 101. *Source*: Authors' collection.

final implementation was the responsibility of service providers. Although the function keys could be made to perform a variety of tasks, following the DGT's recommendations helped orient new users and was therefore in the best interest of most service providers.[42]

An additional set of terminal functions was accessible via the keyboard, but not documented on the surface of the device itself. Rather, these functions were listed deep in the technical documentation, out of view of the nonspecialist. These additional functions included taking a screenshot and sending it out via the serial port, switching between the videotex and ASCII display modes, disabling the error correction software, setting the serial port's transmission rate, and "flipping" the modem for a high-speed transfer. To activate these special functions, one pressed a combination of the "Fnct" key and a letter followed by a second key. This unusual sequence of actions seemed designed to limit the possibility that a user would trigger one of these special functions accidentally.

Other Features and Functions

The formula "modem + keyboard + screen" describes the foundation of the Minitel terminal equipment, yet the basic terminal was designed to be a starting point for telematics. The DGT hoped that Minitel would be used both in the home and at the office. Toward this end, the Minitel 1B included a serial port, or *une prise péri-informatique*, expressly to support the integration of Minitel with new and existing computing equipment. Two common uses for the serial port were to connect a printer (*une imprimante*) or smart card reader (*un lecteur de cartes à puce*). Crucially, both peripherals served a data storage function. Prior to the introduction of memory cards, the primary way to capture the information that one encountered on the network was to print it out. Printers were available from multiple suppliers including Epson and France Telecom itself.

Card readers were a less common class of peripherals than printers, but their unique qualities and potential social implications merit a moment's consideration. Smart cards were already in wide use in France as bank cards and prepaid phone cards. The prototypical Minitel card reader was the LECAM, produced around 1987 and rented to Minitel users by France Telecom for a monthly fee. The reader was the same width and depth as the Minitel 1B, and designed to be clipped to the top of the terminal. The reader contained a generally programmable computer that could run software stored on smart cards. This promised to extend the functionality of the standard Minitel in a variety of ways, including turning it into a point-of-sale terminal for processing credit and debit card payments. This application was especially notable at a time when most US merchants still used manual "zip-zap" carbon imprinters to record card payments.

In addition to payment processing, the LECAM documentation suggests a number of other communication applications for the Minitel-connected smart card reader:[43]

- Connecting to a Télétel service automatically
- Authentication and verification of identity to limit access to a server
- Certifying, or electronically "signing," official documents
- Encrypting and decrypting messages sent over the network

Pascal Chours, author of a set of programming tools for LECAM, recalls the smart card reader as a peripheral full of unmet promise. Joking that the designer must have been a "madman," Chours remembers that the Minitel transfer rate of 1,200 baud was too slow for large applications.[44]

If one were willing to purchase or rent equipment, France Telecom offered a variety of Minitel terminals with a greater range of features than the Minitel 1B. The Minitel 12, for instance, included an integrated telephone and special telephony features, such as an account of missed calls and an option to respond to incoming calls automatically with a string of text. Later models such as the Magis included an integrated smart card reader, color screen, and faster modem.

Les serveurs

In contrast to the standardized Minitel terminal equipment, service providers (les fournisseurs de services) were granted a great degree of flexibility in the technical design of their systems. Any hardware or software was permitted as long as its output conformed to the guidelines of the Télétel standard (and even this requirement could be relaxed, as we will see). Indeed, from the perspective of the rest of the platform, the server was effectively a black box with a network interface. Data went in, and data came out. Whatever happened inside the black box was the responsibility of the service provider.

The DGT attempted to encourage the creation of new services by publishing high-quality documentation of the Minitel standard as well as pamphlets detailing design patterns for efficient, user-friendly systems. The investment in developing Télétel services was further protected by the stability of the system. The core characteristics of the platform stayed constant for the system's life. In contrast to the rapidly changing

Figure 2.6   Minitel Magis video terminal with built-in smart card reader. With this particular model, inserting a smart card also woke the Minitel from its sleep state. *Source*: Authors' collection. Photograph courtesy of Jeff Jamison.

microcomputer market, a Minitel service written in 1985 would continue to function, unchanged, in 2012.

The adaptability of Minitel to many different types of servers presents a paradox for our platform-oriented analysis. While a mass-market device like the Minitel 1B offers a stable object for close study, Minitel servers were idiosyncratic, bespoke systems. Documenting the range of different server hardware and software used to host Minitel services is neither practical nor theoretically necessary. Instead, we briefly discuss two exemplary types at opposite ends of the scale—one larger, and one smaller—to outline the range of different server configurations.

A Typical Server

The typical Minitel server was built on a minicomputer running a multi-tasking operating system such as Unix. The capacity of a server to handle multiple simultaneous connections was limited, on the one hand, by its network interface and, on the other hand, by its host software.

Before Minitel rolled into full-scale production and ran over the public data network, Transpac, servers were connected to the telephone network by a bank of modems, each of which could handle one user at a time. Gretel, the service often cited as the origin of messageries, opened in 1981 as an experimental online complement to *les Dernières Nouvelles d'Alsace*, a daily paper covering the region around Strasbourg in the northeast corner of France.[45] Gretel became a platform for real-time discussion thanks to an unexpected appropriation of its support system by local tweens.[46] And yet in spite of its reputation and place in Minitel mythology, Gretel could accommodate only as many simultaneous users as its bank of modems: thirty-two.[47]

To serve greater numbers of simultaneous users, servers needed a direct connection to Transpac, France's public data network. Transpac was a packet-switched network running the X.25 protocol, which was largely based on the work of CCETT researcher Rémi Després.[48] Founded in 1978 as a public information infrastructure, Transpac provided the underlying infrastructure for a number of public and private utilities, including the electronic phone book and interbank check clearing.[49] Connecting to Transpac required service providers to purchase special network interface hardware—namely, an X.25 modem—and use an operating system with support for the X.25 protocol.[50]

Micro-serveurs

Building even a modest Télétel service with a minicomputer and multiuser operating system was more expensive than most individuals and small organizations could afford. For experimenters, enthusiasts, and nonprofits, microcomputers offered an alternative. Just as a PC could be used to host a bulletin board system (BBS), a microcomputer with a modem (or repurposed Minitel) could function as a videotex server.[51] These small-scale systems were generally connected to the standard switched telephone network (*le réseau téléphonique commuté* [RTC]) and accommodated one user at a time.

Known as "micro-serveurs" or "serveurs RTC," microcomputer hosts became more common in the late 1980s, in parallel with the diffusion of BBSs across Europe and North America. Accessible host software packages like Stut One for Atari ST or Cristel for Apple II were written in familiar programming languages like BASIC, C, and 6502 assembly.[52] While most host packages were designed for single user operation, *des serveurs monovoie*, a more powerful micro with a multitasking operating system like the Amiga could interface directly with Transpac and host a fully functional Télétel service.[53] From 1988 to 1996, *Amiga News* covered updates to Amigatel, a commercial Minitel host software package maintained by four developers and sold for a thousand francs.

Minitel service providers took a range of approaches to the construction of their host systems. Whether running a mini- or microcomputer, with a single- or multitasking operating system, connected via RTC or Transpac, the common feature of all Minitel services was an adherence to the videotex specification published by France Telecom. Once a server was programmed to "speak" the language of videotex, it could reliably communicate with the millions of Minitel terminals installed throughout the country. The question that remained was how to connect the terminals to the servers.

Les réseaux

At the start of Minitel, *videotex* was not yet a standardized technology. Terms like *videotex*, *teletext*, and *viewdata* were used somewhat indiscriminately to refer to an emerging family of information services. All these neologisms reflected a sociotechnical imaginary informed by the mass adoption of television and telephony. The promise of videotex/teletext was a convergence of these media—a digital system that combined communication and information retrieval.

Unlike the British implementation of videotex where the production of content and its distribution were completely integrated, the CCETT separated the network protocol (which developed into X.25) from the protocol controlling the visual display of data (Antiope). By separating these two layers, the CCETT videotex system was effectively "medium free."[54] In other words, the French standard for videotex/teletext did not proscribe one or another medium for transmission. Some videotex systems broadcast over the air, and others used wireline telephone or cable television networks. The medium-free quality of videotex contributed to the lingering ambiguity around the terminology. Previously, new communication technologies were defined by their carrier media—consider the role of medium in the description of two-way radio as "wireless telegraphy." The emergence of videotex as a supposedly medium-free medium marked the start of a decades-long period of convergence, culminating in the diffusion of ubiquitous mobile broadband.

In practice, of course, videotex requires a medium to carry information between terminals and servers. The choice of medium has a profound effect on the types of services that can be implemented in a given system. Many of the national projects initiated contemporaneously with Minitel opted for a broadcast model. Systems like Ceefax, operated in the United Kingdom by the BBC, were essentially one-way electronic publishers, distributing content via broadcast that could be decoded and displayed on a home television. Viewers could not transmit back to the broadcaster, nor communicate with one another using the set-top teletext receiver. Nothing like a messagerie could emerge via Ceefax.

Minitel involved a combination of new and old media. In the course of a typical Minitel session, data flowed through both the existing analog telephone system (RTC) and newly implemented public data network (Transpac). The apparent seamlessness with which data flowed between terminals and servers disguised the sequence of encoding, modulating, demodulating, and decoding required to continuously maintain communication over the network. In the ideal case, this chain of transformations felt no different from a direct connection by wire.

Le point d'accès Vidéotex

The final component in our disaggregated Minitel platform is a boundary keeper. The points d'accès vidéotex, or PAVIs, were specialized computers sitting in the logical center of the platform responsible for overseeing the exchange of data between old and new communication media. They were programmed to play gatekeeper, guide, interpreter, and accountant, sitting at the multidimensional crossroads of old and new, analog and digital, telephone and computer, terminal and server, public and private,

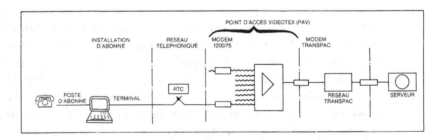

Figure 2.7 The path from a home terminal to a remote server. Note the crucial role played by PAVI as a gateway between the analog and digital networks (réseaux). Direction générale des télécommunications, *Spécifications techniques d'utilisation du point d'accès* Vidéotex (Paris: Ministère des Postes et des Télécommunications, 1987). *Source:* Orange/DGCI.

open and closed. The moment-to-moment operation of Minitel depended on the autonomous supervision provided by the relatively invisible PAVI.

PAVI is a technical term and not widely used in colloquial speech, but the PAVI was an unavoidable part of the Télétel experience. When one first picked up the phone to dial "3615" and begin a Minitel session, it was the local PAVI that answered the call and established a connection with the local terminal. In practice, the PAVI functioned like a computerized switchboard operator.[55] A service running on the PAVI instructed the user's terminal to display a simple interface indicating the cost of the connection, and invited the user to enter either a mnemonic code (for example, PLNUIT) or the number of the service they wished to reach. If the service was found in the PAVI's database of known and approved services, it would attempt to establish a virtual circuit between the caller and remote server.[56] If the service was accessible, it would either connect the user straight away or prompt one to enter a password. If the service was inaccessible or not found, it would return an error message and return the user to the main menu.

To provide a gateway function, the PAVI was composed of five interfaces: a user-facing directory service, a database of known Télétel services, a database of known subscribers, an RTC modem, and an X.25 Transpac modem.[57] The PAVIs were installed in regional switching stations throughout France. Dialing a Télétel short number such as "3615" routed your call to the PAVI located in your regional switching station. Each PAVI was built on an Alcatel-CIT E-10 switch.[58] Whereas the Minitel 1 is a small, approachable device, the E-10 is massive, filling six large cabinets in a temperature-controlled environment.

Beyond its technical function as a gateway router between the RTC and Transpac, the PAVI was the point at which the larger apparatus of the DGT oversaw the activity on Télétel. The PAVI automatically monitored each virtual circuit to facilitate the billing and accounting structure known as "kiosque." It was in this capacity that Minitel operated as a true multisided market, connecting end users to service providers while extracting a toll.[59] The PAVI also played a part in the enforcement of Télétel censorship. If a service was found in violation of Télétel rules, the PAVI would be programmed to refuse to connect incoming callers. The PAVI determined, call by call, which servers were accessible, to whom, and under what conditions.

Les branchements alternatifs

As a cultural phenomenon and because of the platform's modularity, Minitel was not limited to the services accessible through Télétel. Although

Figure 2.8 Photograph of an Alcatel-CIT E-10 gateway. Direction générale des télécommunications, Spécifications techniques d'utilisation du point d'accès Vidéotex (Paris: Ministère des Postes et des Télécommunications, 1987). *Source*: Orange/DGCI.

the PAVI provided access to a range of convenient features, it was not the only option for service providers. Just as the micro-serveur offered an alternative to minicomputer-based host systems, some service providers opted to use the standard switched telephone network rather than register their service with Télétel. Of course, not all RTC services were hobbyist micro-serveurs or privacy seekers trying to evade surveillance. Some large institutions, such as la Banque de l'Union Européenne, advertised both Télétel and RTC access numbers.

Conclusion

As a computational platform, Minitel was composed of three components: terminals, servers, and the network infrastructure to interconnect them. Unlike the videotex/teletext systems being assembled elsewhere in Europe, Minitel was designed to encourage the development of privately owned third-party services. In this respect, Minitel was an early example of a technical platform intended to support an economic platform or "multisided market" by bringing together potential user-consumers with service providers while extracting a small rent for making the match. From a technical standpoint, the platform encouraged the development of both sides of the market in two ways. First, a user-friendly core set of terminal functions was specified and implemented in a device that was distributed to users free of charge. Second, potential service providers were free to choose the hardware and software of their choice as long as their output conformed to a clearly documented protocol.

The full range of services and peripherals built atop the Minitel platform during the 1980s and 1990s could not have been anticipated by the platform's designers in the late 1970s. The technical complexity, thematic diversity, and scale of adoption represented by social computing services like 3615 PLNUIT and la Voix du Parano demonstrate the generativity of the Minitel's minimal design. From the simple combination of "modem + screen + keyboard" to the straightforward videotex protocol, Minitel provided nonspecialist users with an accessible point of entry into the world of remote computing and virtual community.

In the course of everyday use, however, it was easy to overlook the defining role of the PAVI in facilitating the Minitel platform. The Télétel project was intended to modernize French telecommunications, and the often-overlooked PAVI represented the boundary agent negotiating the transformation of data from the analog telephone system to the digital Transpac network. The PAVI was also the site at which policy met technology. The centralized systems of addressing, censorship, billing, and accounting all depended on the PAVI for implementation and enforcement. To understand the tensions between open and closed, centralized and decentralized, public and private that we explore throughout this book, it is necessary to understand the practical function of the PAVI.

In the next chapter, we turn to the political affordances of the network protocols governing the connection between terminals and servers on Minitel. Through this close examination, we uncover the distinctly French character of Minitel.

8:00 p.m., May 10, 1981. The big election night. With the riveted attention of all of France, television screens throughout the country went black in anticipation of the results. From the top of the screen, a seemingly abstract sequence of blue, white, and red lines began to appear—a drawing of the new president elect, rendered in the fuzzy aesthetic of Minitel. At 1,200 baud, the revelation was agonizingly slow. As the image unfurled line by line, viewers shouted out their guesses, filling the houses, apartments, city halls, and cafés of France with excitement. Finally, enough horizontal lines appeared to reveal with certainty that Socialist Party candidate François Mitterrand had won, defeating Valéry Giscard d'Estaing of the center-right Union for French Democracy.

The Minitel screen was a fitting medium for the announcement of France's new president. Profoundly French, from the design room to the users' fingertips, Minitel stood proudly as the pinnacle of centralized State power at work—the poster child of a coming telecommunications renaissance in France.[1]

For France, Minitel represented more than an innovation in data communications. From the start, State policy and national identity were woven deeply into the design and implementation of the system. This chapter discusses the relationship between specific features of the Minitel platform and the French political tradition of centralization. The Post, Telegraph and Telephone Ministry (PTT) at the center of all networked activity plays as a leitmotiv against a backdrop of economic and infrastructure development (the renovation of the phone network and the

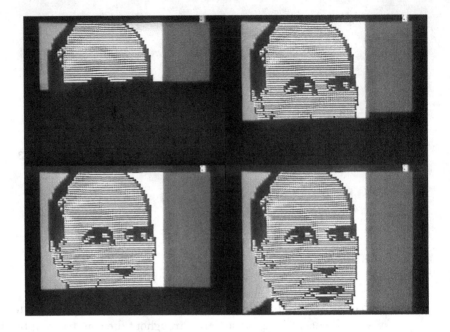

Figure 3.1 In 1981, the election of François Mitterrand was announced on television by way of a videotex portrait of the president's face. Antenne 2, "Election présidentielle 1981: Mitterrand élu," Paris, May 10, 1981, accessed September 18, 2016, http://www .ina.fr/video/I00002041. *Source*: Institut national de l'audiovisuel (INA).

jump-starting of a computer industry) as well as foreign policy antago-nism, with IBM in the role of the US villain.

French Political Tradition of Centralization

In France, the State has historically played a central role in the organiza-tion of social and economic life. This tradition was reflected in the archi-tecture of the Minitel system. From the start of the Capetian dynasty in 987 up to arguably the beginning of the twentieth century, France in many ways had been a fragmented country.[2] As historian Peter McPhee observed, while the 1789 French Revolution sought to overthrow a monarch seen as absolute, "the claim of the royal State to its territory [had been] contra-dicted by ethnic and linguistic diversity." It took hundreds of years for the State to embed centralized power through its institutions and finally be perceived "as the administrative arrangements of an older, deeper univer-sal entity claiming an almost timeless reality."[3] The national myth of an inevitable French universalism implied that humans be identical in all places.[4]

The French State produced a sense of unified, universal nationhood through centralized control of language and enforcement of linguistic rules. Historians Hervé Le Bras and Emmanuel Todd describe France since the revolution as

> a unified administrative system, wonderfully centralized, obsessed with rationality. ... One follows with a manic precision uniform grammatical and orthographic rules recognized as sacred. Nowhere else in Western Europe, is the State more powerful, more dirigiste. Indeed, the State is strong in France because it must ensure the survival of a decentralized anthropological system.[5]

As French Marxist philosopher Etienne Balibar noted, the institution of language is rooted in "the process by which monarchical power became autonomous"—that is, in France, through progressive extreme centralization.[6] James C. Scott remarked that "the imposition of a single, official language" is a crucial element that supports the imposition of vertical State control, for "language represents a formidable obstacle to State knowledge, let alone colonization, control, manipulation, instruction, or propaganda."[7] Centralized control of the French language was enacted through a myriad of institutions. At the top of the pyramid sat Paris along with its ministries, schools, and academies, including the ultimate authority on the French language, l'Académie Française.[8] The centralization of language and culture, quipped Alexandre Sanguinetti in the late 1960s, "permitted the making of France despite the French."[9]

One of the key institutions in the production of modern France was a stratified public educational system topped by the *grandes écoles*—university and graduate-level schools where future civil servants were trained to serve the State and learned the virtues of centralization.[10] Prior to the revolution of 1789, centralization efforts culminated under the leadership of Jean-Baptiste Colbert, Louis XIV's finance minister, whose influence was such that the word *Colbertism* has come to symbolize the process of top-down state planning and mercantilism. Following the French Revolution, the graduates of the grandes écoles would go on to lead the State's infrastructure projects, further unifying the nation through the post, telegraph, telephone, and roadways.[11] It is no surprise, then, that the political tradition of centralization was embedded into the design and implementation of national communication networks.

During the nineteenth and twentieth centuries, several interlocking networks for communication and conveyance were laid atop the geography of France by the State. The tradition of centralization was clearly

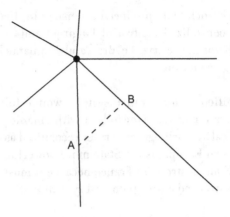

Figure 3.2   Diagram of a Colbertist road network in which Paris is the central traffic hub, and direct travel is impossible between points A and B. Adapted from James C. Scott, *Seeing Like a State: How Certain Schemes to Improve the Human Condition Have Failed* (New Haven, CT: Yale University Press, 1998), 75.

observable in the topology of the resulting road networks (see figure 3.2). Newly built pathways enabled convenient transit between the countryside and Paris while smaller, regional hubs remained largely isolated from one another.[12] Predigital communication networks were designed to facilitate communication to and from the capital city, where control over the entire system was exercised.[13] Scott argued that the "centralizing aesthetic" common to French infrastructure projects preserved strict hierarchical control at the cost of cultural and economic development.[14] Echoing Eugen Weber, Scott concluded that the centralized topologies of these systems were developed principally to serve the needs of government.[15] In Scott's words, the political tradition of centralization was "hardwired" into France's transit networks.[16]

The Plan to Digitize France

The Minitel adventure began as one of France's *grands projets*—ambitious blue-sky efforts designed by State engineers and carried out by domestic industry with little regard for the bottom line. At the start of the 1970s, France was faced with a pair of related problems. The first problem was a crumbling telephone infrastructure in desperate need of attention. The second was a sense of competition with the computer industries in the United States, particularly IBM.[17] Minitel emerged within a grander plan intended to address both problems.

The plan to improve the nation's telecommunications infrastructure was itself driven in part by an existing system on the verge of collapse. At the end of the 1960s, France had one of the worst telephone networks in the industrialized world.[18] The waiting list for a copper pair installation for 90 percent of clients was three years while at the same time in the United States, 99 percent of installs were completed within three days.[19] In 1971, the penetration rate in France was equivalent to that reached by Denmark in 1930, Sweden in 1935, the United Kingdom in 1956, and Italy in 1964.[20] By the mid-1970s, the forty-seven million people living in France were still served by fewer than seven million telephone lines—a penetration rate comparable to that of Czechoslovakia.[21] Rural networks continued to be switched by manual operators; the automation rate in 1971 was equivalent to that of West Germany in 1947, the United Kingdom in 1959, and Japan in 1962—a situation famously mocked in 1955 by comedian Fernand Raynaud.[22] In what remains a favorite skit in France, the comedian joked that the manual switching system was so inefficient that to place a call from inside Paris to the suburbs, the call had to be switched through New York (notice again the anxiety about the US role in controlling French telecommunications).[23] The average wait for urban customers to have a line installed in their homes in fact kept increasing, such as to sixteen months for Parisians in 1972.[24] The situation appeared to be worsening.

In 1975, the government decided to overhaul the country's patchwork telephone network and replace it with a completely automated system. Consistent with the ambition of previous grands projets, the new plan—dubbed "A Phone for Everyone" (un Téléphone pour tous) explicitly sought to provide universal service to both voice and data. For data, a high-speed public packet-switched network was necessary.[25] An upgrade of this magnitude was expensive, however, and the fees generated through telephone calls alone would not be sufficient to cover the added cost.[26] Instead, it was necessary to not only improve on the existing network but also develop novel revenue-generating services that could recoup the heavy investment.

Minitel provided one solution to the steep cost of upgrading the telephone network. As a user-friendly system, Minitel offered a satisfying demonstration of the value of digitization. In addition to this symbolic function, the consumer-oriented Minitel created new streams of revenue for the PTT. Just as the long-distance calling needs of business users generated significant revenue, the profit-seeking services running on Minitel paid fees for their use of the network.

But Minitel was not simply intended to increase traffic over the network or raise revenue. The story of Minitel plays against a backdrop of international relations—in particular, French–American relations in the fields of telephone equipment, computers, information networks, and content creation. The domination of US companies—chiefly IBM—in this set of interconnected fields was perceived as a threat to national sovereignty. President Giscard d'Estaing stated in 1974 that "for France, the American domination of telecommunications and computers is a threat to its independence in the crucially significant if not overriding area of technology and in the field of culture, where the American presence, through television and satellite, becomes an omnipresence."[27] The United Kingdom was also of concern in the teletext and videotex fields. As early as 1974, the State's joint television and telephony research center (the CCETT) began developing Antiope, its own standard for the display of information on video screens, to combat UK efforts to impose its Ceefax and Viewdata standards. In 1976, Giscard d'Estaing tasked Simon Nora and Alain Minc, two top French civil servants, with the production of a report that would address the concerns over the lack of digitization of France, the British threats, and the US threat embodied in IBM.

Nora and Minc's influential report, *The Computerization of Society*, recommended that the French State focus its resources on *telematics*, the meeting of telecommunication and computers. In a society defined by centralization—"publicly criticized and secretly craved"—the authors predicted that widespread telematics would significantly alter the economic, cultural, and political relationships within the nation. New circuits of communication, within and across the nation's borders, threatened to fragment the "social consensus" traditionally maintained by the State's central position in society.[28] In Nora and Minc's account, the development of telematics in France was inevitable. The only question that remained was the role that the State would play.

The conclusion reached by Nora and Minc was that France should enter into the field of telematics without hesitation. IBM, they argued, was undergoing a transition from manufacturing data processing machines to building mass-scale telecommunications networks. IBM posed a challenge that was not simply a matter of competition among national industries, as was previously thought, but rather concerned the administration of a global information infrastructure.[29] Whereas a mainframe computer might be adapted to any number of uses, they contended, IBM intended to maintain administrative control over the networks it was developing. In the absence of a strong national telematics policy, this sort of corporate oversight was likely to come into conflict with the State's interest in maintaining central control over telecommunications. Furthermore, IBM was seen as an agent of US hegemony. Resisting Big Blue was crucial to preventing US influence from taking ahold of France and, by extension, the world.

The future envisioned by Nora and Minc in *The Computerization of Society* was as unsettling as it was exciting. Telematics, by necessity, drew public life into an uncertain space between private industry and the State. The implications that this ambiguity might have for the social life of the nation were yet unknown. "Care must be taken to prevent any portion of the computer industry from dominating any other part," asserted Nora and Minc," and to prevent the industry as a whole from dominating business and the citizenry." Faced with the encroaching forces of industry from abroad, the authors were unequivocal in their support for firm action on the State's part to preserve the nation: "to improve France's position in a contest with competitors not under her sovereignty, the authorities must make unrestrained use of their trump card, which is to decree."[30]

And decree, France did. In 1978, the executive branch of government approved an experimental videotex project.[31] Nora and Minc provided the political impulse. The Direction générale des télécommunications (DGT) was ready to build on several years of fundamental and applied research conducted through the CCETT (Antiope) as well as its own research center, the CNET, which had already developed functioning remote computing systems using the phone network for transmission ("Tic-Tac").[32] So started Minitel.

Centralization in the Architecture of Minitel

The system that became known as Minitel was comprised of multiple interlocking components developed in parallel during the 1970s and maintained throughout the following three decades. The first area of development was in planning and constructing a nationwide digital network; the second was in the design and mass production of terminal equipment for the French citizenry as well as mainframes and minicomputers to host the services; and the third was in the creation of a new administrative institution to regulate the system. Each of these aspects of the system was realized through cooperation between State agencies and private industry while keeping with the tradition of centralization.

The Télétel network featured a hybrid architecture involving both centralized and decentralized characteristics. Users accessed the network through gateways, the PAVIs, which were centrally controlled by the DGT, the telecommunications branch of the French PTT. The number of PAVIs varied over time to alleviate the load on each gateway, but this number is irrelevant for purposes of our analysis: since all gateways were controlled by the monopoly operator, and followed the same access-control rules determined by the operator, access was logically centralized. On the other hand, the servers that hosted content were all privately owned as well as decentralized to the edges of the network.[33] This stood in contrast to the other European videotex experiments, particularly those in England, Germany, and Switzerland, where all content was hosted on centralized servers operated by the monopoly PTT operator. In those systems, potential content providers rented space on a shared central server.[34] In France, however, it was left to the content providers to purchase and administer their own servers. These privately operated machines were then added to the edges of the network through a digital data line leased from the State-controlled public data network, Transpac. In this sense, servers on Télétel were decentralized even as user access points were not.[35]

Data were routed through the Télétel network using the X.25 packet-switching protocol, a standard adopted by the ITU but developed largely in France by the CCETT, a standard that would end up competing with and losing to TCP/IP, the protocol that undergirds most of today's Internet.[36] Routing was handled on Télétel differently from both the X.25 and TCP/IP networks of the period.[37] While the standard X.25 protocol enables all hosts on the network to act as routers, or packet switches, the DGT implementation of X.25 did not.[38] In this nonstandard variant of X.25, therefore, the DGT deliberately prevented the decentralized, privately owned servers at the edges of the network from acting as routers.[39] Only the operator-controlled nodes were allowed to route packets. This meant that virtual circuits that would have been possible using a standard X.25 implementation were prohibited, thereby forcing all user traffic to pass through one of the State-run gateways (see figure 3.3).

The deliberate choice by the DGT to restrict routing to centrally run servers had major implications from the standpoint of economics and free speech. From a practical angle, the main implications are twofold. First, for a server to be accessible by the user, it had to establish a direct connection to one of the gateways. If the DGT decided not to allow a virtual circuit to be established from the gateway to the server, then the server remained inaccessible to end users, effectively "silenced" by the network administrators. This would not have been the case had the DGT allowed privately run servers to act as routers and create virtual circuits that did not pass through one of the PAVI. With regard to free speech, such a technical choice enabled the implementation of the censorship system discussed later in this chapter. By preventing direct, lateral connections

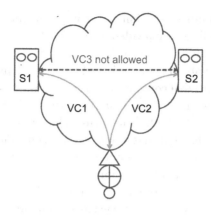

Figure 3.3 Télétel network architecture.

among privately run services, the DGT precisely controlled who was allowed to run a server, and by proxy, who could publish content and provide services.

The second implication of Télétel architecture on the culture of Minitel concerned the interaction of servers with each other. The nonstandard implementation of X.25 prevented a service hosted on one server from directly embedding content or accessing services hosted on another server without first requesting assistance from a PAVI. Thus, in the flow of data among different privately run servers, the PAVIs acted as intermediaries. France Telecom described this functionality as "rerouting," and the intermediary role of the PAVI was clearly documented in materials provided to the developers of new services. This feature placed the DGT at the center of the network's economic activity and enabled it to mediate what would otherwise have been uncontrolled lateral ties—in other words, the nonstandard implementation of X.25 on Télétel reproduced, in digital France, the star-shaped topology of the Colbertist road network (see figure 3.2).

Centralization and Economies of Scale

The Télétel network was just one component of the plan to place a newly digitized France at the forefront of the global telematics industries. Indeed, a crucial justification for building the high-speed data network was to create demand for French-made servers and terminal equipment. The antagonist in this high-tech drama went by three letters, IBM, and the battle played out against the backdrop of intense Franco–American rivalry across many strategic sectors.[40] By aggressively building Minitel, France hoped to jump-start a domestic computing industry and become a leader in the rapidly growing videotex market.[41]

To enable the nascent French computing industry to compete with established players like IBM, the State actively primed the pump by creating programs that commissioned large number of terminals from domestic manufacturers.[42] For example, in 1985, 120,000 desktop computers made mainly by Bull, Goupil, and Thomson were installed into French schools, under an initiative known as *Le plan informatique pour tous*.[43] Such a strategy is particularly effective in an industry like computer hardware that benefits from what economists refer to as "economies of scale."[44] With State programs creating reliable, high-volume demand, French computer makers enjoyed lower average costs to manufacture their products.

As with all communication technologies, realizing the potential value of the Minitel network depended on mass-scale adoption by end users. Indeed, there is a strong feedback mechanism at work in most telecommunication systems. As more people log on, the existing participants benefit as well: chat rooms become livelier, content providers have larger audiences, games have more players, and on and on.

The central problem for attracting users to Minitel was a lack of suitable videotex equipment. At the start of the 1980s, few people in France owned a home computer, never mind a modem or specialized telecommunications device.[45] To overcome this barrier and stimulate use of the system on a mass scale, not only did the DGT forego any sort of basic subscription fee, but it also decided to subsidize the cost of providing a simple terminal to *every single citizen in France*. This highly unusual arrangement ensured mass participation and created an immediate demand for hundreds of thousands (and eventually millions) of durable home terminals.

The wisdom of giving away, rather than selling or leasing, Minitel equipment was not immediately obvious to everyone involved. To justify this massive expenditure, the DGT proposed discontinuing the traditional phone book and replacing it with the *réseau annuaire électronique* (digital phone book network), a telephone directory service running over the same infrastructure as Minitel. In fact, early versions of this plan made videotex use compulsory for all citizens wishing to use the phone book.[46] Although the notion that the DGT might altogether cease publishing a phone book on paper in the 1980s was premature, it suggested a grander future in which numerous State services might be provided electronically, easily recovering the sunk costs of building the network. The DGT proposal was a success, and the State began to place orders for vast numbers of terminal equipment to be distributed among the citizenry.

Although private firms were selected to carry out the manufacturing of Minitel equipment, engineers at the CCETT as well as the DGT itself remained intimately involved in the design and realization of the hardware.[47] According to Bernard Louvel, one of the original Minitel terminal engineers, the development of Minitel was a "very strong human and industrial adventure" characterized by mutual trust along with a "technical bond" between teams at the DGT and in industry. Louvel remembers the early days of Minitel as a uniquely productive partnership between public and private sectors, "inconceivable" today.[48] In the end, it was the centralization of the Minitel project management in the DGT that enabled the private industry to flourish.

Centralization and Billing/Accounting

One key feature of Minitel was its novel billing system, Kiosk (*le kiosque*), introduced in 1984. In the late 1970s, telematics was a niche activity, and the designers of new services struggled to find viable economic models. For terminal hardware, the DGT had already made the radical choice to distribute equipment free to users, thereby creating a critical mass on one side of the market to attract entrepreneurs to the network. It was less clear how network services would be financed, especially since by law, only traditional newspaper companies were permitted to distribute classified ads over Télétel.[49] For Minitel to succeed, it needed a means for service providers to generate revenue from their users.

Many contemporary online services opted to charge a baseline subscription fee for access. This model was adopted by both publicly run networks such as Prestel in Britain and privately operated for-profit services such as CompuServe in the United States. In these early days of telecomputing, however, subscription fees were a major barrier to adoption and contributed to the failure of numerous start-up systems. In 1980, even the geekiest of Parisians was not likely to have had direct, hands-on experience with a computer network. As such, it was extremely difficult to convince people to pay up-front for access. Computer-mediated communication was obscure, difficult to understand, and to some, downright strange.

In light of these conceptual and cultural barriers, the DGT adopted a pay-as-you-play model that did not require an up-front payment or recurring subscription fee to get started. In combination with the freely available terminal equipment, usage-based billing allowed curious new users to explore and experiment with Minitel at their leisure. In fact, users were not required to input any payment information at all. The DGT instead would bill users directly by adding a simple "Télétel use" fee onto their monthly phone bills. Since everyone who had a phone line would get a free Minitel, and since both the Minitel ecosystem and public switched telephone network (PSTN) were managed by the DGT, all one would have to do to use the terminal would be to plug in the electric socket, connect the phone line, et voilà, you were online.

The simplicity of Minitel billing encouraged regular usage. Payment was delayed until the end of the phone billing cycle so the cost of today's use was not felt immediately. Furthermore, the various fees associated with the amount of time one spent online and the individual services that one accessed were combined into a single charge: Télétel use. One charge, one check. Both analog voice calls and digital data services were billed as one, despite the fact that each ran over separate backbone infrastructures.

The Kiosk billing system was, in many ways, the "killer app" underlying the runaway success of Minitel.[50] The Kiosk also reflected the French political tradition of centralization found in so many other aspects of the system.[51] Like the PAVI gateways in which it was implemented, Kiosk placed the DGT at the center of all online activity. It was also the reason why direct connections between privately run servers were prohibited on Télétel.[52] Indeed, the only way for the DGT to accurately bill users (and levy its toll to the service provider) was to monitor all the traffic passing through the DGT gateways, like the toll booths on a freeway or central hub in the Colbertist road network (see figure 3.2).[53]

While State-run gateways were necessary for Kiosk to function, the design and implementation of the Kiosk system itself was not an obvious choice. In fact, many would-be service providers opposed the centralization of all billing in a single State bureaucracy. As early as 1980, the service providers' association indicated that it did not want the DGT to be involved in the commercial side of Minitel: "Billing and collection shall be handled by the service providers only, the DGT must only intervene as an information carrier."[54] Billing, it reasoned, was a site of potential innovation and competition best managed by private enterprise.

Instead of Kiosk, early Minitel service providers requested that a chip card payment technology be implemented.[55] Payments through credit cards could have been accommodated in an architecture where content servers were allowed to act as switches, since all the payment information would have been included in the packets being switched. A chip card system, in other words, would have enabled the decentralization of payment on Minitel.[56] By rejecting the chip card proposal in favor of the

Kiosk system, the DGT established itself as the single administrative gate-keeper of all commercial activity on the network.[57]

The development of the Kiosk system reflected deeply rooted cultural beliefs about the role of the State in society. Minitel engineers had been trained in the grandes écoles—as noted earlier, prestigious schools where the State trained its best—just like Colbert's engineers, whose *esprit géométrique* was the "driving intellectual force behind" the road systems "devise[d] to facilitate central control."[58] It is no surprise, then, that late twentieth-century State engineers mapped the same architecture onto the online world. By implementing a centralized billing system, the designers ensured that the State maintained control over the content and services provided on Minitel.[59] As one of the young engineers who worked on the project later remarked, "The State was the boss. ... [I]t is therefore logical that [the network was] centralized."[60]

The Kiosk system positioned the State as organizer, controller, and taxer of all economic activity. As organizer, it summarily and autocratically decided on and imposed an economic model for an entire industry.[61] As controller and taxer, it built on the old adage "administrative highways ... made for troops to march on and for tax revenues to reach the treasury."[62] Kiosk enabled the State to tax all traffic, just like bridges over rivers once enabled local lords to enforce taxation over passing merchants. Where the passing goods used to be grain, a percentage of which would be taken by bridge toll, they were now bits, and a third of their value would be captured by the DGT as a tax to use the network.

Today, the notion that a single State intermediary could tax all data traffic seems anathema to the design of the Internet as a system with no central authority. And yet for the advocates of Minitel, a central billing system like Kiosk was deemed necessary to stimulate economic activity on the nascent platform. Indeed, Gérard Théry, head of the DGT at the time, would later go on to predict that the Internet would not successfully develop a mass market because of the lack of a centralized, Kiosk-like billing system.[63] How else could service providers accept payment from users? And how could the network infrastructure sustain itself without taxation? While Théry's prediction was not entirely correct—the public Internet worked out fine—his concerns were not unfounded. More than thirty years later, the lack of a trustworthy payment system continues to plague users and providers of Internet services.[64] None of the well-known payment technologies, such as PayPal or Bitcoin, offer quite the same balance of advantages and disadvantages as the Kiosk system. And, as we shall see, the payment structure of commercially successful platforms such as the Apple App Store more closely resembles Minitel and Kiosk than the historically decentralized Internet.

Centralization and Speech

Throughout the life of the Télétel network, Minitel service providers were subject to State censorship. While the term *censorship* conjures images of banned books and jailed journalists, Minitel services were censored according to the strictest legal sense of the term—that is, government authorization was required prior to the launch of any new service. The specific implementation of Minitel censorship varied over time, but the principle of Minitel as a censored ecosystem itself remained constant.

From 1982 to 1986, Télétel publication was subject to a prior *authorization* regime. All proposals for services had to be filed with the prefect, the local representative of the executive branch who responds directly to the prime minister and oversees, among other things, the police force of the department at stake. If the prefect did not explicitly agree with the service coming into existence and grant it a seal of approval, the DGT would not connect the server in question to Télétel.[65] It was thereby excluded from Kiosk and inaccessible to Minitel users.

In 1986, the prior *authorization* regime formally switched to a prior *declaration* regime, in which would-be service providers needed only file a description of their new service with the DGT versus obtaining prior approval from the prefect. This change did not end censorship but rather shifted the gatekeeping role away from the local prefects to a different central administrative authority. After declaring its intent to create a new service, the would-be service provider was subject to a formal review by the DGT to assess whether or not it met the code of conduct embodied in the Télétel contract.[66] If the DGT determined that the service was not likely to meet the code of conduct, an opinion was sought from a second administrative authority, the Telematics Council (CST, *Conseil supérieur de la télématique*). If both organizations agreed, then the DGT could refuse to connect the new service to the network.[67] Although the new system resorted to a contractual mechanism, it was still censorship, since publication was still subject to receiving prior authorization from the administration—in this case, the DGT itself.[68]

The Tradition of Speech Control in France

Minitel censorship extended a particularly French understanding of free speech to data communications. Whereas the freedom of speech in the United States is guaranteed by a *negative* command in the First Amendment—"Congress shall pass no law ... abridging the freedom of speech," the law in France grants the government a *positive* role in the regulation of speech. The practical implications of this role are elaborated in the Declaration of the Rights of Man and the Citizen: "Any citizen may ... speak, write and publish freely, except what is tantamount to the abuse of this liberty in the cases determined by Law." Tasked with the protection of social welfare, Parliament is responsible for interfering with speech thought to be injurious to French society.[69]

The positive role of the French government in the regulation of speech is grounded in an assumption that freedom can be abused by some to hurt others and society as a whole, and that the people as a whole trust Parliament to guard against abuses of freedom by some—an assumption that contrasts sharply with the US tradition of popular sovereignty and mistrust in government.[70] In practice, French positive law offers many examples of broad content control. Explicit prohibitions range from broadcasting ideas in languages other than French, to insulting the president of the republic, to presenting narcotics in a positive light—an offense used to prosecute proponents of marijuana legalization.[71] Citizens accept these constraints with the faith that the State will maintain a standard of protection and mutual respect across society.

Given this tradition, the regulation of speech on Minitel was no surprise. The decision to require prior authorization, though, was a departure from tradition. Under the 1881 Press Act, speakers—including, later, the providers of Minitel services—were punished ex post facto for utterances that violated the law. Beginning in 1982 and reaffirmed in 1986, however, Minitel services were reviewed *before* they were connected to the network. Ironically, the push to this stricter standard was the result of lobbying by the print-press industry to stave off competition from the paradigm-shifting electronic press.

The Print Industry Appeals to Fear

As early as 1979, French newspaper and magazine publishers acutely anticipated the disruptive effect that a system like Minitel might have on their industry. But rather than extend their print businesses to include digital publishing, influential existing publishers endeavored to put regulatory hurdles in place to slow down potential competitors. At the forefront of this effort was the regional press, and especially François-Régis Hutin, the powerful editor in chief of *Ouest-France*, the country's largest-circulation daily. To curry public opinion, representatives of the press crafted an appeal to fear. An unregulated Minitel, they argued, was a platform for antisocial speech and State surveillance.

Coverage of early, small-scale Minitel experiments warned that the "lack of a rulebook" for online service providers would bring about "a certain State of anarchy" in which "everything was permitted and possible."[72] Such worrisome rhetoric rested on a belief that social stability depends on centralization. Remember Sanguinetti's argument that centralization enabled "the making of France despite the French."[73] And recall the "hardwiring" of the political tradition of centralization into France's transit networks.[74] In the realm of speech, this tradition of broad content control was similarly hardwired into the Minitel architecture through the combined action of the censorship system and centralization of technical power in the DGT. Proponents of the censorship system had their way because of the positive role of Parliament set forth in the Constitution: "Any citizen may ... speak, write and publish freely, except what is tantamount to the abuse of this liberty in the cases determined by Law," which implies that freedom can indeed be abused and needs to be curbed by Parliament.[75] According to this logic, tight control over the network was not only reasonable but also essential for the preservation of social harmony in France.

The press lobby, in a brilliantly schizophrenic move, split its public relations campaign in two. It at once called for greater State control of the system, arguing that an uncensored Minitel would lead to anarchy, and ran a parallel campaign warning that the little Minitel boxes represented an incursion of State surveillance into the home, a sortie by a telematic Big Brother. In short, the lobby demanded both that the project be killed and more regulated. And in 1981, Big Brother was not an abstract threat: the shadow of the USSR loomed large in the French imagination.

Hutin led the charge against Minitel in print. In an infamous series of editorials published from May 1979 to May 1981, Hutin warned of the risks that the online age would bring. He also argued that replacing the paper phone book with an electronic one could open France to totalitarianism. "There is no phone book in Moscow," he observed. "An authoritarian power or an invader could very well shut down the electronic phone book." Further, Hutin claimed, for the State to endanger the economic future of the printed press through the development of a State-controlled electronic publishing platform would call into question "the very existence of democracy in our country"—a move (again) reminiscent of "totalitarian States." Calling for regulation, Hutin stated, "Freedom oppresses, regulation frees."[76] Even though Hutin's argument was incoherent at best because it claimed that both anarchy and Big Brother would triumph lest Minitel be regulated, he successfully leveraged deeply rooted political beliefs about the dangers of freedom and importance of regulation. The censor-ship system for Télétel was implemented as a direct result of the mounting political pressure and general sense of unease instilled by Hutin and others in the regional press.

Print publishing was not the only established media industry to exert political pressure on Minitel. In late 1970s' France, both television and radio broadcasting were overseen by a State-run monopoly. Under the umbrella of the Ministry of Information, *Télédiffusion de France* (TDF) remained a staid operation, with an organizational culture descended from the autocratic norms of colonial administration.[77] In parallel with the Minitel project, TDF was planning its own nationwide data network. Unlike Minitel, however, TDF conceived of electronic media as yet another medium for one-way, broadcast communication. Its project, based on the CCETT's Antiope technology, was a simple teletext system. In effect, the DGT and TDF—"hereditary enemies," in the words of one former administrator—were building two different futures for information net-works in France.[78]

The regulation of speech was a key fault line in the conflict between the two agencies. While Minitel was designed for widespread participation by ordinary citizens, the broadcasting agency envisioned data communi-cations as another tightly controlled channel for the centralized distribu-tion of information. The conflict was embodied in the leadership of each agency. Théry, head of the DGT, remembers a visit from Jean Autin, head of TDF. During the meeting, the antagonism between the two agencies settled on the social effects of uncensored public speech. "They came to lecture me," Théry recalled in a recent interview. He believed that televi-sion specialists simply "could not conceive" of building a network to transmit anything other than "administered images," or preapproved material. The broadcasters seemed to believe that an unregulated network would be a race to the bottom. "If you open the Pandora's box," Théry recalled Autin stating, "it will be smut."[79] Rebuked by the DGT, TDF brought its concerns to Hutin, who in turn reiterated the broadcasters' agenda in the pages of *Ouest France*. In the memory of Théry, rising moral panic came to a head as Autin argued, "You will transform France into one giant porno theatre!"[80]

For Minitel advocates, there was more at stake in the regulation of online speech than an ideological commitment to free expression. In France, speech violations are a criminal matter. Well before Minitel reached mass adoption, administrators of the system worried that they would be held responsible for the speech acts of their users. Indeed, in recent interviews about his role as Minitel project lead, Jean-Paul Maury affirmed a legitimate fear of being imprisoned if illegal content was found flowing across the circuits of a public data network.[81]

For the designers of Minitel, one figure appears to have had a surprising influence on the realization of a centralized censorship system: Jean-Jacques de Bresson, head of the Telematics Commission and one of the colonial "old guard."[82] De Bresson made a career as a lawyer in the colonies, in the Ministry of the Interior, Ministry of Information, and then as director of the Office de radiodiffusion-télévision française, TDF's precursor. According to Maury, de Bresson repeatedly threatened him outright with personal liability for the content found on Minitel. De Bresson was said to holler at the engineer, "Monsieur Maury, you will end up in jail!"[83] Michel Baujard, a former member of the Telematics Commission and former president of a Minitel service providers lobby, corroborates this analysis, and describes de Bresson's personality as a "key" to understanding the ways in which the DGT implemented Télétel. In Baujard's account of the period, de Bresson was adamant about the need for censorship. "He was a guy immersed in censorship," recalls Baujard. "He could not reason in any other way than through censorship."[84] These anecdotes underscore the many ways that the French tradition of central control drove the implementation of censorship into the Minitel project at both micro and macro scales.

Chilling Effects

The day-to-day effects of centralized control over Minitel could be hard to spot. By and large, the overwhelming majority of content found on Minitel fit neatly within the bounds of legality. The censorship regime was carried out along two levels: on the regulatory level, all new services were subject to prior administrative review, and on the technical level, all traffic passed through one of the centrally controlled gateway servers. These two prongs seemed to have been sufficient barriers to keep most potential lawbreakers at bay. Likewise, if it appeared that a preapproved service was overstepping the bounds for which it had been reviewed, France Telecom would simply "turn off the faucet," to borrow an expression from Minitel engineer Bernard Marti.[85] In other words, State administrators retained the power, through the design of the PAVI, to simply stop connecting virtual circuits to a remote, privately run server. There were many violations that might lead to disconnection—such as intellectual property violation and administrative technicalities—but the most commonly cited reason was the use of chat rooms by sex workers to pursue new off-line clients.[86] Solicitation of this sort was not only illegal but also caused embarrassment to the State, which was now accused of supporting prostitution. As a result, sexually explicit chat services were monitored and shut down by France Telecom with great zeal.

It may surprise readers from the US to learn that State censors did not otherwise curb the use of Minitel to transmit adult services and content over the network. Indeed, Minitel gained quite a reputation for its adult offerings, dubbed *Minitel rose* or *pink Minitel*. The lively circulation of text-based porn nicely illustrates the character of censorship in the newly computerized France. In practice, Minitel censorship meant only that services could not come online without prior administrative authorization. Typically, the types of services that were blocked were those likely to circulate content that could offend the political sensibilities of the government elite or upset social consensus. The fact that Minitel was the 1980s' kingdom of online pornography—the world's first mass adult market—simply indicates that pornography was not considered by the French executive branch as something that should receive priority attention.

Once approved, however, the providers of adult services needed to vigilantly monitor the activity on their systems lest they run afoul of local censors and find their "faucets" shut off. Pioneers of Minitel rose hired paid staff members to hang out in chat rooms around the clock, and steer conversation away from criminal or otherwise politically volatile topics. Sexually explicit conversation was tolerated—indeed, encouraged—but the boundary between sexy fun and subversive speech was not always clear. This ambiguity was especially difficult for services catering to kinky or queer communities. Daniel Hannaby, cofounder of the popular 3615 SM site, who also leased space on its server to other pink Minitel services, pointed out that censors paid particular attention to gay sadomasochist chat rooms such as the ones hosted on his servers.[87] Jean-Marc Manach, a man who, as a college job, posed as a female guest on multiple Minitel rose chat rooms, described his twin roles as a host tasked with "livening up" discussion while at the same time monitoring the chat rooms and disconnecting undesirable users.[88] These undesirables included prostitutes who used the Minitel rose chat rooms for solicitation—something that could and did at times create criminal liability for the site operators.

But adult services were not the only areas of Minitel affected by the ambiguities of the censorship system. Censorship also created barriers to entry that repelled entrepreneurs whose content was perfectly lawful—indeed, services were often stymied by the bureaucracy involved before they were ever connected to the network. Consider the story of three jobless yet enterprising individuals who in 1985 attempted to launch a Minitel site. Dubbed Amphitel, the proposed site consisted of an online guide for the city of Grenoble and featured online travel services for tourists.[89] The site's founders partnered with the Sopra corporation, a major information technology services provider, and secured funding from Credit Agricole, one of the largest French banks. They were, however, puzzled by the process of getting approved to go online. They first wrote to their congressperson, one Bernard Montergnole, to request assistance in navigating the Minitel regulatory framework. The congressperson, not up to speed with that aspect of the law but eager to support digital innovation in his district, wrote to the minister of communications, M. Georges Fillioud, on February 4, 1985, requesting an opinion as to what authorization must be secured by the enterprising trio in order to roll out their service onto the Minitel network. The communications minister, though, was not up to speed either and had to request an opinion from his legal department. On March 26, 1985, almost two months from the congressperson's letter, the answer came from Jacques Vistel, a State Council justice delegated to the communications ministry, to explain to the minister that if the service is a mere e-mail system, then no authorization was required, but that if the service used electronics as a means of transmitting information to the public, then the entrepreneurs must retrieve official authorization forms from the local prefect and formally request an authorization to provide their service over the network.[90] The prime minister's legal service archives, where this exchange was recorded, do not indicate whether or not this politically correct service ever made it online. Yet the story is indicative of the very real chilling effects created by the centralized censorship system, even for mainstream speakers.

Conclusion

The design and implementation of Minitel reflected a commitment to the political tradition of centralization widely held across French society. Throughout the interplay between different State actors (the PTT, various ministries, administrations, and representatives of the judicial and legislative branches) and members of civil society, the State remained at the center as a micromanager of social relations. The prominent role of the State in jump-starting a telematics system was by no means unique to France—contemporary state-sponsored networks in the United States formed the basis of today's Internet—but Minitel took on an unusual symbolic position in French politics. Struggles between different ministries and their constituents, and high-level arbitrages, indicate that Minitel was used to promote certain industries over others, and fine-tune social equilibriums as France proactively engaged in the "computerization" of society. As such, Minitel was not just the result but also an instrument of centralized State planning, and its architecture reflected century-old traditions of State–society relations.

For many, Minitel was a natural extension of the existing French media industries. Stakeholders in the traditional publishing industries argued that Minitel should be subject to the same broad content restrictions as newspapers, radio, and television. The notion that information "published" via Minitel might be unregulated was not only a challenge to their economic position but also a threat to the stability of French society as a whole. In the French legal tradition, the State is responsible for protecting society from abuses of free speech. Why should Minitel be any different?

The print and broadcast publishers were not alone in their call for centralized State control of Minitel. Labor unions, which generally saw telematics as a driver of industrial growth and job creation, also insisted that telematics be driven by centralized forces. In 1982, the Confédération Force Ouvrière, a communist-leaning union, demanded that the Ministry of National Education provide training at all levels of telematics in order to raise the skill level and international competitiveness of the French industrial sector. The union's demands extended to the content of Minitel as well, warning that a neoliberal "laissez-faire" network would be dangerous to society. Instead, they argued that State regulators should grant authorization to provide services based on considerations of the common good.[91]

More important, the desire for centralized governance of Minitel was shared within civil society, even among groups traditionally separated by ideological differences. Early Minitel users agreed explicitly with the call for central oversight, albeit more tamely than some of the more inflammatory voices. An association of users of Télétel 3V, a small-scale Minitel experiment conducted in 1982, gave technical reasons for the State regulation of Minitel. Faced with the complexity of databases assembled from many different sources, the association reported that the organizational logic of databases and means of accessing them needed to be harmonized, "which is incompatible with total freedom left to service providers. A *central* organization stating minimum common rules seems to be required."[92] This radical statement went beyond the option eventually taken by the DGT, which chose to support Minitel service providers with educational materials concerning intuitive user experience design, but stopped short of mandating any particular structure or interface.

The deeply rooted perception that centralization and a paternalistic State were necessary for harmonious social order was also visible in the organizational relations between different institutions within the State. Ironically, this role is best exemplified by a 1983 report from the prime minister's office discussing the role that videotex should play in supporting decentralization—a move dear to newly elected President Mitterrand. "Telematics must become the instrument of a true regional, departmental, and local information politics, and serve decentralization," read the report. Further, local entities were themselves responsible to "conceive, implement, and manage their own information systems" on the new network. But in France, decentralization was imposed from the top and responsibilities moved downward by the grace of the centralized State. In doing so, the centralized State ensured that uniformity remained the rule, despite the move toward decentralization: "The State has initiated or supported experimental projects. It is now desirable, in the interest of all, that [the State] be present in the development phase. It is also necessary that each region harmonize the different initiatives that will come to light." Local representatives of the central State were therefore called on to coordinate these regional initiatives, and prevent "disorganized development," waste, and other inefficiencies.[93]

In retrospect, the virtues of centralized planning are clear. Minitel was fabulously successful domestically. By 1989, there were approximately five million Minitel terminals in use, leading James Gillies and Robert Cailliau of the European Organization for Nuclear Research (CERN, where the World Wide Web emerged) to describe France as "the world's most 'wired' country" in their published account of the period.[94] Efforts to prime the pump for local industries led to the creation of the iconic Minitel home terminal and created a platform for hundreds of small-scale entrepreneurs to experiment with online commerce. This nascent digital culture industry was further supported by Kiosk, a system that shifted the burden of billing and accounting from the start-up companies to the State, and supplied a reliable, trustworthy method of payment for curious users. In contemporary terms, Kiosk acted much like the Apple Store—offering a central repository of preapproved sites and services along with a convenient means to pay and be paid. Of course, unlike the Apple Store, which is run with the characteristic opacity of a profit-seeking enterprise, Kiosk was run by the State with the public interest as its top priority.

Centralization was not without its faults, of course. By routing all traffic through the State-run PAVI gateways—a prerequisite for the functioning of the Kiosk system—every bit of Minitel traffic was subject to State control. This technical feature facilitated a degree of gatekeeping and proactive censorship on the part of State administrators that would not have been possible were the network run atop a more decentralized implementation of the X.25 internetworking protocol. Lastly, the limits of Minitel censorship and State oversight were rather poorly defined as the wild success of Minitel was largely unexpected and led to mostly ad hoc, pragmatic, behind-the-scenes arbitrages. Undoubtedly, the resulting ambiguity led some users to self-censor as well as refrain from speech that might have been perfectly permissible according to the letter of the law.

US scholars often liken Minitel to a gated community or walled garden, but these comparisons offer a distorted picture of the Minitel platform.[1] Likewise, attempting to demonstrate the benefits of openness by pitting the French model of *dirigisme* against an American model of venture capital overlooks the many features of Minitel that enabled experimentation and entrepreneurship.[2] In fact, Minitel was not a completely closed system but rather a computational and economic platform that displayed many features of openness. The production of new Minitel services was not directed or micromanaged by the State. Rather, the development of Minitel followed a pattern similar in many respects to that of the commercialization of the World Wide Web: public subsidy programs created a platform and drove its exploitation by private industry. We will now discuss four ways in which the State supported openness on the *Télétel* platform, which in turn catalyzed a creative and dynamic private sector for videotex.

A Novel Hybrid Architecture

The development of a vibrant, independent Minitel enterprise during the 1980s depended on a platform architecture that combined elements of centralization and decentralization. Some degree of centralization was necessary for features such as the routing and addressing systems, micropayments system, and privacy protections. Decentralization was also essential, however, to open up the ecosystem to third-party developers. Although it did not quite follow the "end-to-end principle" characteristic of the present-day Internet, the design of Minitel nonetheless afforded freedom and autonomy to the nodes operating at the edges of the network. This combination of centralized and decentralized architectural features has so far been largely ignored—if not altogether denied—by the relevant literature on Télétel.[3]

The push for decentralization was a departure from the French tradition of centralization, both from a liberal ideological standpoint and as a practical means to develop industry. Policy experts Simon Nora and Alain Minc explicitly advocated the transition, and convinced the president of the republic to launch a mass-scale telematics project. They made their case in an influential report titled *The Computerization of Society*, which we excerpt at length:

> Telematics ... allows the decentralization or even the autonomy of basic units. Better still, it facilitates this decentralization by providing peripheral or isolated units with data from which heretofore only huge, centralized entities could benefit. ... It reinforces the competitiveness of the small and mid-size business vis-à-vis the large enterprises. ...
>
> It would, however, be unrealistic to expect computerization alone to overturn the social structure and the hierarchy of power that governs it. The traditions and the cultural model we have inherited from our history favor centralization and administrative proliferation, hierarchic rigidity in big business, and the domination of small business by big business. Our traditions stand in the way of the initiative and adaptability required by a society based on communication and participation. Only a deliberate policy of social change can both solve the problems raised by telematics and utilize its potential. Such a policy implies a strategy based on the balance of powers and counter-powers and on the capacity of the government to favor development rather than impose it. ...
>
> Authorities will develop tools to make their policy work ... by restricting their action and decentralizing when the needed changes require other groups to take the initiative. ...
>
> Anything that increases access to information facilitates dialogue on a more flexible and personal level, encourages increased participation and more individual responsibilities. ... [W]ill we know how to enhance adaptability, freedom, and communication in such a way that every citizen and every group can be responsible for itself? ...

The authorities will no longer be able to call upon the old methods and objectives, which are almost certain to fail. Preparation for the future implies inculcating a freedom that will cause even the most deep-rooted habits and ideologies to lose their validity. This requires an adult society that can enhance spontaneity, mobility, and imagination. ... [I]t also requires a government that—while openly exercising its prerogatives—acknowledges that it can no longer be the only star of the social drama."[4]

With the caveat that foreign server manufacturers benefited much more than French ones, the decentralization of Télétel hosts to the edges of the network achieved just what Nora and Minc foresaw. By allowing private industry to freely exploit the public platform, the telematics program enabled the government "to favor development rather than impose it."[5] In practice, the decentralization of Minitel fostered the development of private industries in hardware, software, and content. Hardware manufacturers were doubly bolstered by this arrangement. First, the State's plan to provide millions of Minitel terminals to the general public created economies of scale in the production of terminal equipment, and second, the requirement that service providers maintain their own servers stimulated the demand for host computers.

In refusing to enter the content industry, and leaving it to the service providers to create, organize, and manage the servers and databases however they wished, the State fostered a new industrial culture characterized by spontaneity, mobility, imagination, and individual responsibility. This was the transformation that Nora and Minc envisioned. The hybrid network design, part centralized and closed, part decentralized and open, contradicts the reductive depictions of Minitel as a top-down, closed, controlled, and inflexible dirigiste system that suffered no nuances. The hybridity of the Télétel architecture is especially pronounced when compared to the architectures of contemporary videotex networks developed in other countries, both by public investment and private enterprise.

Télétel and Its Videotex Contemporaries
In the realm of public systems, the monopoly PTTs in Britain, Germany, and Switzerland, among others, all opted for fully centralized architectures. Videotex content was hosted on servers that were owned, controlled, and managed by the PTT itself. Space on the servers was leased to content providers, which would periodically upload pages on the state-run servers to be published on the state-run network.[6] This arrangement provided no

opportunity for a third party to develop novel software or services for the system.

In contrast to Minitel, the decision to centralize videotex elsewhere in Europe created demand for a few large mainframes as opposed to many smaller host servers.[7] The reason for centralization was simple and political: both the hands of the British and German PTT were guided by mainframe maker IBM.[8] Indeed, in the mid-1980s, sociologists Renate Mayntz and Volker Schneider wrote that the German system as a whole was "designed and implemented by IBM," whose strategy was "to create [and host] one single big database."[9] From the point of view of a mainframe manufacturer, complete centralization was merely common sense. This had been the standard approach to institutional computerization throughout the postwar period.[10] In fact, when the French Direction générale des télécommunications (DGT) designed its only online information service, the electronic phone book, it also centralized all the content on a few PTT-run servers. But Télétel was different. Instead of sponsoring one hardware manufacturer that would also maintain all the databases, the French government aimed at giving the means to multiple hardware manufacturers to compete and thrive.

The decentralization of Télétel unleashed private innovation in the development of content and services. "The most striking difference between Télétel and the other systems," concluded Mayntz and Schneider, was "its complete decentralization" at the level of content providers. This difference in design had "far ranging implications for the flexibility of adapting to the users' changing needs."[11] It is a lot easier for a service provider to constantly update its content when it has control over its servers than when it needs to request that the PTT implement changes on its behalf in a central IBM mainframe.

The autonomy of service providers is particularly important for enterprises that succeed or fail based on the timely distribution of information. The bottleneck on content creation hardwired into the architectures of centralized videotex systems certainly played a large role in their failure to develop a private industry.

The problem with the British, Swiss, and German videotex systems was centralization, not necessarily public control. This subtle distinction is illustrated by a comparison between Télétel and a failed attempt by France Telecom to implement a similar system through a private corporation in the San Francisco Bay Area in 1991 under the name 101 Online. There are many reasons why this experiment failed, but a major problem was that France Telecom abandoned the hybrid architecture of Télétel. Instead, the implementation of 101 Online more closely resembled Prestel,

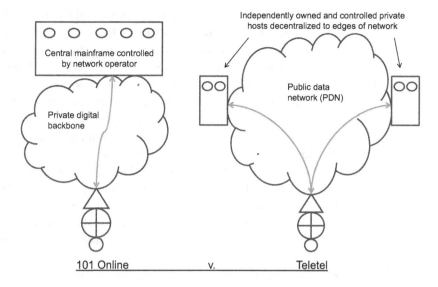

Figure 4.1 Comparison of 101 Online and Télétel network architectures. Julien Mailland, "101 Online: American Minitel Network and Lessons from Its Failure," *IEEE Annals of the History of Computing* 38, no. 1 (January–March 2016): 6–22.

BTX, and US videotex systems such as CompuServe and the Source.[12] Instead of distributing the servers to the edges of the networks as it had done in France, and thus fostering independent entrepreneurship, 101 Online centralized all content on a mainframe it controlled.

The design of the 101 Online network was very much operator centered. Third parties were welcome to create content for 101 Online, but they were afforded little autonomy. Indeed, every time that a service provider wished to make a change to their content, someone had to physically travel to the 101 Online office in downtown San Francisco and ask the 101 Online editor to make the changes in the mainframe on their behalf. This was not quite a conducive environment for spontaneity, mobility, imagination, and individual responsibility, to once again borrow from Nora and Minc. As decrypted in retrospect by a lucid Jean-Eudes Queffélec, 101 Online's director of sales and marketing, "We did not create an ecosystem enabling anyone but us to make money." In contrast, in France, the DGT was part of something bigger: a plan decided by the president of the republic himself to boost private enterprise—hence, the decentralization of the hosts to the edges of the network. This comparison is particularly relevant because the network designer is roughly the same in both the Télétel and 101 Online cases: the DGT in France, and a France Telecom affiliate in the United States.

Beyond the French servers operating at edges of the network, Télétel also provided gateways to data networks, public and private, emerging elsewhere in the world. This interconnection contradicts the portrayal of the system as an exclusively national network.[13] The design of Télétel followed a clear goal of the Nora and Minc report insisting that French telematics policy should "improve [France's] ability to compete [globally] and open new markets."[14] From an export perspective, Télétel was accessible to users in foreign countries using either a Minitel terminal or a PC outfitted with a software emulator through a dedicated French phone number. From an inbound perspective, the Télétel ecosystem was open to and interconnected with foreign public data networks, and open to foreign content. The short code to access the international gateway portal was 3619—from there, one would type in the region and then the specific code of the service. For example, one could access the nascent Internet from a French Minitel for 2.19 francs per minute by dialing 3619 ETATS - UNIS + USNET.[15] Newspaper *Libération* even published a joke article giving a tutorial for finding the phone number for the Pizza Hut of Wichita Falls, Texas, through the 3619 Siriel international gateway service.[16]

Let us not overstate the simplicity of becoming a participant in the ecosystem, however. While Minitel was completely plug and play for the end user, it was somewhat more complex for service providers. Daniel Hannaby evokes his experience actually connecting his servers for his 3615 SM site to the Transpac network:

It was a complicated process. It took a few months because … we were not in this business before. … We went to see France Telecom [and] they had to explain [to] us how it worked, so we went to buy these boxes to connect Transpac in a certain [place] in Paris that was the only reseller of these boxes. And well, it took a few months.

On the economical [side]—the nice thing about France Telecom and Minitel was that they gave this [away] for free. [That] was fantastic because [they were] able to create a nice ecosystem of companies that were able to [make] money [from] it.

It was, for the companies, a bit complicated because they had to create these softwares, specialized software, to connect to Transpac. So, we had at one point black boxes that were in front of the computers to translate the X.25 coming from the lines into something that the computers would understand. But beside that, the architecture was really something—it was a choice between this and, of course, IP, TCP/IP, but it did a really good job. So, I can't complain.[17]

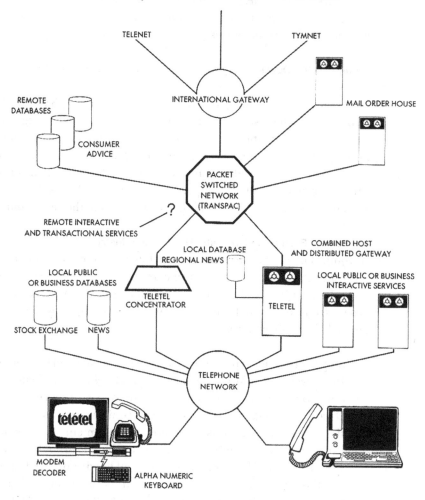

□ Intelmatique
FRANCE

Complete Teletel Videotex Network

TELENET

TYMNET

INTERNATIONAL GATEWAY

MAIL ORDER HOUSE

REMOTE
DATABASES

CONSUMER
ADVICE

PACKET
SWITCHED
NETWORK
(TRANSPAC)

REMOTE INTERACTIVE
AND TRANSACTIONAL SERVICES

?

COMBINED HOST
AND DISTRIBUTED GATEWAY

LOCAL DATABASE
REGIONAL NEWS

LOCAL PUBLIC
OR BUSINESS DATABASES

TELETEL
CONCENTRATOR

LOCAL PUBLIC OR BUSINESS
INTERACTIVE SERVICES

TELETEL

STOCK EXCHANGE   NEWS

TELEPHONE
NETWORK

télétel

MODEM
DECODER

ALPHA NUMERIC
KEYBOARD

Figure 4.2   Expanded diagram of the Télétel platform including gateways from Transpac to Telenet and Tymnet, two commercial public data networks based in the United States. Intelmatique, *Télétel Videotex*, February 1982. *Source*: Orange/DGCI.

All in all, the French content industry was highly successful domestically, and decentralization of the servers to the edges of the network was a key part of that success. The benefits were not limited to the service providers, though. Next, we examine how France Telecom leveraged the hybridity of the architecture to promote the development of private hardware and software industries.

Catalyzing the Development of a Domestic Computing Industry

Nora and Minc chose to portray IBM as the prototypical US villain. Decentralizing the Télétel servers to the edges of Transpac and giving operators "free rein" to assemble their own host systems was meant to catalyze the development of a vibrant French computing industry.[18] The plan worked, insofar as industry development is concerned. But while domestic enterprises flourished in the development of software and consulting services, foreign manufacturers like IBM quickly dominated the server industry.

Challenges Facing the Domestic Hardware Industry

In 1989, Bull was the flagship of French hardware manufacturing. It was the leading manufacturer in Europe and the seventh-ranked manufacturer worldwide.[19] And yet at the same moment, Bull was conspicuously absent from the Minitel scene. As summarized in 1988 by Marie Marchand, a France Telecom researcher,

> Steps were taken to promote what French industry had to offer by using Honeywell Bull's Mini 6 computer, Intertechnique's Réalités 2,000 and 5,000 models, and Thomson's Microméga. France's Agency for Data Processing, the ADI, had taken a similar tack by subsidizing the first videotex operations using French equipment. But despite such backing, French manufacturers would not be able to hold on to the host systems market, from which they have all but disappeared in 1987.
>
> From the outset foreign manufacturers carved out a share of the market. IBM, DEC, Hewlett-Packard, ATT/Olivetti, and McDonnell-Douglas supported systems and software houses in their approach to videotex. They knew how to adapt to market trends; they had a range of marketing techniques and product lines that meshed with the needs of service providers. When in the early going, high-capacity host computers were called for, they had just what the doctor ordered. When around 1982–83, microcomputers were needed, they were able to meet the demand, and in 1984 they supplied the megamachines necessary for seeing through a mass-market strategy.[20]

Beyond marketing, another set of factors was driving the adoption of US computers: the preferences of the programmers and system administrators tasked with building Minitel services. During the 1980s, a generation of software engineers and system administrators were trained on campus computer systems running Unix, and they carried a preference for this "open" operating system into their professional lives.[21] As US computers tended to accommodate more operating systems and programming languages than their French counterparts, US manufacturers came to dominate the field of Télétel hardware. Hannaby, for example, recalls choosing AT&T servers to host his site specifically because the French-made Bull systems did not handle Unix: "We had to go onto something that was using Unix because our system was Unix based. We found that AT&T was using these 3B2 and 3B5 computers, Unix based, and they were sold by Olivetti [the Italian company] at that time."[22] Taranis, another consulting and hosting firm, similarly relied on Unix-compatible minicomputers from Texas Instruments—namely, the BS 300, 600, and 800 models—for its infrastructure.[23] In contrast, Marchand notes, "Other host systems remained tethered to the [Bull] Mini 6 or equivalent hardware [that was not Unix compatible] and dropped out of the consumer videotex market one by one."[24] By allowing service providers to build their own host systems, the State may have stimulated the growth of third-party services, but it was up to French hardware manufacturers like Bull to exploit this opportunity by meeting the demand for Unix among technical professionals.

Many Minitel services were built by consulting firms specializing in videotex rather than by in-house developers. As a result, the preferences of busy consultants had an outsized impact on the market for Minitel hardware. Jean-Louis Fourtanier was one such consultant who preferred Unix "both in terms of quantity and quality."[25] Fourtanier's consulting and hosting business, CTL, was used by many of the largest Minitel sites, including Crac, Aline, Anabelle, the public television station FR3, and eventually all the properties of Le Nouvel Observateur, one of the top promoters of services.[26] Since Fourtanier swore by Unix, he "invested in hardware that operated under Unix"—in this case, Hewlett-Packard.[27] Once a machine gained a reputation as a reliable platform for a Minitel service, it was more likely to be used in the future. Hannaby remembers noticing that Olivetti started selling many Unix-compatible AT&T 3B15 minicomputers after he used one to build a Minitel server.[28] Large institutions were even more likely to stick with familiar brands. When Crédit Foncier de France, the first French bank to offer its services over Minitel, had to choose a system, it went with something "muscle-bound … an IBM 3081 CPU with two front-end communications units and 400 access points."[29] Apparently no one was ever fired in France for buying IBM, either.

Opportunities for the Domestic Software Industry

In contrast to their hardware industry counterparts, independent French companies in the realm of software and database consulting as well as those (often the same) that offered hosting services were able to reap the benefits of the openness features of the Télétel platform. In addition to the traditional powerhouses such as SAGEM and Capgemini, a plethora of midsize and small software consulting houses thrived in that market. A ten-page France Telecom directory from April 1986 listed over 230 such firms.[30] By April 1990, that directory's pages would number seventy-seven.[31]

The hybridity of the Minitel platform, with decentralized hosts operated, designed, and maintained by private parties, exhibited a kind of openness that was not present in the other videotex systems of the time. By operating as an open platform, Minitel supported the development of dynamic and competitive hardware and software industries. Let us now observe how the State, far from being dirigiste, applied a venture capitalist approach to catalyze what would become a booming and wealthy private content industry.

Venture Capitalism à la Française

With Minitel, the State built a generative platform for developers through the combination of the *kiosque* billing system and the distribution of free terminal equipment. By threatening to discontinue the phone book and provide an electronic phone book service instead, the State forced free terminals onto the populace and the pump was primed on the user side of the market. The resulting base of potential consumers was enough to attract service providers to the platform. But the State also spared no expense in priming the service provider side of the market as well. The goal was to catalyze the development of a domestic content industry to rival the global hegemony of the US media industries. The DGT supported potential service providers in four ways: intensive, large-scale testing; openly sharing design research and expertise; sponsoring professional education in the realm of videotex; and subsidizing select services in ways that resembled the public–private partnerships that led to the rise of Silicon Valley and subsequent dot-com industry.[32] All in all, the State acted much like a venture capitalist, offering financial support and organizational guidance to budding Minitel service providers.

The Circulation of State-Sponsored Research

Following the executive decision in 1978 to launch the telematics program, the DGT initiated two live experiments. First, in the region of Ille-et-Vilaine, it provided twenty-five hundred users with various experimental terminals hooked up to an online phone directory. Second, in the cities of Vélizy, Versailles, and Val de Bièvre, in the suburbs of Paris, it recruited another twenty-five hundred users who would connect to eighty services providing a total of thirty thousand pages of videotex content. This project was named Télétel 3V, or T3V, after the three cities.[33] The two experiments would provide fruitful lessons in computer ergonomics and human–computer interaction. For example, some of the keyboards were laid out in alphabetic order to test the hypothesis that users unfamiliar with typing would find it easier to input commands. As it turned out, new typists were agnostic to the layout, whereas experienced users found it more difficult to use, as they were accustomed to an AZERTY layout.[34]

The experiments in graphical user interface design were published in the form of a book, *Communiquer par Télétel*, which targeted potential service providers and gave them advice ranging from organizing the logical tree structures of sites to best practices in color coding.[35] It is worth noting that where the DGT had single-handedly imposed the choice of the X.25 network protocol, in contrast, it never required the service providers to use a particular structure or interface design at the application layer. Unlike, say, the 101 Online venture, service providers were free to organize their services and content however they liked. But France Telecom offered its recommendations as a means of helping the new, independent industry succeed. France Telecom then produced a number of free brochures on a variety of topics, including becoming a service provider, designing a messaging system, and building an interface as well as general information and statistics regarding the T3V experiment.

Over the course of the Minitel years, France Telecom published a large number of sophisticated brochures, printed on appealing glossy paper, covering a range of topics from recommendations on graphical user interface standardization to full technical specifications for every piece of the platform: terminals, PAVIs, protocols, and so on. France Telecom also published a quarterly newsletter, *La Lettre de Télétel* (Télétel letter), informing industry participants of the latest technical improvements to the platform and business experiments by service providers. This large corpus of reference material and market research was available free of charge to support third-party service operators.

The combination of centralization and decentralization in Minitel enabled France Telecom to develop and circulate expertise regarding the

Figure 4.3 Technical documentation for designers of videotex services. Direction générale des télécommunications, *Spécifications vidéotex de visualisation et de codage* (Paris, France: Ministère des Postes et des Télécommunications, circa 1980). *Source:* Orange/DGCI.

design and maintenance of videotex operations at a pace that was not possible elsewhere. First, it was easy to gather information about services and their users on a large scale via the PAVI. Second, because the network operator was not competing with the service providers, it openly shared the results of its analyses. This openness and cooperation stood in contrast to the contemporary situation elsewhere on both counts. For instance, the myriad of small-scale videotex services in the United States did not benefit from the experience and know-how that France Telecom was able to develop through lengthy tax-funded experiments and mass-scale

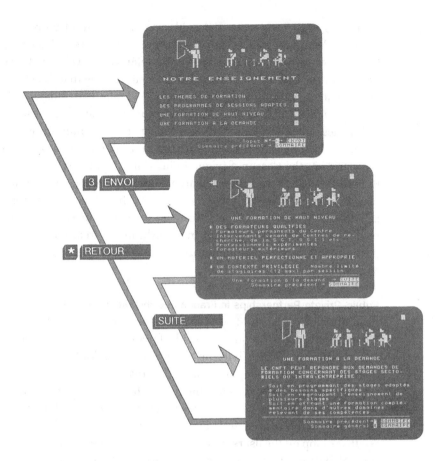

Figure 4.4 France Telecom documentation included detailed examples demonstrating how to design videotex services that would be easy for users to navigate. In this picture: the tree structure and use of function keys suggested for Télétel sites. Ministère des PTT, *Recommandations aux partenaires Télétel*, (Paris: Ministère des PTT, 1986), 11. *Source*: Authors' collection, donated by Jean-Luc Beraudo De Pralormo.

adoption by users. Even when they did gather information on a large scale, companies like the Source or CompuServe had no incentive to share it with their competitors. In this respect, then, the centralized, state-funded nature of the Minitel platform enabled an element of openness with regard to design expertise and directly contributed to the blossoming of private, for-profit operators. And because every Télétel connection generated revenue for the DGT, the State stood to benefit from the success of any service using the platform. Venture capitalism, *à la française*.

In addition to openly publishing research, recommendations, and statistics about its experiments, the State supported a number of initiatives to directly train and guide would-be Minitel entrepreneurs. France Telecom created a school for Minitel developers called the Centre national de formation aux usages de la télématique (National Training Center for the Use of Telematics). It provided training that closely resembled what an executive graduate program looks like today, including courses in the fundamentals of network economics, and practical training in business plan development, legal aspects of telecommunications networks, and applied electrical engineering and computer science. It located the school in the Cesson-Sévigné industrial zone that was already home to both the CCETT and DGT research centers as well as major industrial players such as Thomson and Transpac.[36] The DGT itself occasionally acted as an ad hoc incubator. During trade shows, for example, the DGT hosted small service providers in its exhibition area, and supplied all participating service providers with hardware and other equipment, free of charge.[37]

Public–Private Partnerships in France and the United States

Beyond the training and free research, a number of Minitel service providers received a direct public subsidy. Financing for these entrepreneurs was supplied by France Telecom itself; the *Caisse des Dépôts et Consignations*, the French development bank that invests in private ventures "in support of the public policies implemented by the State"; and public banks such as the Crédit Lyonnais.[38] These monetary infusions further primed the pump on the service providers' side of the market, creating a positive feedback loop on the users' side: more services attracted more users. This form of State intervention did not involve central control over the creation of content, however, nor did it otherwise bear the mark of dirigiste micromanagement. Quite to the contrary, public subsidies for new service providers supported the development of an unbridled private industry, from mainstream information applications to the frequently edgy *messageries* (chat rooms).[39]

From the standard Silicon Valley perspective, it is tempting to assume that because third-party service providers were subsidized by the French State, then the overall Minitel ecosystem must have been State-controlled or strangled by bureaucracy. On closer inspection, though, the public–private partnership driving the development of Minitel looks very much like the public–private partnerships that led to the commercial exploitation of the packet-switched Internet in the United States.[40] Indeed, the rhetoric surrounding US information infrastructure projects of the 1980s and 1990s mirrors many of the ideas developed by Nora and Minc. When then US senator Al Gore explained the significance of the

High-Performance Computing and Communication Act in 1991, he emphasized the importance of information infrastructure for the future of US hegemony: "The nation which most completely assimilates high-performance computing into its economy will very likely emerge as the dominant intellectual, economic, and technological force in the next century."[41] This rhetoric justified the allocation of billions of federal dollars to the technology sector and the creation of a venture capitalist investment firm by the Central Intelligence Agency that financed over 180 private firms.[42] Evan Sutherland, vice president of Sun Microsystems Laboratories, later acknowledged that the thriving tech industries were facilitated by "decades of consistent federal investment in information technology research," and Marc Andreessen, founder of Netscape, bluntly stated that if development had been left to the private sector, "it wouldn't have happened."[43]

Certainly, the DGT was more hands-on than the Advanced Research Projects Agency (ARPA) or the National Science Fountation (NSF), as it required Transpac to use a network protocol that it had developed itself rather than leaving the decision to either the preferences of researchers or forces of market competition. But extending the meaning of this intervention to say that the whole Minitel ecosystem was subject to dirigiste forces, or worse, was "doomed by ... excessive culturalist policies," as one scholar put it, is inaccurate.[44] Likewise, using the fact that the taxpayer paid to build the Transpac network to distinguish the US and French models is a fallacy; the US taxpayer subsidized several networking projects including ARPANET and NSFNET. Indeed, the hybrid architecture of Télétel requires a more nuanced description of State intervention than simply calling it *dirigiste*. While intervening *à la française* at certain levels, for example, by picking the network protocol and centralizing certain aspects of the platform, the State also very much acted like a venture capitalist, investing in emerging service providers and thereby enabling private sector innovation at the edges. And in spite of its investment, the State did not guide the hands of private developers but instead left them free to create and promote their own content and services (to wit, the rise of the pink messageries).

Walled Gardens, Gated Communities, and Shades of Openness

Minitel has been dubbed a gated community, and compared to "walled garden" services like CompuServe and America Online.[45] While there certainly are elements of closedness in the platform—chiefly, the State gateways and censorship regime—the description of Minitel as "open" or "closed" requires some clarification. Just as the technical architecture of Télétel was not strictly end-to-end but still fostered innovation from the edges, content circulated on Télétel was censored and open at the same time. In spite of the censorship regime, Minitel service providers certainly enjoyed greater freedom than their US videotex counterparts—perhaps even more so than later entrepreneurs working within twenty-first-century walled gardens such as the Apple App Store.[46] The comparison between Télétel and US-based walled gardens makes clear that the mere existence of a censorship regime did not mean that Minitel was in thrall to a totalizing form of authoritarian state control, as is often believed. Indeed, the practical experience of content regulation on Minitel underscores the need to approach the theoretical concept of "openness" with nuance.

There is no technical definition of *walled garden* (also known as *gated community*) in the realm of information networks.[47] Yet in the United States, *walled garden* is a colloquialism that refers to an information system in which the service provider exercises final authority over the content and services accessible to users. In that sense, a *walled garden* is a censorship regime (where the prior approval of the network operator needs to be secured before information is published) as well as a regime where a central operator can kick content out of the gated community *ex post facto*, at will. This filtering may be based on legal grounds (e.g., the removal of unlawful content), but it may also be based on any number of criteria such as quality or business grounds elaborated in a "terms of service" agreement. Facebook's behavior in this respect is a good illustration of a platform that, albeit seemingly open at the user level, exhibits features of gated communities.[48]

The walled gardens model is also associated with centralized systems such as the videotex networks emerging outside France at the same time as Minitel, such as Prestel, BTX, and 101 Online. In the 1980s, CompuServe centralized the hosting of services that it had picked as part of business negotiations with external content providers, and such negotiation often led to certain content being removed or replaced. In 1983, for example, the online version of the twenty-volume *World Book Encyclopedia* was simply removed from the CompuServe walled garden and replaced with the Grolier electronic encyclopedia.[49] Overnight, CompuServe users lost access to the *World Book* content. Likewise, the Source (the online arm of *Reader's Digest*) hosted all its content in a central facility in McLean, Virginia. In March 1983, the Source announced a new policy for curating the content on its platform: "THE SOURCE notes that new products are receiving close scrutiny based on likely long-term usage rates, as opposed to 'attention-getter qualities.' This relatively new policy has led to decisions to drop a number of previously anticipated new products, such as an electronic encyclopedia."[50] By taking an active editorial role licensing and soliciting content and services, early online services like the Source acted more like newspapers or radio stations than platforms.

The walled garden model and associated censorship regimes are not unique to early online systems. Since opening the App Store in 2008, the Apple iOS ecosystem has exhibited a hybridity similar to Minitel's. Third-party developers build applications for Apple devices that can only be accessed through a centralized platform. Nearly all third-party apps are sold through the App Store where Apple acts as an intermediary, handling payments and taking a percentage of all sales. As part of the platform operation, Apple vets all potential applications and reserves the right to unilaterally remove any app or developer.

While the App Store has created a new commercial opportunity for small-scale software enterprises, Apple's autocratic control of the platform routinely leads to conflicts with developers. In 2010, Apple removed the WikiLeaks app from its App Store, making it more difficult for iPhone users to access content published by WikiLeaks. The decision by Apple to block access to WikiLeaks through its platform was not motivated by any legal mandate—WikiLeaks was protected by the First Amendment—but rather by public relations considerations. Vice President Joe Biden had called WikiLeaks founder Julian Assange "more like a high-tech terrorist than the Pentagon Papers," and Apple did not wish to be associated with that image.[51] Unlike Minitel, with its implied commitment to the French public interest, privately run platforms like CompuServe and the Apple Store are governed by an opaque, centralized form of authority—gated communities à l'Américaine.

To understand Minitel as a kind of a walled garden, it is useful to directly compare Télétel with US walled gardens along four dimensions: the motivation for censorship, implementation of censorship, recourse available to censored service providers, and censorship of individual users.

First, the only element of the Télétel platform common to a walled garden is the censorship regime. In practice as well as policy, prior authorization from the executive branch of government (and later France Telecom) was required before a service could be connected to Transpac. The prior authorization regime, however, was not part of the original design of Télétel and was imposed solely because of pressure from the existing media industries, which were concerned (rightfully, it turns out) by the competition from electronic publishers. Originally, the DGT wanted to apply common carrier principles to the network and implement the policy we now refer to as "net neutrality"—that is, to not discriminate against packets based on the identity of the speaker or the content at stake. Until the election of Mitterrand in May 1981, internal notes from the prime minister's office focused on common carrier and content neutrality principles as cornerstones of the nascent network's organization. F. Froment-Meurice, of the government general secretariat, asserted in 1980 that "we do not find any legal basis under which the administration could impose to TÉLÉTEL's 'service providers' a 'code of conduct' containing clauses relative to the content of data transmitted, to a right of reply, etc."[52] Similarly, one month before the election of Mitterrand, Pierre Huet, a State Council justice and the head of the ad hoc Telematics Commission, stated, "The administration must also respect the principle of equality of users."[53] In June 1981, debriefing the new, Mitterrand-appointed PTT minister, Huet reasserted and detailed the implications of this principle, noting, "The PTT Code applies: it grants the telecommunications administration a monopoly of transmission of mail correspondence, and in turn the administration is bound by public service obligations (freedom of access, mail secrecy)."[54] The analogy used by the justice rested on the traditional-mail common carrier principle: a monopoly is granted to the carrier, which in turn cannot look into the content being transmitted over the network, and cannot discriminate based on content or user group.[55] Ultimately, the pressure of the press lobby was such that the executive branch, and then Parliament in 1982, imposed a censorship system in order to reach a truce with the lobby and be able to move on with Télétel.[56] The only walled garden aspect of Télétel, therefore, was not the result of a desire to control the network on the part of the State, as is often maintained. Quite to the contrary, the censorship regime was the result of lobbying by one private industry sector trying to prevent the emergence of competition from another, emerging private industry sector.

Second, because of the requirement of due process to which the State is bound, even with the censorship system in place, access to the Minitel platform was much more open than in the typical walled garden scenario. In the United States, because the censorship takes place in the private realm, there is no legal recourse for service providers that are shut out of a walled garden. If Apple does not want an app to be part of the iOS ecosystem, the developer of the app cannot sue Apple. In contrast, because Télétel was a public platform managed by the State, French service providers were afforded due process. Only illegal content could be rejected, not content that the platform operator did not like. Thus, the public management opened the platform up in ways that have not been realized elsewhere. In contrast, apps like WikiLeaks get rejected by Apple based on business considerations, even though their content is protected by the First Amendment.[57] The administrative process through which the censorship system was administered, although complicated, was also transparent. If a service provider was not satisfied by the outcome of the administrative process, it could sue the State in court. So while the platform was not fully open and chilling effects certainly existed, due process principles ensured that legal content could eventually make it through—a level of openness that has never existed on the prototypical walled gardens built in the United States.

Third, once the service provider was approved, it could not get kicked out of the ecosystem lest the content turn out to be illegal. This again is an element of fairness—not to mention openness—that contrasts with US gated communities.

Finally, in the context of the messageries, once the provider of a messageries service was approved by the DGT, all the users of that system became de facto content producers. *Publishing*, in this sense, included all the messages posted in the chat room from thousands of individuals connecting via their Minitel terminals. Individual users were not subject to State censorship, and as a result, Minitel became an important platform for fringe political and cultural activity.[58] For instance, during the massive antigovernment student demonstrations of 1986, Minitel became "a peerless tool for information and communication" used to organize the protests.[59]

As these examples demonstrate, the Télétel platform exhibited various characteristics of openness that exceeded walled gardens such as CompuServe or Apple. The contrast between these French and US illustrations provides yet another counternarrative to the portrayal of Minitel as a dirigiste, closed, parochial, and centrally controlled platform. In practice, Minitel was open in ways that should push us to think with greater nuance about the "shades of openness" in information and communication platforms.

Conclusion

Cesson-Sévigné may not be as sunny as Silicon Valley, but the public–private partnership that undergirds the French telecom capital is not all that different from the military-industrial complex that initially spurred the growth of the US tech capital. Over the years, many scholars have come to see Minitel as an icon of centralized State planning, the epitome of dirigisme, and the ideological opposite of US entrepreneurialism. Not only is this portrayal inaccurate—dirigisme implies a certain microman-agement that is absent from the Minitel case—but it also overlooks impor-tant decentralized characteristics of the Minitel architecture that are useful for thinking with greater nuance about the openness of the systems we rely on today. Indeed, while some aspects of Minitel were kept under centralized State control, the provision of end user services was left to independent enterprises positioned at the edges of the network. The State further stimulated the growth of this private sector by providing billing and account services, high-quality technical documentation, training in the design and management of information resources, and detailed research on large-scale public videotex experiments. By combining ele-ments of centralization and decentralization, the architecture of Minitel invited mass-scale participation as well as encouraged widespread entre-preneurship and experimentation.

The plan to create Minitel was motivated in part by a vision of telemat-ics put forth in 1978 by Nora and Minc. The two researchers hoped that by decentralizing the provision of services, French telematics might enable a kind of entrepreneurial "freedom" to unsettle long-standing political traditions in the country, causing "even the most deep-rooted habits and ideologies to lose their validity."[60] On reflection, it seems that while a certain amount of freedom may have been realized at the edges of the network, the system could not wholly undermine the French tradition of centralization.

In 1994, Gérard Théry was tasked by the French prime minister with studying ways in which France could benefit from the develop-ment of the international information superhighway. In his report, Théry opined that the Internet could not successfully develop in France without State sponsorship because it lacked many of the centralized features of Minitel—namely, a comprehensive directory of users along with a reli-able system for billing and payment.[61] Instead, Théry envisioned that there would be two Internets: "one Franco-German internet [driven by the French and German governments], and another one [the legacy of ARPANET and NSFNET]."[62] Théry's failure to foresee the commercial success of the Internet suggests that he did not believe that a network ecosystem could be viable unless it was designed and managed by a top-down state-like entity. Rather than challenge the political tradition of centralization, the Minitel experience seemed to reinforce a belief that centralization was a necessary precondition for the success of the Internet in France.

Freedom—in the Nora and Minc sense of the term—was felt most strongly at the edges of the Télétel network, among those users and service providers that built and occupied the services that gave life to Minitel. The hybrid architecture offered a generative platform for these private stakeholders to experiment and play with the possibilities of widespread telematics. In the next chapter, we examine the creativity of the private entrepreneurs who introduced online services, software, and hardware that extended Minitel in ways that the designers of the network could not have envisioned.

In the mid-1980s, computer geeks traveling to Paris were confronted with glimpses of a telematic future. By 1986, advertisements for Minitel services were ubiquitous on the highways and high streets of France. All along the dark, gloomy taxi ride from the airport to the city, colorful billboards implored drivers to *tapez*, or "type," inscrutable alphanumeric sequences into their home terminals. Crossing the Porte de la Chapelle, one of Paris' thirty-eight "doors," a remnant of fortified Gallo-Roman communication networks, the visiting geek would see yet more Minitel advertisements plastered on the city walls. While some ads sported recognizable brand names, such as national newspaper *Le Monde*, others featured startlingly erotic photos of nude women and men, gonzo illustrations, and piercing neon graphics, all tagged by similarly mysterious strings: 3615 ALINE, 3615 CRAC, 3615 ENCORE, and 3615 ULLA. Further into the Latin Quarter where students, hipsters, and intellectuals crowded along the Boulevard Saint-Germain and the UGC Danton cinema was still playing *Retour vers le Futur*, the visitor would encounter a little newspaper kiosk with a towering poster trumpeting "3615 SM." Our geek has found "le Minitel."

These were the 1980s: appointments were made over landline calls, there were no pagers or cell phones, and yet advertisements for commercial online services pervaded the visual culture of the city. By the time writer Howard Rheingold arrived in Paris in the early 1990s, Minitel was fully domesticated, a bare fact of everyday life through the cities and towns of France.[1] Billboard advertisements—as common in rural towns as metro cities—materialized the emerging online frontier. Unlike in the United

States where online services operated largely out of sight of the general public, everyone living in France was peripherally aware of the network thanks to the omnipresence of Minitel advertising in print and public, on television and the radio. Indeed, even the most dedicated Minitel users spent more time staring at Minitel ads than sitting in front of their terminals. For while many people brought terminals into their homes, the high per minute cost of actually using Minitel precluded the kind of permanent connectivity that most of us enjoy today. In a very real sense, the cultural memory of Minitel is largely shaped by its representation in commercial advertising. Billboards and television ads enjoyed a pervasiveness that the actual consumption of services did not, and defined Minitel both in material and cultural terms.

The billboards that stuck in the memories of tourists and citizens alike were advertisements for the sexually explicit services, known locally as *Minitel rose*. With their libertine use of sexual innuendo and naked skin, the pink advertising made a strong impression on French society. In Rheingold's account of the period, "the churches and many citizens looked on in horror" at the proliferation of rose imagery through the city.[2] Surprisingly,

Figure 5.1 A woman walks by a billboard in Mulhouse advertising 3615 ULLA, one of the most famous messageries, August 1987. *Source*: Authors' collection.

however, a majority of private citizens and government officials took the pink services in stride—a surprisingly sexy quirk of the information society.

In spite of their memorable ads, however, the pink services were just one slice of a lively culture of entrepreneurship and commercial experimentation supported by the Minitel platform. With its built-in billing system and population of users, Télétel provided a generally low-risk environment—a primed pump—for would-be online service providers. Far from being an impediment to innovation, as it is often characterized, the State instead encouraged free enterprise by actively sharing its own taxpayer-supported research on human–computer interaction and online consumer behavior. The positive feedback loop in this two-sided market attracted a cohort of wild, young entrepreneurs who were poised to see a reliable stream of revenue in the short term—a key distinction from the more widely publicized dot-commers who floated on venture capital a decade later. The decentralized aspects of the architecture of the platform enabled service providers to experiment with a variety of business models, frequently anticipating models that would surface later as web services and mobile phone apps.

Within a few years, Minitel was deeply enmeshed within popular culture and public life in France. Over time, the thematic range of Minitel services expanded—from hobby sites and niche fetish communities to a variety of information databases and targeted business services—drawing more and more of the French population into the online world. This increasing integration of Minitel into quotidian French life was reflected in the lyrics of pop songs, plots of television dramas, and other ephemera that would otherwise not be seen as "techie" or "geeky."

In this chapter, we explore the breadth of commercial services that were assembled atop the Minitel platform. In the first half of the chapter, consistent with the cultural memory of Minitel, we begin with a deep dive into the profoundly successful phenomenon known as Minitel rose. Not only were pink services adopted widely across French society, they provided a massive stream of revenue to traditional institutions—from the telephone company to major newspaper publishers. Without this novel financial opportunity, the media ecology of late twentieth-century France would have developed quite differently. In the second half of the chapter, we detail several notable Minitel-related businesses that represent the commercial diversity of the platform. From home automation and online banking to e-commerce and virtual assistants, many of the experiments taken up by Minitel entrepreneurs are only beginning to take hold on the web thirty years later.

In the hands of third-party developers and nonspecialist users, Minitel developed in ways that Télétel engineers and early advocates could not have anticipated. As sociologist André Lemos reflected in 1996, Minitel came to life, achieving a "technical vitalism" as a result of the unpredictable interaction between diverse social forces and new media technologies.[3] The very existence of the *messageries*, or chat rooms, is the result of that vitalization process. The messageries' founding myth attributes their appearance to a teenage boy nicknamed Big Panther, who, the story goes, used his TRS-80 to hack into the internal messaging system of Gretel, an experimental Minitel system run in the city of Strasbourg by Les Dernières Nouvelles d'Alsace beginning in 1981.[4] The story was best told by Michel Landaret, manager of Gretel, at a wake in honor of Minitel in June 2012:

> The first messagerie, the first chat, we set up in 1981, and of course it immediately went awry, as you could have guessed. How did it start? Simply put, someone hacked a system. You know, at the time, we weren't concerned about hackers. So we had a menu that went 1, 2, 3, 4, 5, and I set-up a .99, and of course someone found it [laughter]. Well at first it was cute, it was nice, one would use it to order croissants from the boulangerie, on Saturday night, for Sunday morning delivery, and then the first smutty moniker appeared. ... it was *Peggy La Cochonne*.[5]

That first "smutty moniker" on Gretel presaged the subtle, bawdy humor and innuendo that would characterize much of the discourse around the pink Minitel. Peggy La Cochonne is a direct translation of the Muppet character Miss Piggy. In French, though, Peggy La Cochonne has a salacious connotation, as the word *cochonne*, literally "female pig," is also a slang term for a promiscuous woman. The moniker thus suggested something a little naughty without coming right out and saying it.

Revenue Rose

Pleasure, play, sexuality, and anonymity swirled together on the new system, and there was no stopping the inflow of money. Landaret remarked, "[Minitel was] made on gaming and sex, as usual, just like all technological innovations, including the Internet."[6] Adult-oriented services were not cordoned off or marginalized; Minitel was infused with sexuality and innuendo. As Landaret wryly noted, "All messageries are pink."[7] Sexy chat may not have been part of the original plan for Minitel, and not everyone was happy about the emerging culture, but Télétel administrators did not want to stanch this new stream of revenue. Landaret remembers hearing conflicting messages from Minitel administrators. At a France Telecom conference, Direction générale des télécommunications (DGT) representatives admonished the gathered service providers, calling adult services an "abomination." In private, however, DGT project lead Jean-Paul Maury displayed greater equanimity toward Minitel rose, reassuring Landaret: "but above all, do not stop, it is the only thing that brings in money."[8]

And money, they brought. The Gretel messageries were used on average 22.08 hours per day, and one had to dial in repeatedly for 1.02 hours on average before actually being able to connect, as the lines were constantly busy. The record for the highest phone bill on Gretel (over a two-month billing cycle) was FF225,000. One Telic-Alcatel employee managed to spend 520 hours on the messagerie over a one-month period (which has 720 hours in total). The longest continuous messagerie activity by one user was 74 hours; someone finally noticed the incongruity of the situation, Landaret says, "and we had to send an ambulance."[9] Other entrepreneurs tell the same story. Daniel Hannaby, cofounder of 3615 SM, said, "I remember one person sending us a letter that she was asked by France Telecom a bill of 30,000 Francs; so it was a lot of money at the time, 30,000 Francs it was really huge. And so she was asking for us to reimburse but well, we couldn't do that."[10] A 1986 study calculated that a small messagerie, averaging 150 hours of connection per day, would gross 173,250 francs per month—that is, over 2 million francs per year.[11] It reported that in May and June 1986 only, 14 million calls were made to Télétel numbers for 1.7 million hours of total connection time, of which 70 percent was spent on messageries. Assuming these numbers are correct, at 61.60 francs per hour of connection charged to the end user, this would amount to 73.3 million francs for that two-month period for the messageries—averaging these numbers over twelve months, the entire messageries industry would have made 879.6 million francs for the year.

Starting shortly after the introduction of the kiosk system, and for several years thereafter, the high cost of Minitel to the user became a recurring theme in the popular press. Newspapers and magazines frequently published horror stories of humongous phone bills showing up out of the blue, either because the unsuspecting customer had not realized how much time they were spending, or how much money was charged per minute, or because children explored the new electronic frontiers while their parents were at work. For headline writers, riffing on the name of the system must have been irresistible. In 1985 alone, two different articles appeared with the title *"Minitel, Maxi-Prix"* (Minitel maxi-price).[12]

So what exactly went on in the messageries? What was it about these plaintext chat rooms that so compelled users and turned 3615 into such a cash cow? It varied, but many, many messageries were organized around sexual fantasies and virtual play. While few services retained logs of their chat channels, the advertisements printed in magazines, newspapers, and Minitel directories during the late 1980s offer a snapshot of how the messageries appealed to potential users.

Advertising the Messageries

The advertising for pink messageries varied widely, reflecting a diverse array of personality, theme, and promise. Some services overtly advertised hard-core discussions with erotic imagery and unambiguous references to sexual activities (see figure 5.2). Others preferred humor and innuendo to advertise explicit services. Some focused on fringe fetishes: 3615 ANDI, for example, self-identified as "a convivial space for handicapped people and their friends," while La voix du parano (the voice of the paranoid) was promoted as a "non-conformist messagerie."[13] Some appealed to misogynistic patriarchal values while others promised female empowerment through sexual liberation (see figures 5.3 and 5.4).[14] In some cases, the names of the messageries themselves referred to sex acts, even if the advertising did not. Libération, a major newspaper, named its messagerie 3615 TURLU, in reference to the word turlute, French slang comparable to "blow job."[15] 3615 SM exploited the ambiguity of its short mnemonic, branding itself as a serveur médical, a database for doctors that happened to have messageries attached—but even its streamlined, minimalist ads left little doubt as to the real nature of the service.

Not all messageries made appeals, either explicitly or implicitly, to sexual play in their advertising. Some systems, such as FUNITEL, did not even always mention sex, but Landaret was not alone in his belief that "all messageries were pink."[16] Without regard for context, it seemed that the use of the messageries for sex was inevitable. Even the very serious Le Monde, made purposeful, humorous reference to the use of its messageries for sex. An ad began, "We're mostly IQ," and then proceeded to list all the things you could do on 3615 Le Monde: challenge your IQ with games, keep up with the news, find weekend activities for the kids, manage your stock portfolio, search for your dream apartment, and order groceries from home. All this wholesome activity was punctuated, however, by a small drawing of a Minitel terminal appearing at the bottom right-hand corner of the ad. The Minitel screen depicted a pair of pixelated buttocks printed in the same pink color as the letters IQ in the title. For French readers, the connection was clear: phonetically, Q sounds like the word cul (butt). The

Figure 5.2 This ad for the Magix messagerie is rife with puns and innuendo. The subscript (*tapez sur nous, on aime ça!*) translates literally as "hit us, we like it!"—a play on the double meaning of the verb *taper* for "hitting" and "typing on a keyboard." *Minitel Magazine*, no. 19, January–February 1987, 83.

prevalence of casual innuendo in advertisements ranging from niche hard-core services to the national intellectual newspaper of record reflected the diffusion and acceptance of Minitel rose across popular culture.

A Return of the Masquerade

Not all chat was crude or even aimed at sexual satisfaction, however. One recurrent pattern of use highlighted in magazines and newspapers was the online masquerade (see figure 5.6). As Rheingold reported in his early

Figure 5.3 This ad for the SeXtel messagerie situates the Minitel rose in a longer tradition of patriarchal heterosexuality. The illustration invites a historical comparison between Minitel and earlier uses of new media for sexual exploration such as boudoir photography. *Revue du Minitel*, no. 8, November–December 1986, 47.

work on virtual communities, many in the Minitel industry believed that their users were attracted to the liberating feeling of fantasy play:

> It was a chance to step out of their normal identity and be superman or a beautiful woman and say all the things that they only think about in their most secret fantasies. You are a nobody at work. You have to fight a commute to work and back. You are lonely, or you are married. Indulging in an hour of sex chat is a crude but effective way of creating a different self.[17]

Horriblement draguée
et ça la fait marrer !

Quel trafic le soir sur le service dialogue de Funitel ! Des milliers
de connexions dans tous les sens, de toute la France. Mot de passe FUNI.
Branchez votre Minitel, inventez-vous un pseudo et c'est parti !
Attention, sens de la répartie exigée, on s'aborde en direct. Drague dure
ou drague douce, c'est égal, tant que l'humour est au rendez-vous.
Et à ce jeu-là, l'amour aussi y trouve son compte. Alors, à très bientôt.
Faites le 36.15, tapez FUNI.

FUNITEL
50 jeux pour vous marrer avec votre Minitel.

Figure 5.4 FUNITEL portrays the Minitel rose as a more egalitarian space for sexual play, inviting women with an implicit promise of pleasure and empowerment: "She gets hit on a ton, and she finds it hilarious." *Revue du Minitel*, no. 8, November–December 1986, 39.

The belief that the online masquerade offered a momentary escape from the drudgery of everyday life was widely held among *minitelistes*. In 1987, Marie Marchand described Cécile Avergnat, founder of the popular Crac messagerie, as having "a conviction that today's world generates seas of solitude." To Avergnat, then, videotex services like Crac represented a countervailing force, a means of bringing strangers back into communication. In Marchand's words, the messagerie could be "an effective means of limiting the damage" wrought by social isolation.[18]

Avergnat was not alone in her view of the messagerie as a bulwark against the atomization of French society. Hannaby of 3516 SM also

Nous c'est plutôt le Q.I.

36.15 tapez LEMONDE. Un Monde branché le jour et la nuit. Histoire d'exploiter votre Q.I. 25 heures sur 24.

Un Monde qui bouge tout le temps, colle à l'événement, sort les enfants le mercredi et change d'air le week-end.

Pour prendre la température de votre portefeuille boursier, ou celle de Bourg-en-Bresse. Pour flasher sur l'information ou sur l'appartement de vos rêves.

Pour jouer aux jeux de l'intelligence et du hasard, passer vos nuits blanches en couleurs ou croiser la plume sur le dernier Goncourt.

Pour savoir où souper à la mode. Pour faire vos courses dans un fauteuil ou recevoir une bouteille de Chivas à minuit.

36.15. Tapez LEMONDE

Le Monde sur Minitel

Figure 5.5 The rose phenomenon was not limited to explicitly sexual services. At first blush, this advertisement from *Le Monde*, a major mainstream newspaper, offers to engage your brain ("We're mostly IQ"), but the illustration depicts another part of the body altogether. Further, the letter *Q*, when spoken aloud, sounds like the word *cul*, meaning "butt." *Source*: Authors' collection.

emphasized the value of the messagerie to people "bored with their lives." When asked to confirm that messageries were used mostly for sex-oriented chat, his response was emphatic: "It was not porn. It was not porn." In Hannaby's experience, the messageries offered a dynamic social experience that ran the gamut of adult sociality. To reduce them to "porn" was to overlook the grander social experience unfolding on systems like 3615 SM. Indeed, Hannaby saw the messagerie as a space of identity play and experimentation, set apart from the everyday world:

Figure 5.6 The playful, pseudonymous discourse of the messageries was often compared to the traditional masquerade ball. *Minitel Magazine*, no. 19, January–February 1987, cover.

People were able to pour all their fantasies on the system, just saying whatever they were not able to say in their real life … [Some had] five different or maybe ten different personas on the system and [were] maybe sometimes chatting on two Minitels having two different nicknames. … [W]e were able to see that these people were trying to experiment many ways of chatting, so a lot of people were simply genuine but a lot of them were taking a mask and trying to, I don't know, seduce or chat or just have fun on the system. … It was an equivalent of Facebook today, a way for people to connect together … they were able to chat about their problems at work, anything; what happened last night with friends during a date and it was a bit of sexy talks but not only that. It was a lot of friendly talks. Being able to find a friend; someone you can talk with, you can spend time just talking about your fantasies.[19]

Referring to the phenomenon as "social innovation," communication scholar Josiane Jouët also stresses the new opportunities to break free from classic social relations and meet new people from extremely diverse social backgrounds—not an easy feat in off-line life. Oftentimes, she notes, the minitelistes she interviewed "insisted that even if it did not end up in a hook up, it was always interesting to have a drink with people we didn't know, very different people whom we would never have met through the day-to-day routine."[20] Despite their pink reputations, then, the messageries provided a context for meaningful communities to develop. In some cases, dedicated users organized off-line parties similar to the face-to-face get-togethers hosted by Echo, the WELL, and other US-based systems with less sexually explicit reputations.[21] In Hannaby's recollection, long-time users maintained the system's social norms by helping to acculturate new users:

> There was the core, a very strong core of users that knew each other and there was all these people added by the ads we had at one point, in the subway, in the magazines and so on. I think the core of users were happy to see all these new people coming in. I think that this core taught the way of using and interacting with the system. So it created a strong bond between the users, because they were using the same way of interacting that was taught by the first users. So of course, it was chatting, dating of course. People used that to date and myself, I used it to date. At one point, I had a girlfriend that I found with the system. So there were a few people that were able to marry using the system. Because of the popularity of the system, we started to organize parties. These parties gathered maybe a few hundred people at one point, so that was not too bad. I remember one of the parties was organized at the Moulin Rouge in Paris. We rented the whole space at the Moulin Rouge, so people came and had their dinner and danced, and it was fun.[22]

To see the messageries as a masquerade (rather than, say, a bathhouse) reveals the social complexity of these text-only spaces. While some pink systems were little more than engines for sexual release, many messageries offered a novel social space for strangers to meet—part nightclub, part salon. Just as scholars would later observe on Internet services like Usenet and Internet Relay Chat, the groups of people drawn to messageries formed bonds and relationships that gave rise to lasting communities, and perhaps to the surprise of system administrators, many were eager to extend these online interactions into their off-line lives.[23]

At Work in the Messageries

A key role in the commercial success of the masquerades as well as the cruder version of the messageries was played by *les animatrices*, employees of the service provider.[24] Their job was to pass for actual users and tease the real users into chatting with them for as long as possible. In the words of one, since the business was the "economics of attention," animatrices were, literally, "attention whores."[25] The animatrices were often young men—mostly college students—who passed as women, at least on the straight sites.[26] They would juggle multiple connections/personas at once, either by using multiple terminals or through PCs enabling them to manage multiple virtual Minitels on one screen. They also served as compliance officers for the site; they were present 24/7, monitored all conversations, and would disconnect users breaking the law (such as prostitutes soliciting on the sites or blatant pedophiles). Some of them seemed to enjoy the work quite a bit. Hannaby remembers recruiting some of his animatrices from his user base: "They did it because they liked it." In fact, two of his particularly enthusiastic animatrices wound up getting married. Working in the same room, surrounded by Minitel terminals, the husband-and-wife team would even chat to each other over the Minitel.[27]

But not all was rosy in the Minitel rose factory. Jean-Marc Manach, a college student at the time, recalls feeling like a "whore" who was not selling his body but rather his words. While some messageries encouraged friendship and community, Manach worked for a more frankly utilitarian service:

> My boss, who was gay and had as much female psychology skills as a dry oyster, would yell at us when we started chatting one-on-one with the users. He wanted us to just dump lewd scripts on them, to perform strip tease, to offer blow jobs and facial ejaculations, while yelling "Oh yeeeessss! More! I'm cooommiiiiiing!" As a result, these guys would jerk off, and in a few minutes it was over. It was a slaughterhouse. I did not like it.[28]

The assembly-line sexuality of such messageries led some of the workers to a sense of disillusionment. As another animatrice concluded: "At the end of the day, those encounters were pretty sad, because they reflected our times: everything is communicated, but there is not physical touch."[29]

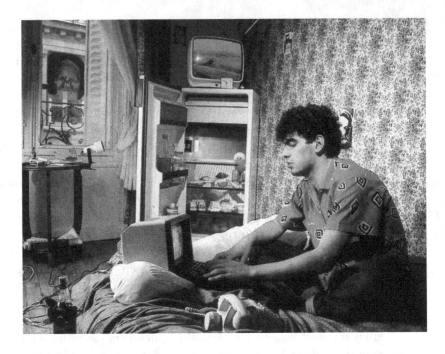

Figure 5.7   A trade magazine's reenactment of an *animatrice* at work depicts "Koka," a male college student presiding over a *messagerie* from his bedroom. Notice the empty fridge and bottle of whiskey in the foreground. "Koka, the Telematics 'Disc-Jockey,'" *Revue du Minitel*, no. 8, November–December 1986, 47.

Minitel Rose in Public Life

It would be easy for the US reader unfamiliar with 1980s' France to *under-state* the pervasiveness and social significance of Minitel rose in the French *cité*. Minitel rose was *everywhere*. With messageries accounting for up 50 percent of all traffic, revenue was enormous.[30] And with the top twenty sites garnering 85 percent of pink connections, visibility was key.[31] The result was a feedback loop that incentivized the messageries to put out more and more ads, in more and more public places. By the late 1980s, ads for Minitel rose were pervasive on the streets of Paris. Short codes such as 3615 SEXTEL appeared on any surface that could carry an ad— billboards, buses, subway stations, magazines, and television. *Everywhere*. Most ads were playful rather than crude; they were, after all, displayed in public for eyes of all ages. But while their level of explicitness varied, there was no question what was being advertised.[32] The PTT minister would even comment that the public displays versus the services themselves were "the most shocking element of this affair."[33]

It is worth noting that the press industry, past its initial reluctance, embraced the Minitel golden goose, and not just as a platform to publish news. In fact, it had an edge in this business since the legal framework put in place to regulate Minitel gave the incumbent press industry a monopoly over access to the Kiosk billing system.[34] For example, popular newsprint magazine *Le Nouvel Observateur* notoriously became the promoter of many a pink service such as the highly successful 3615 ALINE under the leadership of legendary entrepreneur Henri de Maublanc. Le Nouvel Observateur and Le Parisien Libéré, two large press corporations, were in constant competition for the number one rank of 3615 promoters, all services combined.[35] Landaret, who himself ran Gretel on behalf of a regional newspaper, went as far as stating that certain publications such as *Le Nouvel Observateur*, *Libération*, and *Le Parisien* only survived thanks to the 3615: "It was considered a cash machine."[36] And as far as the sites themselves were concerned, the messageries systematically topped all other services in the various rankings produced by industry publications.[37] As we have noted in the introduction, the accuracy of these data is tainted, in this case because they were self-reported by the promoters themselves, but the rankings nonetheless offer a view of how the industry understood and represented itself. Regardless of which particular service was in the top slot, the messageries were the dominant form of activity on Minitel, providing a huge stream of revenue to both their owners and the State. A far cry, perhaps, from the electronic telephone book, Minitel blossomed culturally and commercially thanks to the widespread adoption of adult-oriented chat.

The Pink Workplace

Pornography is an undisputed driver of new media technologies. VHS took movies inside the home, and provided countless people with the privacy a visitor to an actual porno cinema wished they'd had. Minitel, unlike the Internet, was private by design, and the privacy features of Minitel took sex chat into the workplace. Minitel flows were anonymized both on the upstream and downstream. On the host side of the platform, service providers did not see from what number users were calling. This precluded later Internet innovations such as user tracking and micro-targeted advertising, as well as prevented service operators from getting an accurate head count of their client base.[38] On the user side of the platform, connections were anonymized as well: the phone bill would only list connection minutes in bulk, without detailing either the specific times of connection or destination addresses. The privacy features were key in helping the DGT move forward despite popular opprobrium in the early days of Minitel; remember that the regional press has cried Big Brother in its campaign to kill the high modernist project. Full privacy was therefore a crucial public relations tool for the DGT.

Privacy features on the user side of the platform enabled the messageries roses to enter both the home and the office. They did not prevent curious children from being disciplined for running up a large Télétel bill without permission. However, because the bill did not detail the services that had been accessed, spouses could discreetly explore the messageries under the guise of ordering food or browsing train schedules while their better half was away.[39] Similarly, the aggregate billing system enabled workers to sneak in a bit of relaxing chat into the workplace. Minitels were widely used by small, midsize, and large businesses alike to manage inventories, order supplies, fulfill orders, check rates or corporate records, book trips, and so on. In fact, professional apps such as Agricom, used by swine traders, remained active until the end of 2012, when the closing of the network left many in distress.[40] With all digital destinations anonymized on the bill by the DGT, it was easy for Minitel-enabled workers to escape the gloom of the workday for a few minutes here and there, and ramble into rosy paradises. Visually, the text-mode interfaces of these digital frolics also made it difficult for a zealous boss to discern the specific nature of the computing act from a distance. Just in case a compliance officer happened to pop in, some sites built in a feature that enabled the user to display a fake, "clean," home page at the touch of a button.[41] And as an added forbidden pleasure, self-employed business owners could even write off the not-so-rosy phone bill as a business expense.

Minitel rose at work was a real issue for French bosses, not for moral reasons, but financial ones. One study suggested that 15 percent of work connection time was spent on the messageries.[42] Systems emerged that enabled corporate "Minitelmasters" to block access to 3615 services—but by the same token, blocking access to messageries also blocked access to useful professional sites.[43] Bosses faced a somewhat-unsolvable conundrum. The press reported many stories about extravagant bills being run up at night by janitors and other blue-collar staff, also known as the "syndrome of the Minitelist night-watchman."[44]

During the daytime, workers took Minitel breaks instead of hanging out by the watercooler. One office worker, known as "Wild Stallion," was said to have written to his online counterpart, "If you called to administer a survey, please speak to my secretary. She has felt lonely since I've become a minitelist and started neglecting her."[45] As usual, France Telecom tried to minimize the impact of pink Minitel on the workplace. Maury, the Minitel project lead, declared that what was reported in the press were individual cases amplified by the media—"we surveyed 200 companies,

Figure 5.8 Minitel was a fixture of many workplaces, from the office to the shop floor. This photo appeared in a feature on the use of telematics by the auto industry: "[Along] with the 12" wrench and the hub puller, Minitel has become a vital tool for the car mechanic." *Revue du Minitel*, no. 7, September–October 1986, 26.

not one brought up 3615 as a problem."[46] Meanwhile, the DGT as well as other ministries such as the Foreign Affairs Ministry blocked 3615 access for their workers.[47] Landaret recalled being grateful to Telic employees for the time they spent on the Gretel messageries.[48] And Hannaby noted, "You know, people were paying a lot but I think a lot of money came from the companies that were having Minitels and maybe France Telecom had a lot of Minitel and people in France Telecom [were] using them [*laughs*]."[49]

Beyond simply blocking access to whole categories of sites, more sophisticated access control systems emerged around 1987. Unlike filtering software à la Net Nanny that came to existence in the mid-1990s to filter the downstream flow of Internet traffic, Minitel filtering systems offered upstream control mechanisms. *Maya*, a board connected to the Minitel through the peripheral DIN output, could limit upstream connections to a select forty sites as well as offer time limit controls.[50] Despite France Telecom's denial that the pink workplace was even a thing, four thousand Mayas were said to have been ordered in the first month. In an editorial comment on the popularity of the new control mechanism, *Minitel Magazine* remarked on the conflicting interests of workers, managers, and the DGT: "Minitel at work? A great deal for the 3615. Dynamic white-collar workers are keen on exchanging tender words the second their boss turns around. A boss sometimes has an urge to put the terminal under lock and key."[51]

Filtering systems aside, one man almost killed the golden goose. Ironically, it was the man who had engineered the platform in the first place. Maury, a typical engineer preoccupied by technical performance more than by policy, law, or social impact, devised a unique digital identifier similar to a web browser "cookie." Using an eight octet sequence stored in the terminal's memory, a disconnected user could log back onto a server and pick up where they left off.[52] To speed up the reconnection, the last visited page would reload the next time that the terminal was switched on. Unfortunately, this clever function left unsophisticated users vulnerable to being tracked by anyone with access to their terminal equipment, be it a spouse or boss.

News that Minitel might gain a memory prompted social outrage. *Que Choisir*, a leading consumer report magazine, reacted with an article titled "Un mouchard chez vous" (a snitch in your house). The piece opened with the provocative line "Big Brother has arrived."[53] A second leading consumer reports magazine, *50 Milllions de Consommateurs*, similarly expressed discontentment, and in 1985, angry users physically returned three thousand units to the PTT's storefront.[54] France Telecom immediately killed the cookie feature, saving the pink goose that it denied existed in the first place.[55]

Une panique morale? Non!

To the US reader unfamiliar with French customs, the prevalence of the messageries both on- and off-line might sound baffling. In a country where comedian George Carlin was once arrested for disorderly conduct for uttering the words *shit, piss, fuck, cunt, cocksucker, motherfucker,* and *tits* as part of a political comedy routine, where radio station Pacifica was reprimanded by the Federal Communications Commission (FCC) for broadcasting the same routine in violation of indecency regulations, and where the brief sight of Janet Jackson's nipple caused over half a million complaints to be filed with the FCC, advertisements for pink services would not have seen the light of day.[56] They would have been confined to specialty magazines hidden high up behind the register, veiled in dark plastic covers—not a rosy pixel in sight.

But no such moral panic occurred in France. Certainly, the Minitel rose was the source of some controversy, and crimes involving Minitel were sensationalized in the news. In one case, a user reportedly "borrowed" the moniker of someone who had gone on vacation and used it to harass other participants of the messagerie. On their return, the original moniker user became ostracized from the community and ended up committing suicide.[57] In another case, a newspaper reported that a woman was raped "after meeting her torturer on the grey screen."[58] As with so much of Minitel culture, these stories of tragedy by Minitel prefigured the moral panic about meeting strangers online that gripped the United States in the late 1990s.

Just as *Time* chose to highlight "cyberporn" as a key threat to US children in 1995, the sexually explicit messageries were a focal point of Minitel controversies in France.[59] Attempts to shut down pink services were justified under the guise of protecting minors and "other weak members of society."[60] Rather than mainstream, heterosexual pink chat, however, regulatory scrutiny fell mainly on sex workers, queer users, and the services they frequented. For example, it was well known that prostitutes used the messageries to solicit clients, and several services were shut down on that basis.[61] Critics also targeted France Telecom because it cashed one-third of all Minitel revenue in its role as network operator—something both the media and General Auditor (a quasi-judicial agency that audits the executive, legislative, and administrative branches) found problematic.[62] Associations of Catholic families became active in initiating complaints and lawsuits against what became dubbed "the pimp State," and other critics would raise the alarm about "the moral decadence of the State and of the high administration."[63] The criminal code was even amended in order to increase penalties for the crimes of "offense to good morals" (*outrage aux bonnes moeurs*), "incitement to debauchery" (*incitation à la débauche*), and the publication of messages that "adversely affect human dignity" (*porter atteinte à la dignité humaine*) when the target of the messages are under fifteen years old—the legal age of consent in France.[64]

Messageries appealing to gay users came under the strongest attack during this period of moral outrage. In 1986, a mainstream daily newspaper published an exposé about solicitation and teen prostitution on Minitel. The opening paragraph called special attention to gay services: "Minitel is used as a modern pimp and meeting point to all amateurs of teenagers under 15. Since Minitel exists in a legal vacuum, the 'gay' servers are having a field day." The article printed the full text of several personal ads, all of which were reportedly found on a gay service: an adult seeking "little boys," a thirty-five-year-old offering free rent for sex, and a fifteen-year-old "awaiting financial offer."[65] In the same vein, the ultraconservative and ironfisted Charles Pasqua, minister of the interior, singled out a gay pink chat room called Gay Pied that ironically had been financed by the State's sovereign fund, the Caisse des Dépôts et Consignations.[66] While preventing the sexual exploitation of children was a reasonable goal, it seems clear that gay systems were unfairly targeted and grossly misrepresented. As a result of the conservative pressure, gay messageries were more actively monitored than their straight counterparts—by their own editors and the hosting services that hosted them.[67]

In spite of these alarmist reports, it is important not to overblow the significance of such outrage. As Marie Marchand, a France Telecom researcher, noted,

There is no point in exaggerating! Since the dawn of time communication has been used as a vehicle for sex. This should come as no great revelation; it is common knowledge that the phone has long served the same purpose (Paris' renowned tarts of the turn of the century, denizens of the Bois de Boulogne, were among the first to subscribe to the telephone!), but that the telephone is put to such use is a fact of life and does not upset many.[68]

In fact, despite the stir, by and large the messageries remained the most popular of all Minitel services. The loudest critics often were not the most representative of public opinion.

The general public's attitude toward the playful chat rooms was mostly benevolent; a 1991 poll found that 89 percent of the population was against Pink Minitel prohibition.[69] And while a few politicians such as Pasqua (who would incidentally later twice be convicted of corruption) were vocally opposed to the pink services, this was far from the case for all of them. PTT minister Gérard Longuet, who thought that the content of the messageries was much less shocking than the billboards themselves, declared that he simply did "not want telematics to have its image tarnished by the exclusive use of fornicative fellowship."[70] In retrospect, this was wishful thinking. As competition among the pink services increased, so did the overall visibility of pink advertising in public. Ultimately, that same PTT minister would concede, "We are not going to ban hotels because there is prostitution, or public bathrooms because there is graffiti."[71] Also quite telling is a June 1987 interview with Philippe Séguin, a prominent right-wing politician who would later become the head of the General Auditor, at the time minister of social affairs, in the racy men's magazine *Lui*. The discussion with the interviewer, famed television anchor Yves Mourousi, goes as follows:

Yves Mourousi:
—*There are newspaper kiosks in [your town of] Epinal ...* [where the minister was also the mayor]
Philippe Séguin:
—Of course!
—*And on them, there are billboards of young girls who give their phone number or Minitel access code?*
—As is the case everywhere
—*Today, when you drive around Epinal or Paris, is this a spectacle that bothers you?*
—Not at all
—*Do you know how to use a Minitel?*
—Yes, in fact we uploaded 3,000 e-government pages in Epinal
—*With a messagerie?*
—With a messagerie indeed.
—*Did anyone explain to you that it is the messagerie that makes money?*
—With a messagerie, we take full advantage of interactivity. Our relationship with citizens goes through Minitel. They can send us their grievances—a broken sidewalk, or anything else. And our rule is to answer them within 48 hours.
—*When certain members of your government say that we must control Minitel, because it can be used for sexual outburst or nocturnal fantasies. ... In Epinal, do you have such controls in place?*
—If we go down this route, we'll have to ban the telephone too?
—*Are the messageries something that revolts you?*
—Not one second. And if it helps popularize Minitel, then why not? Minitel is a fantastic invention.[72]

That the minister of social affairs himself would take such a position is telling of the overall benevolence—even affection perhaps—with which French society as a whole approached the rosy side of Minitel.

Finally, a rather-bizarre editorial sums up the French attitude toward the messageries quite well. In the summer of 1986, *Minitel Magazine*, under the heading "DECENCY," declared that it would from now on refuse to publish any advertisement that "directly and crudely called upon sexuality."[73] At stake, explained the editor in chief, was the reputation of telematics: "There are people who understood quite quickly that one of the juiciest market[s] was sex. ... [A]nd porn, trust me, is very strong. So of course since they make money, they advertise ... maybe a little too much. We're not going to censor, that's not the issue, we're just saying that telematics is not just [sex]."[74] While sexually explicit services sparked early interest in Minitel, videotex advocates like the editor of *Minitel Magazine* were concerned that the stigma of porn would stymie the potential for telematics to grow beyond the messageries. "French telematics is recognized everywhere as a great success," continued the editor. "It must therefore not become tainted in bright pink if it wants to continue in the direction of success and not become a specialized network. A few services must not jeopardize the image and the formidable potential of Minitel. This deserves some prudishness."[75]

Both the editor of *Minitel Magazine* and the aforementioned PTT minister were concerned that Minitel was becoming known exclusively for its pink services. They were not worried about the content of the messageries but rather the outside world's perception—a serious issue given that France was busy trying to export Minitel.[76] In spite of the editor's call for "decency" and "prudishness," *Minitel Magazine* did not cease running sexually explicit advertisements. In fact, the very same issue that called for a ban was itself riddled with ads for pink services.[77] Telematics enthusiasts may have been concerned by the overwhelming attention paid to the messageries roses, but they certainly were not willing to give them up.

New media technologies are often sites of moral conflict, and telematics was no exception. In the mid-1980s, a loud conservative fringe in France reacted with moral outrage to the pink services on Minitel, but there was no widespread moral panic like the one that would form a decade later in the United States. Instead, French society seemed generally bemused by the unexpectedly risqué turn taken by their telematics system, and the flow of pink revenue was certainly welcome by Télétel administrators. Was it any coincidence that France Telecom printed a user manual with a glowing pink terminal on the cover?

Digital Innovations

The range of Minitel services was huge.[78] With over twenty-five thousand sites at its peak, Minitel provided a depth and breadth of data and services, from general to niche, that only the World Wide Web would rival. Rather than making a list, we have selected a few innovations that prefigured what the post-1995 Internet would offer. Data published by France Telecom

Figure 5.9 This ad for 3615 RS—*Rencontres Sympas!* (friendly meetings)—features a satirical cartoon by Georges Wolinski. A nude woman lying on a bed cries out, "Damned be this Minitel of doom!" to which a man seated nearby answers, "But it is to it that we owe our happiness!" Ironically, the ad appeared in the same issue of *Minitel Magazine* as an editorial proclaiming the magazine would no longer publish advertising that "directly and crudely called upon sexuality." *Minitel Magazine*, no. 16, August–September 1986, 26.

indicated that the top services, by category, remained fairly constant over the years: banking, gaming, transportation, e-commerce, general information, and "the press" (which includes both traditional media sites and the messageries they hosted).

Data published by France Telecom offer a sense of market dynamics, but must be taken with a grain of salt. First, France Telecom did not use the same service classifications every year, which makes accurate

Figure 5.10 A glowing pink Minitel on the cover of a technical documentation suggests a winking recognition of the popularity of the messageries. Direction générale des télécommunications, *Réseau Minitel: Spécifications techniques d'utilisation* (Paris: Ministère des Postes et des Télécommunications, n.d.). *Source*: Orange/DGCI.

Table 5.1 Proportion of Users Accessing Various Types of Services during the Previous Year

	1986	1988	1994
Banking	24%	33%	51%
Gaming	—	—	55%
Travel	18%	28%	4%
E-commerce	28%	28%	14%

Source: Orange/DGCI.

comparison over time impossible. Second, it seems clear that the books were cooked when it came to reporting Minitel rose. For example, in 1987, France Telecom reported that the messageries accounted for 16 percent of traffic. But in 1988, after Minitel rose became somewhat scandalous, it retrospectively reported that the messageries were only visited by 5 percent of users in 1986 and 9 percent in 1988 while also introducing "the press" as a distinct category (with 25 and 16 percent participation, respectively). Splitting the messageries and press into separate groups was an obvious attempt to minimize the impact of the messageries since the chat rooms were the primary reason that many users visited the press sites. The press category therefore should have been taken into account as a noisy measure of Minitel rose activity. In subsequent publications by France Telecom, messageries would sometimes appear (in 1992, 6 percent of users reported accessing *messageries de charme*), and sometimes not (in 1997, only "the press" was a category, with 7.1 percent of users visiting). And when messageries were reported, the data were inconsistent. France Telecom, for instance, reported that only 1 percent of users visited the messageries in 1994, but in July 1999, in a special issue discussing why Minitel was better than the Internet and should be kept by users as their primary online venue, it reported that 21 percent of users were still using the messageries. Rather than paying too much attention to these rankings, then, we now describe a few services that prefigured what the web would later offer.

Before There Was ...

The history of Minitel offers early glimpses of many of the social and political issues that surround the Internet today. Examining how these issues played out in the context of Minitel supplies a new perspective for thinking about current-day design and policy challenges. Similarly, Minitel provided an early platform for minitelistes to experiment with business ideas that would later become staples of the Internet ... for good or bad. Some of the early practices we document in this section are trivial but worth mentioning for their entertainment value; some provide provocations for thinking about policy conflicts and business models in new and future online ecosystems. Before there was ...

Before There Was Webvan, There Was ... 3615 TMK (Tele-Market) In 2008, Webvan was dubbed "one of the most epic fails in the dotcom bubble fiasco ... a cautionary example of how not to start your Web business."[79] This online grocery store, the business model of which still remains unclear, "went from being a $1.2bn company with 4,500 employees to being

Figure 5.11 Françoise Marceau, Tele-Market's head of client service, poses with her Minitel in front of her "Minitel-Van." Tele-Market Minitel-Van," *Revue du Minitel*, no. 2, September–October 1985, 18.

liquidated in under two years." Before there was Webvan, however, there was Tele-Market.

Tele-Market promised to deliver food to the Paris area and offered same-day delivery. It competed with several other companies; a 1987 guide lists four different services focused on delivering to the Paris area, and twenty-three total in France, enabling one to order from large stores, specialized wine retailers, or straight from local farms.[80] The story does not tell whether any of these businesses were successful (we know that they never made the top list of the industry magazines). But at least, unlike Webvan, they drew revenue from the per minute fee that the user had to pay while browsing the catalog over a 1,200 baud connection, which, all things considered, did not make these ventures unreasonable gambles, considering these sites offered up to two thousand products each.[81]

Before There Were Emojis and Text Messaging Slang, There Was ... Messagerie Slang   In a country where language is highly codified and placed under the protection of the *Académie française*, the messageries provided a welcome playground for those who wanted to free themselves from conventions and could not handle a huge phone bill: contractions, phonetic language, and symbols were much quicker to type—a crucial advantage for users billed by the minute. While the practice of butchering language raised some eyebrows, it was mostly looked at with amusement and benevolence by the specialized press.[82] Conversely, other authors noted that some users actually developed highly sophisticated styles, some even writing poetry using verses; since no pictures were available, the power of words were the ultimate tool of seduction.[83]

Before There Was SETI@home, There Was ... Cosmos Art Initiative Before the University of California at Berkeley launched SETI@home, a "scientific experiment that uses Internet-connected computers in the Search for Extraterrestrial Intelligence (SETI)," in 1999, Minitelists were able to chat with aliens, or at least send them messages, through the Cosmos Art Initiative, "the first intergalactic messagerie."[84] Messages typed on the Minitel screen were beamed into space through the Nançay radio telescope, another jewel of the post–World War II French technological renaissance. Things would turn full circle when said radio telescope joined the SETI program.[85]

Before There Was Ask Jeeves, There Was ... Minitel Artificial Intelligence The France Telecom telephone directory, known as *Le 11*, featured a natural language interface. Name searches could be successfully completed even when the name or address was spelled wrong, and the yellow pages sections of the State-run directory as well as the Minitel online directory *MGS* offered powerful natural-language search capabilities. For example, one could search for "reservation of theater tickets in Paris" or "residential real estate rentals in Lyon." By May 1991, France Telecom would boast a 98 percent rate of accuracy in the search results.[86]

In addition to natural-language interfaces, the private sector also experimented with on-demand personal assistants and semantic search. Before Apple's Siri or Microsoft's Cortana, Minitel users could chat with Claire or Sophie. Claire provided administrative information, while Sophie answered questions on Parisian cultural activities. But Claire and Sophie were not powered by artificial intelligence software; there were real, live people on the other end of the connection, referred to as "Minitel girls." That was 1984.[87] Truly automated personal assistant services with natural-language interfaces began to appear around 1987, such as 3615 AK, a public-facing database of health information similar to WebMD.[88]

Before There Was Ticketmaster, There Was ... Billetel Several systems were developed to purchase tickets online. *Le Point*, a major French magazine, enabled one to order tickets from the comfort of one's home by simply providing a bank account number (something not nearly as risky as over the Internet thanks to Transpac's advanced security features). Tickets would then be delivered by mail.[89] Fnac, France's main chain retailer of cultural goods, set up public access points connected to Transpac where one could pay by credit card and have the ticket printed. It subsequently attached those points to Télétel, so one could order from home and then go print the ticket at the access point.[90]

Before There Was the Internet of Things, There Was ... *domotique*, **the Minitel of Things** In the early 2010s, many tech companies began to invest in a vision of the future dubbed the "Internet of Things," in which "physical objects, such as sensors or everyday objects like appliances and vehicles ... are capable of structured communication to and from remote databases and between themselves."[91] But this vision of home automation was hardly new. Before there was the Internet of Things, there was a Minitel of Things, or as the French call it, *domotique*, from the Latin *domus* (house) and the French *informatique* (informatics)—in other words, the smart house. Before the Nest thermostat became all the rage in Silicon Valley (with its obligatory billboard on the 101 South Freeway), the French were layering such systems over the Minitel platform. The Minitel terminal—and specifically, its serial port—played a central role in coordinating the domotique network. First, it provided communication to and from the outside world by supplying an interface between the various "smart" devices in the home to the telephone system. This enabled cybernetic devices to communicate with the outside world. For example, a domotique fire alarm could ring the firehouse.[92] Similarly, the Minitel could receive orders sent remotely and communicate them to the control unit. Just as Télétel enabled third parties to independently experiment with new services, the Minitel-enabled vision of domotique was vendor neutral, enabling independent corporations to develop a variety of devices and applications.[93] The present-day vision of the Internet of Things depends on the same openness: devices can be remotely controlled from any computer as long as they both use IP as the network protocol, and the Internet service provider does not discriminate against them. Domotique devices from the 1980s included thermostats, VCRs, security systems, lights, yard irrigation, and even kitchen appliances—although it remains unclear why anyone would want to remotely control a stove, fridge, or supply of laundry detergent or trash bags.[94]

A more successful use of the Minitel serial port was to create a local area network. A strong peripherals industry developed as a result of the terminal's open standards and device neutrality. Peripherals were sold to make data more permanent (e.g., a printer or external storage device) or the terminal smarter (e.g., a computer could be attached to manipulate the data), or turning things around, the Minitel itself could become a peripheral

MINITEL AND HOME AUTOMATION

With LIGNE DIRECTE, home automation comes within the reach of the general public, offering a range of essential and easy-to-use functions, and at a very attractive price.
LIGNE DIRECTE is a family, multifunction, home automation unit which combines two modern techniques :
– interactive and economic communication by Minitel,
– data transmission through the existing 220 V network ("power line carrier") ; this makes it possible to control the devices throughout the home without installing new wires.

comfort

– Without any special installation, the system controls the boiler or

the convectors, through an incorporated temperature sensor. The user modifies the temperature instructions from any Minitel unit, locally or by remote.
– All other electrical devices (water heater, lighting, sprinklers, etc.) can be controlled at wish. LIGNE DIRECTE possesses 20 differents channels.

security

– Smart presence simulation
– Alarm transmission by Minitel. An entirely new feature, the incorporated alarm transmitter is, at the same time : very flexible, since all the parameters can be consulted and modified by

remote (telephone number, instructions, times switches, test, etc.) ; and fully complete, through the facility to transfer all instructions necessary for taking the measures necessary in case of emergency.

Sales prices : FFr 2 950, inclusive of all taxes, for the device, and FFr 350, inclusive of all taxes, per receiver socket.

IDT, who specialises in home automation applications benefits from the cooperation of two partners of high reputation, Finovelec, a subsidiary of IDT and of EDF, and CAT, a subsidiary of FRANCE TELECOM.

IDT
1 bis, rue Gager-Gabillot
75015 PARIS
Contact : Monsieur de SALABERRY
Tél. : 33 (1) 45 67 20 31

FRANCE TELECOM
Direction de Programme Télétel
35, rue du Commandant Mouchotte
75675 PARIS Cédex 14
Contact : Monsieur HAMELIN
Tél. : 33 (1) 45 64 08 61

Figure 5.12 Minitel provided a convenient platform for the production of numerous peripherals. The Ligne Directe system from IDT promised home automation (*domotique*) with remote control via Minitel. Advertisement, n.d. *Source*: Orange/DGCI.

for a computer—that is, a modem—used to download software or communicate through BBSs.[95] The number of peripherals available was large, both in depth and breadth. Products included printers, analog and digital voice recorders, external hard drives, autodialers, voice-mail systems, screens, projectors, systems enabling the sending of signals through coax television cables (similar to today's Slingbox), voice synthesizers, optical disk readers, and electronic billboards. A 1989 guide published by France Telecom listed 266 product lines from 123 independent providers—quite the counternarrative to Minitel as a closed system entirely run by the

State.[96] Though Télétel failed to boost the domestic computer industry, it worked wonders at stimulating a market for Minitel peripherals.

Before There Was E-banking, There Was ... Minitel Banking Banking has historically been a driver of innovation in information technologies, and Minitel became a natural playground. While online banking experiments in the United States such as Covidea in 1985 (launched by the Bank of America and Chemical Bank in cooperation with AT&T and Time, Inc.) and a venture supported by Citicorp in 1986 were failures, online banking became an early staple of Minitel.[97] The first service, Vidéocompte (video account), was launched on December 20, 1983, by CCF Bank (now part of HSBC). But far from being what the *Financial Times* called an "electronic gadget," within a year the service attracted 65 percent of CCF clients who owned a Minitel.[98] Other banks were a bit less successful, for unlike the CCF, they actually charged a monthly fee for the service.[99] A 1991 France Telecom survey estimated that "the penetration ratio (total subscribers/total bank customers) average[d] 8% for nationwide banks and 19% for local banks."[100] Nonetheless, that was enough for banking services to repeatedly be ranked in the top of all services by France Telecom. Services ranged from checking balances and making appointments with bank personnel, to ordering checkbooks and transferring money. Using Minitel as a modem, the home or office accountant could download banking data to further manipulate it using a personal computer.

The contrast between the successful Minitel model for online banking and US videotex failures in this realm highlight the power of Minitel as a neutral, open platform on which private actors could layer their services. In contrast, the fragmentation of US systems made it impossible for banking services to succeed. Different banking applications required separate subscriptions to distinct gated communities and sometimes dedicated hardware.[101] The United States would have to wait for the privatization of the open Internet as a neutral, open platform to see the successful emergence of online banking in the retail sector.

The day trading of securities also became a reality long before the likes of E*Trade would open the US markets to retail investors. Some services enabled the management of mock portfolios as competitive games. For example, FUNITEL diversified its messagerie business, and "launched the Stock Market game in which the trading rates on the Paris Bourse were made available on-line and updated daily. Players managed a fictitious investment portfolio valued at $100,000. The winner took home a sum equal to the amount of money 'made.'"[102] And many services provided actual portfolio management and same-day online trading. As a trade magazine pointed out in 1987, Minitel was particularly well suited to a time when a wave of corporate privatizations, financial markets deregulation, and high volatility required that one be well informed and act fast.[103]

Before There Was Square, There Was ... LECAM Before US merchants could accept secure payments over the Internet, a system named LECAM enabled Minitel users to both send and receive online payments. The system was based on smart chip cards—another invention developed in France and sponsored by the State as part of its digital plan.[104] It enabled secured payments to be made to a merchant from home or a point-of-sale system, in real time. Initially, smart card interfaces were sold as peripherals, but, due

Figure 5.13 A restaurant customer pays her bill using a secure chip card reader connected to a Minitel 1B, circa 1988. With the addition of a smart card reader, Minitel became an affordable point-of-sale system enabling businesses to accept payment cards. Direction générale des télécommunications, *La Lettre de Télétel*, no. 16, Q1, 1989. *Source:* Orange/DGCI.

to the popularity of Minitel-based payments, later models of the Minitel terminal included a built-in card reader (see figure 2.6).

Cultures of Minitel

A testimony to its mass-market retail success, Minitel figured prominently in French popular culture during the 1980s and 1990s. In contrast to contemporary systems in other parts of the world, Minitel use was depicted frequently in French television and film, and referred to in the lyrics of pop songs. Whereas many Americans born in the 1970s would regard a 1980s advertisement for CompuServe as a historical oddity, their French counterparts would react to a similar Minitel ad with nostalgia. The French denizen will associate Minitel with milestone life experiences: the first computer, the first online chat, university registration (which required the use of Télétel), and the first online gaming or shopping experience. And if not memories of an actual online experience, the ad will trigger the recollection of the *possibility* of the experience. The role of Minitel in the cultural memory of France exceeds the actual use of Minitel in the everyday lives of French people.

Billboard, television, and radio and print advertisements were omnipresent. Other, more typically French media formats also made it seem that each and every consumer good now had a 3615 companion. Lapel pins were all the rage in France in the 1980s and 1990s, and pins featuring 3615 services became part of this trend. Phone cards equipped with smart chips were pervasive in France during this same period due to the practical impossibility of making pay phone calls with coins. The disposable cards served as a prime advertising medium for Minitel services, especially since phones and online services were linked both in practice and in the popular psyche.[105] This helped Minitel enter popular culture not only because phone cards were present in everyone's wallet but also because they quickly became trading cards, both in schoolyards and adult marketplaces. Where Americans traded baseball cards and pogs, the French traded Panini soccer cards and used DGT phone cards. As phone cards became part of mainstream popular culture, so did Minitel.

In what appears to have been a positive feedback loop, traditional mainstream media such as books and records in turn appropriated Minitel, this time not as a provider of advertising revenue but rather as a narrative theme in its own right. For example, *Premiers Baisers* (first kisses), a popular television sitcom for teenagers focusing on the trials of young romance, extended its fictional world through a series of books, an early form of transmedia storytelling.[106] One of the books centered on Minitel.

Titled *L'inconnu du Minitel* (The stranger from Minitel), it offered a PG-13 version of the countless erotic stories that revolved around a mysterious Minitel paramour.[107]

The impact of Minitel on society was also heard in the pop music of the period. Songs about online intimacies and the thrill of the digital masquerade contributed to reinforcing the platform's position as a mainstream cultural artifact, even for those who, because of socioeconomic status, age, or choice, continued to reside solely in the analog world. *Minitel ... Miniquoi?* by Liaison is a subtle synthpop record.[108] Les Inconnus, a group of comedians that was a staple of prime-time French television at the time, parodied 1980s' French rock: in "C'est toi que je t'aime" (It is you who I love you), the group narrates the story of a downtown boy courting an uptown girl; to woo her, he promises to be polite with her mother, vote for Jacques Chirac (then right-wing mayor of Paris and future president of the Republic), and stop surfing 3615 ULLA (the most famous of pink messageries).[109] Noe Willer's "Sur Minitel," Marie-Paule Belle's "Mini-Minitel," and Les Ignobles du Bordelais' "Minitel" each discuss the novel challenges and vicissitudes of meeting a lover online.[110] Willer sings about overcoming shyness, and Belle recounts "undressing him with my digital fingers." Les Ignobles du Bordelais narrate the story of a gentleman who meets a young lady over Minitel while his wife, Simone, is at work. After days of electronic flirting, she agrees to speak on the phone. His anticipation peaks as she picks up the phone—she must be naked!—only to discover that the voice on the other end belongs to Simone, who was herself expecting a young stud.

As a testimony to the Minitel pop cultural legacy, in 2014, two years after the termination of the ecosystem, a popular publisher printed a book titled *Minitel and Fulguropoint: Le monde avant Internet*.[111] The title is a reference to both Minitel and the popular cartoon *Grandizer*, and plays on 1980s' nostalgia. It was followed in 2015 by a self-described "nostalgeek party" at a popular Paris theater. Minitel lives on—in the collective memory of premillennial French people.

The book and party were subtitled *The World before Internet*; we subtitled ours *Welcome to the Internet* to suggest that the history of Minitel prefigured the innovation opportunities and economics, law and policy issues, the world now has to grasp. In the conclusion, we will discuss the lessons of the Minitel platform experience along with the ways they can help us devise better Internet policies for the future. But let us now turn in chapter 6 to a consideration of the radical potential of the Minitel system in the hands of a creative populace and show that the seemingly tight grip of the State over Minitel did not prevent fringe uses of the network.

Figure 5.14 The illustrated sleeve for the twelve-inch maxi-single *Minitel ... Miniquoi?* by pop group Liaison depicts a telematic love affair in full-color comic book style. Jointly released by the Kangourou and Musical Force labels in 1987 with catalog number 24.101. *Source*: Authors' collection.

"The street finds its own uses for things."

—William Gibson, *Burning Chrome*

Minitel came into being through the simultaneous efforts of hundreds of engineers, policy makers, designers, and bureaucrats living and working in France during the 1970s and 1980s. These individuals labored away in different labs and offices, reporting to different agencies and producing different components of the system, all in the pursuit of diverse notions of what this new platform might become. In the years leading up to its nationwide launch, Minitel was variously envisioned as a driver of industrial development, demonstration of technical sophistication, expression of State power in modernizing infrastructure, competitor and complement to traditional news media, and medium for public culture. To a large extent, each of these visions was eventually realized in the running system. And yet none of the designers or early champions of Minitel could have foreseen the full range of uses to which their system would eventually be put.

After years of planning and testing, Minitel was rolled into production in 1983, region by region. Deployment began with Brittany (where Minitel had been designed and tested) and the greater Paris area (the densest in France). By 1987, Minitel access was available to all of France using the same standard twisted pair of copper wires that carried voice telephone calls.

The hardware and software may have worked reliably, but this was just the beginning of the system's evolution. Because of its ambitious scale and complexity, Minitel continued to grow and change long after its terminals lost their novelty and faded into the background of everyday life. As Minitel connected ever more homes and offices throughout France, users took an increasingly central role in the further shaping of Minitel. By adapting the system to their own idiosyncratic needs and purposes, Minitel users contributed to defining what Minitel was for and how it should be used.

Once Minitel moved out of the lab and into the hands of everyday French people, it entered into a vast, messy process of ongoing reinvention and change that sociologists and historians refer to as "social construction."[1] Rather than study the "impact" or "effect" of technology on society, social constructivist research traces a reciprocal relationship in which technology and society are mutually constructed.[2] To make sense of Minitel, we must also understand the environment within which Minitel was conceived and implemented. When the Minitel 1 appeared, shiny and new, in 1983, it was more than just a new technology. It was also a political achievement and pop cultural phenomenon, ranking alongside the Walkman, Mitterrand, *Tron*, Reagan, nuclear testing, Thatcher, and Michael Jackson. These political and cultural circumstances shaped how the French people came to understand what the Minitel was for as well as what it could do. The unassuming Minitel terminal, taking up residence in millions of homes, was a tiny synecdoche of the increasingly global, high-tech world of the 1980s.

From BBSs to mobile phones, computer networks have proven particularly generative sites of user-driven innovation, but they are not alone. Time and again during the twentieth century, everyday users have adapted new communication technologies for purposes that were not foreseen by their designers.[3] Today, the telephone, radio, phonograph, and World Wide Web are each best known for such unexpected uses.[4] That we no longer think about the radio as a "wireless telegraph" or the World Wide Web as a tool for trading research papers is evidence of the power that users have to reshape their technological environments.

Unlike the telephone, Minitel was designed explicitly to support the creation of new services by third parties. The unique Kiosk system and detailed technical documentation lowered the technical and economic barriers for entrepreneurial developers that wished to hang a shingle out in cyberspace. Indeed, as we discussed in chapter 5, close to ten thousand services were deployed within the first five years of service, eventually peaking at over twenty-five thousand. But users took Minitel in directions that its early champions could hardly have expected. From bawdy adult *messageries* to political protest, it seemed that people from every niche of French society found a home on Minitel. That process took creativity, experimentation, and persistence as well as a good amount of jockeying with various State entities, not to mention several lawsuits, in order to get and remain on the platform. Further, while most fringe uses took place within the Télétel platform itself, some users borrowed certain Minitel modules—namely, the terminal and its modem—and took them outside the Télétel platform, exemplifying both the complexity and versatility of the overall ecosystem. We now consider fringe uses within the system by entrepreneurs and end users (in ways that sometimes blur the lines between the two), and then look at fringe Minitel uses outside Télétel.

Fringe Uses within Minitel/Télétel: The Entrepreneurs

Making Money before the Kiosk

The early 1980s was a period of tremendous business experimentation in France, thanks to Télétel. Third-party Minitel services began to appear as early as July 1981, when the first large-scale videotex experiment, T3V, was launched, featuring thirty thousand "pages" of online information published by eighty service providers.[5] But one key part of the platform was not implemented until 1984: the Kiosk. Until the Direction générale des télécommunications (DGT) made the State-run micropayment system available to independent entrepreneurs, it was difficult for third-party service providers to get paid. As a result, early entrants were forced to experiment with new mechanisms for raising funds and making money—a preview of the frenzy that would later characterize the early commercial web.[6] Some tried subscription models, similar to US systems of the time, but as the CEO of FUNITEL, one of the largest messageries, soon found out, the "Minitellers were decidedly adverse to subscribing to services."[7]

Just as print media had long relied on advertising, pre-Kiosk Minitel services also experimented with ad-based business models. Service providers, however, soon learned that users and advertisers alike found Minitel poorly suited to advertising. The limited bandwidth of a 1,200 baud connection meant that an advertising message that might have seemed like a minor disruption in theory could be downright agonizing in practice, driving users away from ad-supported services.[8] Medical and health ads were particularly excruciating as service providers were obligated by law to transmit a disclaimer that occupied several screens full of legalese before the ad itself could appear. Meanwhile, advertisers were nonplussed by the transformation of their brand images into the blocky videotex format. Compounding the platform's limited color palette, the freebie Minitel 1 terminal could display only gray scale graphics.[9] Minitel seemed unlikely to take off as a platform for digital advertising. Daniel Hannaby, cofounder of 3615 SM, recalls his pre-Kiosk experiments:

> We invested a lot of the money we had in [the Serveur Médical service] and we were not able to get money out of it, so we were searching for a way to do money with that system and first thing we tried was putting ads on the Minitel pages. We were able to create ads for a *laboratoire* [pharmaceutical lab] so the first one was Organon, so we put an ad for a pill, *un contraceptif* [contraceptive pill]. And we needed to put the *mentions légales* [legal disclaimers] of the medicine in the ad, and it took many pages because the *mentions légales* is [written] very small, and the Minitel sadly was not able to display a lot of characters. So people, when they were checking the ad, had to check, scroll through maybe ten pages [*laughs*], so it didn't work as we expected because people would just disconnect because they were not happy with the fact that they have to display everything. So we tried that. We made a little money out of it and it was not the right direction.[10]

But advertising was not the only revenue opportunity available to early Minitel entrepreneurs. Canal 4, Hannaby's company, created an interactive version of the Minnesota Multiphasic Personality Inventory (MMPI) test for psychiatry patients to take online. The cost of adapting the MMPI test, the most widely used of its kind, to videotex was subsidized by the Ministry of Health.[11] The social security office agreed to pay a fee to the service provider for each user who completed the exam. Yet the bureaucratic process of getting paid by the State undermined the promise of this type of sponsorship. The payment process was messy, slow, and cumbersome, and those who tried this business model abandoned it quickly.[12]

These early attempts at building third-party Minitel services may have failed, but they offered glimpses of the commercial potential of the hybrid public–private platform. With the State overseeing the operation of the Télétel infrastructure, entrepreneurs were free to experiment with new types of information services. Of course, without a reliable payment mechanism, it was nearly impossible to profit from these endeavors. The introduction of State-sponsored micropayments via Kiosk resulted in a bloom of new services and spike in the overall revenue flowing through the system—evidence that the ambitious Minitel project was reaching a successful balance between public and private interests.

Kiosk enabled a range of business models that would not be possible on fully decentralized system. For example, to add a similar payment structure to the World Wide Web would require adding a layer of centralized oversight. And yet the introduction of Kiosk and subsequent flurry of commercial activity did not push out any of the preexisting fringe activities. Rather, the changing economic conditions facilitated the continued growth of new, experimental, niche and special interest sites and services on Minitel. As with many State-run systems, though, the day-to-day administration of Télétel was not always smooth, and getting access to Télétel remained a significant bureaucratic challenge for many would-be service providers.

Jockeying with State Actors

Télétel was a closed system in the sense that while service providers' servers sat at the edges of the network, getting connected required the prior approval and active technical intervention of various State actors. Service providers had to jump through four hoops before the DGT would start connecting virtual circuits from the PAVI gateways to their site: get recognized as an official print-press firm, get the censor to approve their proposed content, get a short code issued by the DGT, and get the servers physically attached to Transpac. Each step required its own brand of maneuvering and creativity, and through the process, service providers needed persistence and a bit of luck.

Getting a *commission paritaire* Identifier The conflict with the press was settled in 1981 by reserving the opportunity to create a third-party service on Télétel for the print publishing industry. To be approved for a short code, the equivalent of a URL on Télétel, a site had to be recognized as an official print-press enterprise, which by rule implied obtaining a *commission paritaire* (CP) number.[13] A CP number, delivered by the administration, would enable the corporation it recognized to obtain a preferred tax status (smaller value-added tax rates to add to the paper's price) as well as other advantages, such as cheaper postal rates for distribution to subscribers. Several objective criteria defined by the tax code had to be met in order for a print-press company to obtain the CP number.[14] These criteria included publishing at least once a quarter, having a maximum of two-thirds of the content be advertising, and actually selling the paper, either by the individual issue through a retailer or via subscriptions. This third requirement prevented leaflets, flyers, or free fanzines from qualifying, and had an impact on how Minitel entrepreneurs without a connection to the print media industries managed to obtain the required CP number to publish with a short code over the Kiosk.

Some entrepreneurs simply leased or bought a CP number from an existing publication. Prices were said to average two to three hundred thousand francs—a practice that created a bit of a stir from some in the print-press industry.[15] Albert du Roy, the editor in chief of print magazine *L'Événement du Jeudi*, would denounce the "scandalous" nature of such "trafficking."[16] Others acquired numbers as part of a more integrated cooperation with the print press. When Hannaby and François Lagarde, two entrepreneurial medical school students, created 3615 SM as a "medical service" geared toward doctors and offered medical journals space on their servers to electronically distribute weekly summaries of the off-line journals' content, the journals—ten of them—agreed to sponsor 3615 SM and certify that the online content was indeed part of the overall journal operation. As a result, Canal 4, Hannaby and Lagarde's venture, obtained not one but ten CP numbers.[17]

Other entrepreneurs took a more direct, if laborious, path to obtaining a CP number: launching their own off-line publications. Bernard Louis, president of one of the Télétel service providers' lobbies, referred to the resulting literature as *les journaux fantômes* (the ghost press.)[18] These publications existed for no other reason than to meet an arbitrary bureaucratic requirement. One such ghost paper was called *Informations rigolottes et étranges* (Amusing and weird news). Launched in February 1986, the paper was effectively a homemade, hand-stapled fanzine that commented on news through puns that poked fun at the corruption among politicians, PTT ministry cabinet members, and the print media industry.[19]

But drafting, typesetting, and printing a paper was not enough to meet the regulatory requirements for a CP number. One also had to prove that the paper was actually sold. This administrative hurdle supplied yet another opportunity for the enterprising Minitel enthusiast. A cottage industry emerged to scaffold the production *and consumption* of new print papers by providing an end-to-end publishing pipeline, readers included. The president of the service providers' lobby himself, Louis, moonlighted to serve the growing population of Minitel service providers seeking CP numbers. Michel Baujard, an entrepreneur who would later succeed an ailing Louis as the lobby's president, recalls Louis selling a paper named *Dans la Valise Diplomatique* (In the diplomatic suitcase). The paper came along with fifty subscribers and fifty occasional buyers, for a total of a hundred guaranteed readers. "I would give Bernard five thousand francs in January each year," Baujard recalls, "in exchange for the paper and its readers, and I would obtain my *commission paritaire* number on that basis, as the publisher of the journal."[20]

In parallel, Louis fought the CP requirement in court on the grounds that it did not have a legal basis. To do so, he attempted to register 3615 PTT, which he said meant *Presses Télématiques et Téléphoniques*—a pun on the PTT ministry's name, but without a CP number. This request was denied by the PTT for lack of a CP number until the courts finally recognized that the requirement had no legal basis.[21]

The irony of Louis's story underscores the occasionally bizarre side effects of Minitel regulation. Here was a man who made his living helping people navigate the State bureaucracy—a system that was illegal at best. Meanwhile, his courtroom efforts at reform threatened the very conditions that provided his livelihood. Shortly after winning the fight against the CP number, Louis passed away.[22]

Getting the Content Approved by the Censor   A second bureaucratic barrier facing aspiring Minitel service providers was that, until 1986, the proposed content of their services was subject to prior approval by the executive branch of government represented by the prefect, and then by the PTT censor after 1986. Even though refusals were subject to judicial review through the administrative courts, the whole process tested the patience of would-be providers, and demanded an uncommon degree of persistence and facility with negotiating administrative complexity. As illustrated by the Amphitel story from chapter 3, this process could be as frustrating for inoffensive, vanilla services as it was for countercultural fare, but the bureaucratic hurdles were particularly challenging for fringe actors, especially those who wanted to use the new electronic platform for radical activism.

In 1983, Jean-Baptiste Ingold, a former activist with le Mouvement des objecteurs de conscience (MOC), decided to create a Minitel site to inform French conscientious objectors of their rights.[23] From 1963 to 1983, French law authorized young men to declare themselves conscientious objectors and avoid the then-mandatory military service, yet the same law made it a crime to distribute information "inciting a third party to benefit from the provisions of the law," with a penalty of up to three years in jail.[24] In 1983, the law changed to make it easier to claim the dispensation, and the incitement offense was removed.[25] When Ingold subsequently attempted to obtain prior authorization to open a Minitel site for the MOC, however, the prefect refused on the grounds that assisting conscientious objectors to claim dispensation from military service was illegal.[26] Through persistence, the MOC eventually obtained its short code, but this episode is typical of the censorship regime discussed in chapter 3. In the face of a frustrating, inconsistent administration, persistence was often the only way to get things done on the fringe of Télétel. Well, persistence, luck, and a friend on the inside.

While every publisher seeking a new short code was at the mercy of the local politburo, finding a friend "in the loop" could significantly accelerate the approval process.[27] Canal 4 was a start-up struck by exactly this sort of luck. One day, as its request for a short code awaited approval, one of the Canal 4 founders, Lagarde, paid a visit to the local DGT field office to register a new service. While there, he noticed that one of the Minitel censors was surfing 3615 SM from her desk. Lagarde struck up a conversation and pointed out that he was the operator of the service she was using. "She loved Minitel," Hannaby recalls. "She was very active on 3615 SM." With her help, the bureaucracy became much friendlier to Canal 4. "It took time," Hannaby says, "it was the PTT [after all], … but once [we were] in the loop, it was okay."[28]

Getting the Short Code Issued by the DGT Obtaining a CP number and getting the site's content approved were only part of the battle. The short code name itself also had to be approved by the DGT—a process reminiscent of getting a vanity license plate issued in the United States. As with many aspects of this process, the evaluation criteria were capricious and arbitrarily applied based on the whims of local administrators. In his capacity as a lobbyist, Baujard learned of a company in Toulouse that tried to register "3615 ELVIS." The Toulouse field office of the DGT rejected the request, ostensibly because the word *ELVIS* contained the syllable *vis*—which in French is phonetically reminiscent of the word *vice*. Two weeks later, a competitor managed to register the same short code through a different DGT field office, in Nancy. For Baujard, this case exemplified the problem that entrepreneurs faced: "I wouldn't go as far as saying that the system was mafia-like, but it was definitely corrupt."[29]

The back-scratching and exchange of favors evident in Baujard's story happened even within the State itself. Indeed, Minitel was as much a political as a technical achievement. In the implementation of Minitel, the DGT had to negotiate the competing interests of external constituents such as the press lobby as well as other ministries and institutions within the State. In chapter 3, we discussed how the broadcast television administration initially attempted to assume authority over Télétel. It took the pragmatism and persuasion skills of Justice Pierre Huet to instead lodge the platform under the Press Act. It also took the negotiation skills of the DGT's boss at the time, Jacques Dondoux, to cut an informal settlement with the press lobby and appease a public relations campaign that nearly killed Minitel before it was even released.[30] In exchange, though, the press lobby had obtained a monopoly over Kiosk access—a promise the DGT was eager to abide by. But that wish and these efforts didn't account for manipulations and other behind-the-scenes chicanery, the details of which largely remain veiled in the clouds of State intrigue and secrecy (as well as many off-the-record conversations with former Minitel actors).

Nonetheless, the impact of backroom dealing on the administration of Minitel was clear. Ostensibly, the popular 3615 family of short codes was restricted to service providers affiliated with a print publication, but the high market value of these recognizable codes made them a particularly ripe site of corruption. Although SNCF, the State-owned train company, participated in early Télétel experiments, it should have been shut out of 3615 due to its lack of any connection to the publishing industry.[31] Yet in 1984, it mysteriously managed to secure a 3615 short code all on its own, and began to operate an online service through which riders could check schedules and book tickets.[32]

For the average French citizen, 3615 SNCF was a valuable, convenient new service. Within the Minitel community, however, 3615 SNCF was a scandal. In the words of former Minitel project lead Jean-Paul Maury, the issuing of 3615 SNCF was the result of a "swindle," plain and simple.[33] The unfair allocation of short codes was a source of considerable frustration—even for people working at the DGT. The incident allegedly lead to the demise of Maury's predecessor, fired by Dondoux due to the SNCF affair, and Maury's promotion.[34] It revealed that jockeying with the Télétel administration was a multilevel game played on an uneven field according to rules that were routinely rewritten, when written at all (remember that the Conseil supérieur de la télématique, the censor in chief, was originally a shadow committee with no legal basis, as the Constitutional Council would later point out when Parliament attempted to subject the World Wide Web to a similar censorship regime).[35] It also reminds us that the state is not a unitary actor, and that the public face of Minitel belied considerable conflict within the administration. As Maury put it decades later, "Minitel was the DGT against everybody else."[36]

To some extent, competition for 3615 short codes presaged the conflicts over domain name registration and the practice of "cybersquatting" that continues to characterize addressing on the World Wide Web. Even prominent politicians were not immune to short code chicanery. Before the infamous porn site www.whitehouse.com, there was a controversy over the short codes 3615 TONTON and 3615 CHIRAC.

The political culture of 1980s' France was defined by the bitter rivalry between Jacques Chirac and François Mitterrand. The left-wing Mitterrand was elected president first in 1981 and again in 1988. In 1986, right-wing Chirac became prime minister, forcing a bitter cohabitation. During Mitterrand's reelection campaign, supporters affectionately took up his nickname *tonton*, or "uncle," and their enthusiasm was dubbed "tonton-mania" by the press. At that time, the DGT allowed the short code 3615 TONTON, an obvious reference to the campaign rhetoric, to be issued. Mitterrand campaigner (and future presidential candidate) Jean-Luc Mélenchon vigorously opposed the issuing of the short code, allegedly phoning Maury personally to complain that he was the one who had invented tontonmania and that the code should be issued to him. Maury declined to intervene in the dispute, and the code was issued to the first requester.[37] Shortly after allowing the issuing of 3615 TONTON, the DGT received a request for 3615 CHIRAC from a different third party. This time, the request was denied for reasons that remain unclear but seem motivated by political sympathies.[38] Evidently, even the most powerful politicians in France were not immune to the bureaucratic games of the DGT.

Getting Connected to the Transpac Network   Being approved for a short code was just one of the administrative hurdles facing would-be service providers. In order to add a privately run server to Télétel, one needed a connection to the Transpac network. Fortunately, thanks to modernization efforts at the end of the 1970s, the process of getting connected to Transpac was not nearly as much of an ordeal as it had been to get a plain old telephone line installed just a few years before. Still, in 1983, when Télétel launched, the typical waiting period for a Transpac installation was more than six months. While the delay dropped to seventeen weeks in 1984 and continued to fall thereafter, the long wait to get a connection remained a hindrance to innovation on Minitel.[39]

The long wait for a Transpac connection was both a technical problem (the DGT did not have the capacity to install lines as fast as needed, thereby creating a backlog) and a bureaucratic one: on this farm, all pigs were equal, but some were more equal than others; not surprisingly, then, entrepreneurs with political connections had the luxury of bypassing the backlog. Christian Quest, a Minitel software and content consultant, whose software Cristel enabled any Mac owner to turn their machine into a Minitel microserver, recalls a peculiar situation that illustrates the flexibility of the Transpac timelines. Quest had been contracted out to build the 3615 site for *La Roue de la Fortune*, the French version of *Wheel of*

Fortune. The site had to be up fast, in a matter of weeks, for the launch of the television game show in early 1987. The primary challenge, in Quest's initial assessment of the job, was not so much to map out the site, write the code, or create content but rather merely to get a Transpac line from the State. In his experience, it was not possible to get connected in so short a time. His employers were not concerned, though, and Quest was befuddled to find that the line was installed in a matter of days instead of months.[40]

Of course, Quest was not building just any Minitel site. *La Roue de la Fortune* was set to become a popular program on TF1, one of the premiere television channels in 1980s' France. Formerly run by the State, TF1 had recently been sold to the powerful Bouygues conglomerate in a wave of privatization following the election of Prime Minister Chirac. Critics decried the sale as a sweetheart deal between Chirac and corporate patriarch Francis Bouygues. The success of new programming like *La Roue de la Fortune* was important to TF1. With these political stakes, ensuring the swift connection of a Transpac server could not have been difficult. Jockeying with Minitel administration took many forms but neither prominent politicians nor their rich and powerful friends could access the network without first dancing with its bureaucratic guardians.

Cheating the Tariffs

Just like the attribution rules concerning short codes were strict yet creatively bendable, so were the financial aspects of the platform. The Kiosk system offered a variety of billing schemes for operators to choose. Each scheme was associated with a different numerical prefix on the service's short code so that potential users would be informed about the general cost of a service before connecting. The prefix 3613 indicated a toll-free service fully subsidized by the content provider—comparable to a 1-800 number in the United States; 3614 indicated a partially subsidized connection; but most short codes placed the full burden on the user. Users of 3615 services paid up to 1.25 francs per minute—one-third of which would be kept by France Telecom and two-thirds rebated to the content provider. Other short codes yielded even higher rates but were strictly controlled. While rates (set by Parliament and enshrined in the Consumer Code) were enforced by the DGT, Minitel service providers were clever, finding numerous social and technical means of turning the rate system to their advantage.

Assigning a billing rate to a new Minitel server depended on the type of service being created. According to the rules set by Parliament, for instance, only professional services such as corporate, legal, or medical databases could charge the highest rates.[41] This restriction set off a cat-and-mouse game between profit-seeking content providers, on the one hand, and the DGT (and its thirty employees monitoring the content of Minitel services at all times), on the other.[42] The operators of sexually explicit Minitel rose services are often remembered for attempting to creatively bend the rules to access higher rates.[43] Some operators applied for higher-rate short codes by posing as a "professional service" provider, as defined in the Consumer Code, only to later reveal their true (pink) colors. Typically, the provider would successfully reap a higher rate for a while until the DGT cat caught the pink, sexy mouse and severed its head (or in the terms of Minitel engineer Bernard Marti, "shut off the faucet").[44]

A more subtle and difficult-to-detect scam concerned the technical operation of Minitel host software. The per minute rates set by Kiosk put profit-seeking entrepreneurs in a bind when it came to technical innovation. On the one hand, a snappy, responsive system would likely attract and retain loyal users who would continue to pay for the service over time. On the other hand, services that loaded quickly for the user actually yielded less revenue per session than less efficient systems. In response to these mixed incentives, less scrupulous service providers purposely built slow systems to exploit the short-term gains. Reflecting on these mixed incentives, Hannaby recalls trying to design the most efficient protocol for the 1,200 baud Minitel modem to facilitate a high number of connections. "We had a very fast transfer rate," he remarked, "[but] there were many things done by other editors to increase, of course, the time spent by users online. It's a game of money, you know. That's it."[45]

A variation on the slow connection scam involved increasing the overall volume of data transmitted per session. The obvious approach to increasing data usage was to organize your service into an intentionally inefficient tree structure. This would require users to continually reload high-level pages before descending back down to the information they were looking for.[46] A more subtle method for increasing the data load involved the use of videotex control characters—signals intended to move the cursor around the screen or change the terminal settings. DGT network engineers routinely discovered third-party servers transmitting these invisible characters in the background of pages. While these special characters served no purpose for the service and did not affect the image produced on the user's display, they would imperceptibly increase the volume of data being sent over the network, resulting in longer connection times.[47]

Efficiency scams benefited from the tendency of users to blame the DGT for poor performance on Minitel. This misdirected criticism was maddening for DGT engineers dedicated to improving the network: "I had scrapped everything in the system to increase efficiency," Maury recalls, but "little pricks" purposefully slowed down the download rate.[48] Of course, this habit also reflected a broader association of the State with inefficiency and complexity. Ironically, the DGT was heavily invested in the continued support and improvement of Minitel. In addition to maintaining the infrastructure, the DGT funded studies and experiments on user interfaces, the results of which were published a series of helpful pamphlets titled *Recommandations aux partenaires Télétel* (see chapter 4).[49] Whether or not third-party service providers chose to follow these guidelines, however, was outside the control of the DGT. Indeed, one might wonder if unscrupulous developers strategically used this information to design their suboptimal, inefficient services, thereby exploiting the DGT's goodwill.[50]

Fringe Uses within Minitel/Télétel: The Users

Hacking the Way to Innovations

The origin story of the Minitel messageries—young hobbyists exploit a customer service system for illicit chatting—is a tale of user-driven innovation: technology adapted to a purpose never intended by its designers. True or false, the story of the messageries hack was not an isolated incident. As Valérie Schafer and Benjamin Thierry point out, the messageries story, which protagonist Michel Landaret has been asked by the media to rehash ad nauseam, is the kind of heroic narrative that is typically found in popular histories of technology.[51] In Minitel historiography, however, the repetition of this story overshadows concomitant experiences elsewhere in France.[52]

Looking beyond the widespread heroic narrative highlights the innovative contributions of many different users through various hacks and other unforeseen appropriations. During the early T3V experiment, for example, enthusiastic users, particularly teenagers, were instrumental in shaping the future of Minitel by requesting functions that the PTT had not imagined.[53] Sex workers were another group of users that pushed the boundaries of the system by repurposing the chat room as a site of solicitation.

But too strong a focus on the messageries obscures a whole range of other creative activities initiated by users, both individually and collectively. In the remainder of this section, we focus on two short case studies: the reverse phone book, and the use of Minitel as a protest tool.

The Reverse Phone Book For years, France Telecom held out the promise of a digital phone book as justification for building Minitel. We'll save trees, they argued, despite objections from the regional press industry. In reality, the print phone book was never discontinued during the life of Minitel. Rather, the print and digital phone books coexisted. To encourage use of the online directory and avoid the impression that a fee was now being charged for a service that was otherwise complimentary, the DGT made the digital phone book free—for the first three minutes of connection.

The three-minute time limit was a clever feature, and users quickly adopted techniques for avoiding the charges. Anyone who lived through the Minitel era remembers racing the clock to use the digital phone book: dialing, connecting, typing as fast as possible, and disconnecting before the first three minutes could run their course. Fortunately for slow typists, there was no upper limit on repeat connections, so one who failed to find the information in the first three minutes could simply hang up and try again, repeating the process as many times as necessary.[54]

The digital phone book also served as an entry-level hacking platform in the sense of a playground for digital experimentation. The combination of a free terminal and free connection time presented curiosity seekers with a platform for playful exploration: finding relatives, searching for homonyms, and so on—a 1980s' version of Googling one's own name. Whether it was intended to be pedagogical or not, free access to the online phone book provided novices with a low-risk opportunity to learn the basic functions of Minitel. For many, the telephone directory was a gateway to more sophisticated (and costlier) services.

Opportunities to hack the online phone book were also not lost on a young entrepreneur named Xavier Niel. In what is a seldom-told story, Niel downloaded the entire phone book from the France Telecom service, using the connection-disconnection-reconnection trick so familiar to the populace at large.[55] The process was slow enough that DGT engineers became aware that something strange was happening. Maury recalls, "I had been warned that some of the [Transpac] access points in the North [of France] were saturated." Although the print directory was distributed free of charge, the DGT regarded Niel's efforts as a theft. "He stole from us," continued Maury. "He set up batteries of PCs and queried the whole database two minutes at a time. ... [H]e stole the entire database from us!"[56] But replicating the database was just half of Niel's hack. In 1987, he successfully rolled out 3617 ANNU, a privately run reverse phone book charging a high connection rate typically reserved for professional services.

Niel's reverse phone book illustrates the extent to which the Minitel platform could be explored, exploited, and extended through the creativity of its users. The idea of creating a reverse phone book was not novel—in fact, a team of DGT engineers had created such a service two years earlier, but their boss refused to roll it into production.[57] Minitel was sufficiently open, however, that a private individual could produce services that would otherwise have been run by the PTT itself. This degree of flexibility and extensibility contradicts the perception of Minitel as a closed platform. Indeed, Minitel offered a uniquely generative platform for experimentation and innovation.

Off the record, many France Telecom executives and high-level engineers acknowledge that the company's unofficial motto has long been, "It is urgent to wait" (*Il est urgent d'attendre*). In contrast, and ironically, the open Minitel platform enabled those who didn't want to wait to move forward and create the services they wished to see. Minitel proved to be a prolific breeding ground for disruptive innovation, as exemplified by Niel's later career. Following the reverse phone book, Niel repeatedly provoked France Telecom to innovate with a series of low-cost telecom products, including fixed line and mobile Internet services. Symbolically, the 3617 ANNU reverse telephone directory is still offered by Free, Niel's company, in the form of an Android app.

Minitel as a Protest Tool

Beginning with the "Arab Spring" protests in 2010 and 2011, considerable scholarly attention has been paid to the role of social media platforms in organizing protest activity. Recent social movements have been dubbed "Facebook revolutions" and "Twitter revolutions" based on a perception of the central role of these systems in the dissemination of protest-related information. In addition to overstating the importance of social media to movement organizers, many observers mistakenly believed that the use of online communication platforms for organizing protest activities was a new phenomenon. Unfortunately, such ahistorical analyses overlooked a long tradition of adapting new media to political organizing, including several cases of radical action organized via Minitel during the 1980s and 1990s.[58]

If the State had desired to exert total control, then in theory the Minitel censorship regime should have squashed radical political speech. In practice, however, censorship was neither universal nor totalizing in its implementation. Speech control in the Minitel ecosystem occurred at two levels. The administrative authorization required to open a new service represented a site of a priori censorship, and the manual oversight of the content of third-party services represented a posteriori control. The gap between these two systems represented a space of freedom for activists.[59] In 1986, mass student protests used the messageries of left-wing print daily *Libération*, one of the main Télétel content providers, to organize the opposition to educational reform led by Minister Alain Devaquet.[60] In 1988 and 1989, nurses organized their protests over the messageries, and in 1992, finance ministry unionists followed suit.[61] While these efforts have seldom been documented, it is likely that there were many more examples of protest activity on Minitel.[62] What could be more French than a top-down social engineering project being appropriated by the street and used to fuel social unrest?[63]

Just as the Arab Spring wasn't a Facebook revolution, the demonstrations of the 1980s weren't Minitel revolutions. But the use of the Minitel platform to disseminate information about the protests was nonetheless significant—an early utterance of youthful activists appropriating online communication platforms to organize. Although this sort of bottom-up appropriation of communication infrastructures was not new—"the street finds its own uses for things" after all—it foretold the widespread adoption of computer networks by political activists and organizers since the late 1990s.

Fringe Uses Outside Télétel: "The Whiff of a Lonely Nerd's Hangout"

The Minitel fringe also extended beyond the boundaries of Télétel/Transpac, into sites and services that were outside the scope of the bureaucratic structures governing the State-run system. Indeed, shifting one's fringe activities outside Télétel involved a mix of advantages and disadvantages.

The advantages of going outside Télétel included a freedom to experiment with technical functions and content that may not have been acceptable within the standard DGT framework. The disadvantages were significant mainly for entrepreneurs: no Kiosk and no easy-to-remember short code. But so long as one didn't mind foregoing the possibility of profit (in the short term), the combination of the public switched telephone network (PSTN) and widely available Minitel terminal equipment provided a ready platform for technical experimentation. Unencumbered by the demands of running a business, young computer enthusiasts repurposed parts of Minitel to build small-scale networks of their own.

Dial-up bulletin board systems (BBSs) were popping up all over Europe and the United States during the 1980s.[64] For some hackers, crackers, and software traders living in France, it made sense to create hybrid

Minitel/BBSs, known in France as micro-serveurs, or "serveurs RTC," a reference to the *réseau téléphonique commuté* or public-switched telephone network.[65] Whereas getting connected to Télétel as an approved content provider required both money and prior administrative authorization, something that hobbyists and experimenters were not always able to secure, the telephone system offered an alternative, accessible network infrastructure. Rather than seek a direct connection to the Transpac network with the assistance of a France Telecom technician, micro-serveurs were connected to the PSTN using the standard jack found in every home. These low-cost servers were hosted on consumer-grade personal computers, such as the Apple Macintosh, Oric Telestrat, Commodore 128, Amstrad CPC, Amiga, Atari ST, and IBM-compatible PCs running MS-DOS.[66]

At a time when PC modems were prohibitively expensive for many hobbyists, the freely available Minitel terminal could be adapted to the task. Each Minitel contained a 1,200 baud modem and a serial port that could be connected to a PC. By running server software on the PC and using the Minitel to connect to the telephone network, often from a college dorm room or teenager's bedroom, a hobbyist could create a relatively inexpensive micro-serveur.[67] Potential users could use the same free Minitel terminals to dial into the system, no PC required. Assuming that both the user and server were located in the same city, incoming callers paid only for the cost of a local call.[68]

Whereas official Minitel services were advertised in magazines and listed in periodicals, the phone numbers of micro-serveurs were distributed through alternative channels. They circulated through word of mouth, fanzines, and even in the graphical interfaces of computer games.[69] For example, Christophe Andréani, a programmer who was active in the RTC scene, developed TURBO GT, an early Atari ST game adapted from the arcade classic Super Sprint. Andréani, known online as CHRIST, inserted the phone number for Pinky, an RTC server run by his friend Godefroy Troude, as a decorative advertisement in the middle of the TURBO GT race track. Later, he inserted a second Pinky easter egg in the Bubble Ghost video game.[70] Evidence of the underground RTC culture was hiding in plain sight.

Compared to Télétel-approved services with Transpac connections and short codes, the hobbyist RTC micro-serveurs were quantitatively a marginal phenomenon, most likely in the low hundreds.[71] Unlike with Télétel, they never reached the critical mass that would have had them shake the existing social, economic, and political order. Through obscurity, then, they remained shielded from the backlash created by the regional press lobby and politicians. Within the DGT, their existence was known, but shrugged off as something insignificant—minor mischief carried out by pimply teenagers and not worth thinking about.[72] To borrow from journalist Katie Hafner's description of contemporaneous and similarly marginalized BBSs in the US, Minitel administrators disregarded RTC servers as systems with "the whiff of a lonely nerd's hangout."[73]

As a result of the dismissive attitude from Télétel authorities, the operators of micro-serveurs (known in that community as "sysops," a term of art borrowed from the transnational BBS culture) benefited from an unfettered freedom to innovate in terms of content. They were never subject to the restrictions imposed on Télétel content creators, such as the censorship regime and requirement to be recognized as an official press company in order to publish. Despite their small numbers, micro-serveurs bonded together a generation of French hackers, some of whom later participated in the development and popularization of the early French Internet.[74]

And while the micro-serveurs had no direct impact on the design and implementation of the Télétel network, they serve to highlight the fact that Minitel hardware and software were open to unauthorized experimentation. This openness enabled the creation of unofficial Minitel ecosystems and user communities that coexisted with the official Télétel network. Today, the legacy of these hobbyist-run systems lives on. With the shutting down of Télétel in 2012, hackers renewed their interest in repurposing the basic Minitel technology and expanding its possibilities. Minitel terminals are repurposed to display videotex art, access Twitter, and monitor Linux systems.[75] As Minitel continues to grow in its retirement, the creativity of enthusiasts demonstrates that the opacity and complexity of the Télétel network were primarily features of its administration rather than the technology itself.

Conclusion

Minitel began as a top-down, State-run project with the ambitious goal of outfitting the whole of France with a cutting-edge digital telecommunications system in less than a decade. The authority of the State was distributed throughout the architecture of the system. Network traffic was routed through centralized State hubs, and would-be service providers required prior approval from State administrators. It would seem that a system like this would offer little tolerance for fringe or countercultural activities. And yet the cultural experience of Minitel was marked by ambiguity, negotiation, experimentation, and exploration.

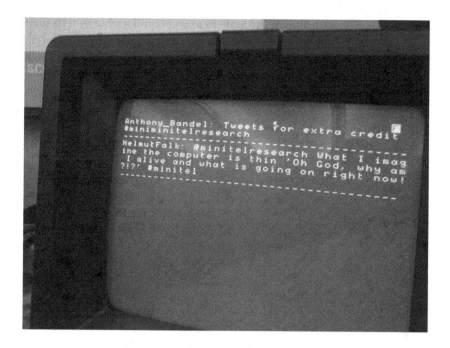

Figure 6.1 Minitel terminal repurposed to display messages from Twitter. *Source:* Authors' collection.

Crucially, Minitel was designed to be a platform for the development of services by third parties rather than a service provider itself. With the advent of the Kiosk system for billing and payment, Minitel supplied a fertile environment for the creation of new services. Unfortunately, these technological innovations were also saddled with a complex administrative structure charged with carrying out a program of universal, content-based censorship. In practice, however, this administrative structure was not a monolith. Favors were exchanged, and backs were scratched. From the power elite to the enterprising upstart, users were as likely to "hack" Minitel's administration as its technology.

Not everyone interested in running a Minitel server was in a position to engage the bureaucracy, however. The mismatch between curiosity and access was particularly pronounced among teenaged computer hobbyists, many of whom had recently come into possession of a PC. Shut out of the official Télétel infrastructure, these enthusiasts used the standard Minitel terminal as a makeshift modem to connect their home PCs to the analog telephone network. The resulting micro-serveurs were a small but lively part of Minitel culture. Their users and operators, meanwhile, would later carry their skills and experiences onto the nascent French Internet.

The ambition of the State to exert central authority tells just one side of the Minitel story. On the ground, Minitel was adopted, explored, hacked, and extended by myriad actors to serve purposes that could not have been envisioned by the system's original designers. The scale and swiftness of the Minitel deployment ensured that users would find ways to bend the rules, circumvent State control, and adapt the new technology to their own ends.

The core of this book provided an in-depth political, social, legal, and business history of the Minitel platform's technological design, implementation, and associated practices. The exceptional Minitel story enables us to grasp subtle shades on the openness spectrum. It also sheds new light on the entangled roles of the state and the private sector in fostering digital innovation in ways that defy conventional Internet policy wisdom. Chapter 2 mapped out the key technical components of Minitel, including its physical infrastructure, routing protocols, addressing scheme, video standard, software interface, and unusual accounting and billing apparatuses. Together, these elements sustained a generative platform for the creation of novel online services and the emergence of thriving virtual communities. Chapter 3 explained how the unique French culture was embedded in the protocols, and how state policy and national identity were woven deeply into the design and implementation of the system. In particular, we discussed the relationship between specific features of the Minitel platform and the French political tradition of centralization. The PTT at the center of all networked activity played as a leitmotiv against a backdrop of economic and infrastructure development. Most Minitel stories, especially on the US side of the Atlantic, stop there. In chapter 4, we showed another side: the hybrid architecture of the Minitel platform, with private innovation decentralized to the edges of the public network. This marked an ideological shift in French policy—one that enhanced spontaneity, mobility, and imagination, to borrow the words of Nora and Minc, and marked a transition from traditional dirigisme to state venture capitalism *à la française*. In chapter 5, we detailed the results of this public–private partnership on content creation, with a particular focus on *Minitel rose* and private-sector digital innovations that the United States would not see appear until after 1995. In chapter 6, we returned to a consideration of the radical potential of the Minitel system in the hands of a creative populace, and showed that the seemingly tight grip of the State over Minitel did not prevent fringe uses of the network.

But if the system was such a success, why did it fail? Taking the concepts of *success* and *failure* with a grain of salt, we now discuss what worked and what didn't work in the Minitel story. We also address what we believe is a much more important question: What do we learn from the Minitel experience that can inform the design and regulation of future information networks to foster innovation and civic participation?

There are many reasons to think of Minitel as a domestic success. Télétel, as a cash cow for the DGT, enabled the State to completely digitize an ailing phone network. Within a few years, France went from having one of the worst phone networks in the industrialized world to leapfrogging into the most "wired" country in the world.[1] By the same token, it enabled an entire country to go online to experiment, play, and work with tens of thousands of innovative services—something unheard of at the time elsewhere in Europe and the United States, where regional bulletin board systems and nationwide online services such as CompuServe were accessible to just a privileged fraction of the population and did not offer the same wealth of information and interaction. So why did Minitel succeed in terms of user adoption and diversity of content and services, while in the United States, privately run walled gardens floundered, only to be swallowed up by a state-funded Internet in the mid-1990s?

Today, Internet service providers in the United States argue that only deregulated, privately owned telecommunication networks can promote as well as protect openness and innovation. In their opposition to "net neutrality" regulations, they suggest that any form of government oversight will doom the Internet. Minitel provides a convenient bugbear for this extreme position. Look, they say, Minitel collapsed because it was regulated! In reality, however, the case of Minitel can be used to argue precisely the opposite point. Public investment and regulation of the Minitel platform did not equal total dirigisme nor did it stifle innovation. Public funding almost wholly supported internetworking research in the United States until the mid-1990s, when the backbone of the NSFNET was turned over to private control and commercial exploitation. In France, public support took a different form: in addition to building the underlying public data network Transpac, the State built a platform layer atop this infrastructure, and strategically incentivized participation on the part of both individual users and service providers.

In economic terms, the Minitel platform consisted of two sides: users and service providers. The State primed the pump on the user side of the market by distributing terminal equipment to the populace at no cost. It also stimulated growth on the service providers' side of the market by supplying Kiosk, a convenient system for billing and accounting. Kiosk, it is worth noting, was not imposed but instead offered on a voluntary basis to the service providers, which as it turned out, embraced it en masse. This multifaceted state intervention catalyzed a private industry of Minitel service providers that had the freedom to innovate from the edges of the network. It also supported the development of a thriving hardware peripherals industry.

So, state intervention in an online system does not necessarily equal a loss of freedom. Quite to the contrary, if well thought out, public subsidy programs can foster creativity and development across the network. In contrast, leaving the private sector solely responsible for organizing a platform can lead to market fragmentation and stagnation, as evidenced by the US videotex experiments of the 1980s.[2]

Some critics of Minitel, including in France, suggest that "success" was only acquired at the cost of a major financial loss for the State. In 1989, the general auditor criticized the DGT and claimed that Télétel was losing money. The minister of the PTT countered, citing a number of independent reports showing massive surplus. Serious authors agree that it is impossible to tell whether or not Télétel made or lost money.[3] Aside from Télétel's own balance sheet, there are too many intangibles that are either difficult or impossible to quantify. Beyond counting the number of jobs created by the telematics industry, how might one quantify the cultural and economic value of leapfrogging into the digital age? Or creating a generation that was tech savvy before most people in the US had ever heard of the information superhighway?

Minitel touched multiple generations, from youngsters who took their first digital steps on the platform and went on to work in the dot-com industry, to older users who were left in distress on the 2012 shutdown. A significant number of elderly people, who appreciated the simplicity of the terminal and did not own PCs, were simply cut off from services they were in the habit of accessing, including the white and yellow pages.[4] At the time of the closure, 3615 ULLA, one of the best-known *messageries*, was still getting twenty-five thousand calls per month—in spite of the wide availability of pornography on the Internet.[5] In Brittany, a major agricultural region, 10 percent of the industry was still using Minitel professionally.[6] Overall, France Telecom estimated that almost half a million users were still active on the platform—a testament to Minitel's ease of use and robustness.[7]

What clearly did not succeed were efforts to export the Minitel model to other national contexts. Spreading the jewels of French technology throughout the world was an explicit goal of Nora and Minc's influential report, *The Computerization of Society*, and France Telecom created a subsidiary, Intelmatique, to do just that. Although France Telecom spared no expense promoting its novel videotex system abroad, foreign countries simply did not embrace Minitel.[8] Efforts to remake Minitel as a walled garden commercial service, such as 101 Online in the San Francisco Bay Area, were never crowned with success and are scarcely remembered today.[9]

Notably, however, certain architectural features of Minitel live on in the form of privately held platforms such as the Apple ecosystem. In almost every way, the Apple ecosystem mirrors the design of Télétel—except that it lacks the transparency and openness of the French system. Like the Télétel Kiosk system, the Apple App Store offers a market mechanism for matching third-party content providers with Apple users. Just as France Telecom took a fee from each Télétel connection, Apple takes a fee from each sale in the App Store. This closed system of micropayments makes it easy for app creators to monetize their products and is certainly a major factor in the success of the Apple platform. Like Télétel, Apple also exercises a form of censorship on its platform. As Wikileaks learned the hard way, one can only distribute software to iOS users with Apple's permission.[10]

Unlike Télétel, Apple is not operating in the interest of the public. Whereas all censorship decisions on Télétel were subject to due process and could be appealed in a court of law, Apple exercises absolute control over the communication that takes place on its platform. The public has no interest, no representation, and no recourse to settle disputes. Likewise, where Télétel published an open standard and allowed any hardware to join the network, the Apple ecosystem is accessible only to Apple's own devices. As a result, Minitel fostered the development of a strong, competitive, private hardware industry at the terminal level as well as the host level, which supported the development of French companies like Alcatel and Matra, and ironically, US companies such as AT&T and Texas Instruments, whereas every increase in Apple's platform penetration mechanically increases Apple—and only Apple's—hardware penetration. The difference in the exercise of control over engineering decisions extends also to the software and services provided on each platform.

Whereas Minitel developers were free to use any technologies to create their services, iOS developers are limited to the programming languages and development tools approved by Apple.[11]

The comparison between Minitel and Apple offers two key lessons. First, openness is not a binary concept. Systems are neither fully open nor fully closed. Rather, openness is a shaded, multicomponent concept. This is important to keep in mind as we analyze the evolution of the Internet, which, it seems, is moving piece by piece toward less openness.

A second lesson of the Télétel/iOS comparison is that sometimes, complete control of network infrastructure by the private sector stifles rather than supports creativity and innovation. Apple controls its App Store content more strictly than France Telecom ever did because, as a privately owned platform, it is not bound by due process or free speech regulations. The prevalence of platforms such as the App Store suggests that targeted government intervention might restore competition and openness in arenas of the Internet where the interests of the private sector and those of the public have fallen too far out of alignment.

Many consider the end of Minitel after thirty years of continuous operation as proof of the success of the Internet over Minitel, and implicitly, the US model over the French one.[12] We disagree. We consider, as Daniel Hannaby has also suggested, that the end of Minitel was simply the end of a cycle in the ongoing process of media change. "I don't think it failed," remarked the French entrepreneur. "Thirty years is a long time in technology. It's a very long time."[13] Indeed, key parts of the platform had become antiquated. For example, the platform relied in great part on its low barriers to entry, particularly the low-cost, user-friendly terminal. What made the platform great, in that sense, is also what killed it. The basic videotex terminal was frozen in time and could not evolve without fundamentally changing the economics of the platform.

Télétel was also accessible from PCs, but by the time French PC adoption began to approach the penetration of Minitel, a wonderful new invention had appeared: the World Wide Web. And here, naysayers see the triumph of private sector investment over publicly subsidized development. But this perspective overlooks two crucial historical details. First, the fundamental technologies giving rise to the web were developed in research institutions across the United States and Europe with public support. As Marc Andreessen described the development of his Mosaic web browser: "If it had been left to private industry, it wouldn't have happened."[14] Second, to argue that the de facto standardization of TCP/IP over X.25 or any other internetworking protocol reflects the success of a specific policy position ignores numerous structural and contextual factors

shaping the diffusion of protocols among academic and industrial computing facilities during the 1980s. The emergence of the web was not a
triumph of US over French policy, otherwise unrestrained competition in
the videotex field in the 1980s would have seen US online penetration
rates trump the French ones. Rather, we may regard the emergence of the
web as the end of a cycle: the replacement of a great technology, videotex,
and a great platform, Télétel, with a more modern and even greater technology and ecosystem.

The end of Minitel prompts us to consider the telematics future spread
out before us. It is a mistake to think that the Internet as we know it will
survive as long has Minitel did. Thirty years is, indeed, a long time. The
Internet has only been accessible to the general public for twenty years,
and most people have only been online for half that time.[15] There is no
reason to think that in ten years, the Internet will be the same as today,
and that the openness characteristic of the early Internet will persist.

As early as the 1990s, Lawrence Lessig pointed out that the Internet
had the potential to become the antithesis of freedom.[16] He was right. Soon
after the privatization of the NSFNET backbone, governments around the
world and corporations alike started moving toward partitioning the open
Internet to sustain their own interests, which are not always in line with
those of the citizenry. Consider, for example, the Great Firewall of China,
or the cyberwalls implemented by corporations such as Netflix and Major
League Baseball to partition the Internet by geography.[17]

The fundamental principles underlying the Internet, including openness and interconnection, have been contested ever since the Internet was
privatized, for a simple reason: the corporations that control the center of
the network have incentives that do not align with those of their users. The
efforts of Internet service providers around the world to impose two-
sided pricing models and violate net neutrality principles is aimed at
shifting control from the edges toward the center of the networks. In real
ways, then, Internet service providers are actively moving the Internet
toward an architecture that more closely resembles Minitel than the
decentralized networks of the 1980s and 1990s. When US Internet service
providers try to charge content providers such as Netflix for privileged
access to their networks, are they not acting like a centralized censor
leveraging their monopolistic or oligopolistic position? Are they not
trying to make the Internet look a little more like a privately run child
of Télétel?

Minitel was not just the result of state dirigisme, nor was the Internet
solely the result of private sector ingenuity. Titling this book *Minitel:
Welcome to the Internet* is not only a reminder that Minitel preceded the

public Internet but also an argument for thinking differently about shaping the Internet's future. As a platform, Minitel was in many ways similar to platforms operated by Amazon, Apple, Google, or Facebook. But whereas today's dominant platforms are operated wholly in the interest of their owners, Minitel represented a complex balance of public and private interests. As platforms continue to enclose the online world, the Internet risks being reduced to a set of incompatible walled gardens. The story of Minitel, with its three decades of continuous operation, offers guidance toward a different future characterized by a commitment to serving the public interest. Unless strategic government intervention preserves the elements of openness and the balance of power between public and private interests that drew so many hackers, entrepreneurs, experimenters, and explorers to the Internet in the first place, the Internet as we have known it since the 1990s may not live to see thirty years.

Appendix: Currency Conversion Table

	FRANCS	DOLLARS	2016 DOLLARS
1983	10	1.3	3.1
1984	10	1.2	2.75
1985	10	1.1	2.43
1986	10	1.5	2.4
1987	10	1.6	3.35
1988	10	1.6	3.21
1989	10	1.5	2.87
1990	10	1.7	3.07
1991	10	1.6	2.8
1992	10	2	3.4
1993	10	1.7	2.82

Source: central banks data compiled by FXTOP SARL; Frink Historical Currency Conversions

Glossary

Term	Description
11, 3611, *Le 11*	Prefix for accessing the electronic phone book.
3613	Prefix for connections fully paid for by the service provider.
3614	Prefix for connections paid for by the user.
3615	Prefix for services paid for by the user at a higher rate than 3614. Most popular culture services, including messageries roses, were listed under 3615.
3616, 3617, 3619	Prefixes for services paid for by the user at a higher rate than 3615.
3618	Prefix used to establish a direct connection from an end user to another end user (Minitel to Minitel service).
Annuaire électronique	Electronic phone book.
Antiope	The videotex display standard used in Télétel.
Baud rate	Bits per second.
CCETT	Centre commun d'études de télévision et télécommunications. The joint research center of the television and telecommunications agencies (ORTF and DGT).
CNET	Centre national d'études des télécommunications. The research center of the DGT.

Term	Description
CST	Conseil supérieur de la télématique. Superior Telematics Council. The administrative agency in charge of overseeing Télétel.
DGT	Direction générale des télécommunications. The branch of the PTT responsible for operating the phone network and Téletel.
Domotique	Home automation.
France Telecom	Organizational identity of the DGT after 1988. Would keep the name until 2013 when it was renamed Orange, by then a fully privatized corporation.
Intelmatique	The France Telecom affiliate in charge of exporting Minitel.
IP	Internet Protocol.
Kiosque	Literally, kiosk or newsstand, but in the context of Minitel, *le kiosque* refers to the system for billing users for their connection time.
Logiciel	Software.
Messagerie	Chat room.
Minitel	Médium interactif par numérisation d'information téléphonique. Literally, interactive medium by digitization of telephonic information.
Miniteliste	Minitel user.
Orange	Legacy incumbent phone operator in France. Formerly France Telecom, which was formerly the DGT.
ORTF	Office de radiodiffusion-télévision française. The State radio and television monopoly operator until 1974.
PAVI	Point d'accès vidéotex. Videotex access point. Gateway between the PSTN and the Transpac public data network.
PDN	Public data network.
PSTN	Public switched telephone network.
PTT	Post, Telegraph and Telephone Ministry.
RTC	Réseau téléphonique commuté. The public switched telephone network (PSTN).

Term	Description
T3V	Télétel 3V. The 3 "V's" refer to the cities of Vélizy, Versailles, and Val de Bièvre, where one of the two large-scale Minitel experiments was conducted.
TDF	Télédiffusion de France. State radio and television monopoly transmission operator after 1974.
Télématique	Information and communication services provided by a computer network. A combination of the words "télécommunications" ("telecommunications") and "informatique" ("informatics").
Télétel	The name of the Minitel ecosystem, combining both analog and digital infrastructures as well as terminal and host servers joined (and billed) by a network of gateways.
Teletext	A noninteractive variant of videotex often used to broadcast metadata and news alongside television programming.
Transpac	The nationwide packet-switched network in France operated by the DGT, France Telecom, and Orange from 1979 to 2012 using the X.25 protocol.
Videotex	An interactive system for the transmission and visual display of data combining telephone and television technologies.
Virtual circuit	Preset path between computers where packets all travel on that fixed route.
X.25	Protocol for packet-switched networks providing virtual circuit connections based on the OSI model.

Notes

Chapter 1

1. Andrew L. Russell and Valérie Schafer, "In the Shadow of ARPANET and Internet: Louis Pouzin and the Cyclades Network in the 1970s," *Technology and Culture* 55, no. 4 (2014): 880–907; Cade Metz, "Say *Bonjour* to the Internet's Long-Lost French Uncle," *Wired*, January 3, 2013, accessed September 14, 2016, http://www.wired.com/2013/01/louis_pouzin_internet_hall/.

2. Marie Marchand, *The Minitel Saga: A French Success Story* (Paris: Larousse, 1988); Valérie Schafer and Benjamin G. Thierry, *Le Minitel: L'enfance numérique de la France* (Paris: Nuvis, 2012), 96–100; Marie Carpenter, *La bataille des télécoms: Vers une France numérique* (Paris: Economica, 2011); Vincent Glad, "Minitel: comment les Dernières Nouvelles d'Alsace ont inventé l'Internet social," *Slate*, November 18, 2011, accessed September 17, 2016, http://www.slate.fr/story/46415/minitel-dna-internet-social.

3. See, for example, Howard Rheingold, *The Virtual Community: Homesteading on the Electronic Frontier* (Reading, MA: Addison-Wesley, 1993).

4. Damien Leloup, "Aux Etats-Unis, le 'modèle Minitel' surprend toujours," *Le Monde*, June 19, 2012, accessed September 14, 2016, http://www.lemonde.fr/technologies/article/2012/06/29/aux-etats-unis-le-modele-minitel-surprend-toujours_1726833_651865.html.

5. "(HZ) France Minitel," AP Archive, June 27, 2012, accessed September 14, 2016, http://www.aparchive.com/metadata/youtube/a9ef10495e306b24603507a56cf2d99d.

6. See Janet Abbate, *Inventing the Internet* (Cambridge, MA: MIT Press, 1999); Paul N. Edwards, *The Closed World Computers and the Politics of Discourse in Cold War America* (Cambridge, MA: MIT Press, 1997); Fred Turner, *From Counterculture to Cyberculture: Stewart Brand, the Whole Earth Network, and the Rise of Digital Utopianism* (Chicago: University of Chicago Press, 2006).

7. In the United States, many fully private online ventures ran concurrently with Minitel using similar technology. But systems like the Source, Viewtron,

Covidea, Trintex, or Keycom failed to attract any significant user base, and the value of getting online was too obtuse for most consumers to justify the steep subscription fees and up-front equipment costs. The services that survived the 1980s, such as CompuServe, Prodigy, and Quantum Link/America Online, only did so by migrating their businesses to the government-funded platform we've come to know generally as "the Internet." See, in general, Jerome Aumente, *New Electronic Pathways: Videotex, Teletext, and Online Databases* (Newbury Park, CA: Sage, 1987), 44–74; Julien Mailland, "101 Online: American Minitel Network and Lessons from Its Failure," *IEEE Annals of the History of Computing* 38, no. 1 (January–March 2016): 6–22.

8. Note that throughout this book, we will capitalize the word *State* when referring to the state apparatus of France as opposed to the noncapitalized generic reference to a state—mirroring the French practice that opposes *l'État* to *un état*.

9. Espace des sciences, "France Télécom et la Bretagne," accessed September 14, 2016, http://www.espace-sciences.org/archives/science/17865.html.

10. On this broad topic, see, in general, Marie Carpenter, *La bataille des télécoms: Vers une France numérique* (Paris: Economica, 2011).

11. For further discussion of network effects in the media industries, see Carl Shapiro and Hal Varian, *Information Rules: A Strategic Guide to the Network Economy* (Boston: Harvard Business School Press, 1999), 180.

12. A small but dedicated cohort of farmers and older folks continued to access Minitel regularly right up to the end. In its final months, journalists were especially keen to seek out these lingering *minitelistes* and brief interviews provided a human-interest angle to coverage of the system shutdown. Scott Sayare, "On the Farms of France, the Death of a Pixelated Workhorse," *New York Times*, June 27, 2012, accessed September 14, 2016, http://www.nytimes.com/2012/06/28/world/europe/after-3-decades-in-france-minitels-days-are-numbered.html.

13. Anne Helmond, "The Platformization of the Web: Making Web Data Platform Ready," *Social Media + Society* 1, no. 2 (July 1, 2015): 2056305115603080, doi: 10.1177/2056305115603080.

14. Bernard Marti, *De Minitel à Internet: 30 ans de services en ligne* (Cesson-Sévigné: Armorhistel, 2011).

15. Paul E. Ceruzzi, *Internet Alley: High Technology in Tysons Corner, 1945–2005* (Cambridge, MA: MIT Press, 2008).

16. Po Bronson, *The Nudist on the Late Shift* (New York: Random House, 1999), xx–xxi.

17. Ingrid Burrington, "Seeing Networks in New York City," 2014, accessed September 14, 2016, http://seeingnetworks.in/nyc/. See also Ingrid Burrington, *Networks of New York: An Illustrated Field Guide to Urban Internet Infrastructure* (New York: Melville House Books, 2016).

18. The practice of "infrastructural inversion" was developed in the work of Geoffrey Bowker and Susan Leigh Star. See, for example, Geoffery C. Bowker and Susan Leigh Star, *Sorting Things Out: Classification and Its Consequences* (Cambridge, MA: MIT Press, 1999).

19. Unless otherwise noted, all data in this chapter, including composite graphs and tables, are sourced directly from France Telecom's official reports, including annual reports (*rapports annuels*), annual surveys (*Baromètre, Bilan et*

Perspectives), and periodic newsletters (*La lettre de Télétel, La Lettre de Télétel et d'Audiotel*, and *La Lettre des Services en Ligne*), published between 1982 and 1997, and available at the France Telecom Archives (Orange/Direction de la Gestion et de la Conservation de l'Information) in Alfortville, France. The relevant boxes at Orange/Direction de la Gestion et de la Conservation de l'Information are as follows: 97030/1, 96030/2, 15078/01, 15078/02, 345, 347, 350, 353, 354, 355, 356, 357, and 358.

20. Eli Noam, "Why the Internet Will Be Regulated," *Educom Review* 32, no. 5 (September–October 1997), accessed September 15, 2016, http://net.educause.edu/apps/er/review/reviewArticles/32512.html; Xavier de La Porte, "Fred Turner: Google, Uber et l'idéologie de la Silicon Valley en treize mots," *L'Obs avec Rue 89*, December 21, 2014, accessed September 15, 2016, http://rue89.nouvelobs.com/2014/12/21/fred-turner-google-uber-lideologie-silicon-valley-treize-mots-256671.

21. Jacques Vallée, *The Heart of the Internet: An Insider's View of the Origin and Promise of the On-Line Revolution* (Charlottesville, VA: Hampton Roads Publishing, 2003), 105.

22. Michael Cusumano, "Technology Strategy and Management: The Evolution of Platform Thinking," *Commununications of the ACM* 53, no. 1 (January 2010): 32–34, doi:10.1145/1629175.1629189.

23. Richard Schmalensee, testimony, United States v. Microsoft Corporation, January 13, 1999.

24. United States District Court for the District of Columbia, "Transcript of Trial before the Honorable Thomas P. Jackson, United States District Judge," January 13, 1999, 81–82, accessed September 15, 2016, https://cyber.law.harvard.edu/msdoj/transcripts/0113b.doc.

25. For a detailed account of the circulation of *platform* during this period, see Tarleton Gillespie, "The Politics of 'Platforms,'" *New Media and Society* 12, no. 3 (May 1, 2010): 347–364, doi:10.1177/1461444809342738; Helmond, "The Platformization of the Web."

26. Richard J. Gilbert and Michael L. Katz, "An Economist's Guide to U.S. v. Microsoft," *Journal of Economic Perspectives* 15, no. 2 (2001): 25–44.

27. Prior to 2005, papers published on two-sided markets used a variety of terms to refer to firms operating a platform: matchmaker, intermediary, and even *cybermediary*. See Geoffrey Parker and Marshall W. Van Alstyne, "Information Complements, Substitutes, and Strategic Product Design" (scholarly paper, Social Science Research Network, Rochester, NY, November 8, 2000), accessed September 15, 2016, http://papers.ssrn.com/abstract=249585; Bernard Caillaud and Bruno Jullien, "Chicken and Egg: Competing Matchmakers" (scholarly paper, Social Science Research Network, Rochester, NY, July 1, 2001), accessed September 15, 2016, http://papers.ssrn.com/abstract=278562; Bernard Caillaud and Bruno Jullien, "Chicken and Egg: Competition among Intermediation Service Providers," *RAND Journal of Economics* 34, no. 2 (2003): 309–328, doi:10.2307/1593720.

28. Mark Armstrong, "Competition in Two-Sided Markets," *The RAND Journal of Economics* 37, no. 3 (September 1, 2006): 668–691, doi:10.1111/j.1756-2171.2006. tb00037.x; Marc Rysman, "The Economics of Two-Sided Markets," *The Journal of Economic Perspectives* 23, no. 3 (2009): 125–143.

29. Jean-Charles Rochet and Jean Tirole, "Platform Competition in Two-Sided Markets," *Journal of the European Economic Association* 1, no. 4 (2003): 990–1029; Jean-Charles Rochet and Jean Tirole, "Two-Sided Markets: A Progress Report," *RAND Journal of Economics* 37, no. 3 (September 1, 2006): 645–667, doi:10.1111/ j.1756-2171.2006.tb00036.x.

30. Helmond, "The Platformization of the Web."

31. Joss Hands, "Introduction: Politics, Power, and 'Platformativity,'" *Culture Machine* 14 (2013): 1–9.

32. Helmond, "The Platformization of the Web."

33. Taina Bucher, "A Technicity of Attention: How Software 'Makes Sense,'" *Culture Machine* 13 (2012), accessed September 15, 2016, http://www.culturemachine. net/index.php/cm/article/view/470.

34. Helmond ("The Platformization of the Web") refers to the simultaneous centralization and decentralization as the "dual logic of platformization."

35. Gillespie, "The Politics of 'Platforms.'"

36. Megan Sapnar Ankerson, "Writing Web Histories with an Eye on the Analog Past," *New Media and Society* 14, no. 3 (May 1, 2012): 384–400, doi:10.1177/ 1461444811414834.

37. Janet Delve and David Anderson, eds., *Gaming Environments and Virtual Worlds*, vol. 3, *The Preservation of Complex Objects* (London: Facet Publishing, 2013); Henry Lowood, Devin Monnens, Zach Vowell, Judd Ethan Ruggill, Ken S. McAllister, and Andrew Armstrong, "Before It's Too Late: A Digital Game Preservation White Paper," *American Journal of Play* 2, no. 2 (October 1, 2009): 139–166; Jerome P. McDonough, Robert Olendorf, Matthew Kirschenbaum, Kari Kraus, Doug Reside, Rachel Donahue, Andrew Phelps, Christopher Egert, Henry Lowood, and Susan Rojo, "Preserving Virtual Worlds Final Report," August 31, 2010, accessed September 15, 2016, https://www.ideals.illinois.edu/ handle/2142/17097.

38. Richard A. Bartle, "Archaeology versus Anthropology: What Can Truly Be Preserved?" in *Gaming Environments and Virtual Worlds*, ed. Janet Delve and David Anderson (London: Facet Publishing, 2013), 92–97.

39. Media scholar Mia Consalvo developed the term *paratext*, on loan from literary studies, to describe the "game-related" materials that accompany a video game's development, introduction, and reception. These include rumors, behind-the-scenes images, previews, and walk-through, many of which are created by players and circulate wholly outside the control of a game's developers. Although Minitel was not principally a gaming platform, we observe similar networks of paratexts growing around new services and peripherals. See Mia Consalvo, *Cheating: Gaining Advantage in Videogames* (Cambridge, MA: MIT Press, 2007).

40. See, for example, Julien Mailland and Kevin Driscoll, "Minitel Terminal as a Twitter Client" (demo presented at the Telecommunications Policy Research Conference, George Mason University School of Law, Arlington, VA, September 21, 2012).

41. Ankerson, "Writing Web Histories with an Eye on the Analog Past."

42. This approach draws on the field of "platform studies," an orientation to the study of media and society that attends to the particular technical features of a system. See Ian Bogost and Nick Montfort, "New Media as Material Constraint:

An Introduction to Platform Studies," in *Electronic Techtonics: Thinking at the Interface* (Durham, NC: First International HASTAC Conference, Duke University, 2007), 176–192; Nick Montfort and Ian Bogost, *Racing the Beam: The Atari Video Computer System* (Cambridge, MA: MIT Press, 2009).

43. Montfort and Bogost, *Racing the Beam*; Jimmy Maher, *The Future Was Here: The Commodore Amiga* (Cambridge, MA: MIT Press, 2012); Nick Montfort and Mia Consalvo, "The Dreamcast, Console of the Avant-Garde," *Loading...* 6, no. 9 (2012), accessed September 16, 2016, http://journals.sfu.ca/loading/index.php/loading/article/view/104; Michael L Black, "Narrative and Spatial Form in Digital Media: A Platform Study of the SCUMM Engine and Ron Gilbert's The Secret of Monkey Island," *Games and Culture*, April 12, 2012, doi:10.1177/1555412012440317; Gillespie, "The Politics of 'Platforms'"; Hands, "Introduction: Politics, Power, and 'Platformativity'"; Eugenia Siapera, "Platform Infomediation and Journalism," *Culture Machine* 14 (2013): 1–28; Ganaele Langlois and Greg Elmer, "The Research Politics of Social Media Platforms," *Culture Machine* 14 (2013): 1–9; Ganaele Langlois, Greg Elmer, Fenwick McKelvey, and Zachary Devereaux, "Networked Publics: The Double Articulation of Code and Politics on Facebook," *Canadian Journal of Communication* 34, no. 3 (2009), accessed September 16, 2016, http://www.cjc-online.ca/index.php/journal/article/view/2114; Taina Bucher, "Want to Be on the Top? Algorithmic Power and the Threat of Invisibility on Facebook," *New Media and Society* 14, no. 7 (November 1, 2012): 1164–1180, doi:10.1177/1461444812440159.

44. We are borrowing *disaggregation* from recent critical platform studies of social media systems, particularly Langlois, Elmer, McKelvey, and Devereaux, "Networked Publics"; Helmond, "The Platformization of the Web." See also Gehl's theorization and application of "critical reverse engineering": Robert W. Gehl, *Reverse Engineering Social Media: Software, Culture, and Political Economy in New Media Capitalism* (Philadelphia: Temple University Press, 2014); Robert W. Gehl, "FCJ-190 Building a Better Twitter: A Study of the Twitter Alternatives GNU Social, Quitter, Rstat.us, and Twister," *Fiberculture Journal* 26 (December 22, 2015): 60–86, doi:10.15307/fcj.26.190.2015.

Chapter 2

1. *Listel: Annuaire des services Télétel*, vol. 5 (Paris: Les Editions Télématiques de France, 1987).

2. Ibid.

3. A virtual circuit is a preset path between computers where "all the data during the data transfer phase travels on this given route. ... The fixed route is called a virtual circuit. ... [T]he billing for the connection is more like what customers expect from PSTN, since the path and the duration of the call is known." Timothy Ramteke, *Networks* (Upper Saddle River, NJ: Prentice Hall, 1994), 246.

4. For more on *disaggregation* as an approach to studying a platform, see Ganaele Langlois, Greg Elmer, Fenwick McKelvey, and Zachary Devereaux, "Networked Publics: The Double Articulation of Code and Politics on Facebook," *Canadian Journal of Communication* 34, no. 3 (2009), accessed September 16, 2016, http://www.cjc-online.ca/index.php/journal/article/view/2114.

5. For a more detailed account of the videotex experiments in Vélizy and elsewhere, see chapter 4.

6. See, for example, Jean Salmona, "La Révolution du Vidéotex," *Le Monde*, March 10, 1979, accessed September 17, 2016, http://www.lemonde.fr/archives/article/1979/03/10/la-revolution-du-videotex_2769676_1819218.html; "Un Annuaire Téléphonique 'Électronique' en 1981," *Le Monde*, March 2, 1979, accessed September 17, 2016, http://www.lemonde.fr/archives/article/1979/03/02/un-annuaire-telephonique-electronique-en-1981_2767824_1819218.html; "Les Progrès de l'Annuaire Électronique," *Le Monde*, January 22, 1982, accessed September 17, 2016, http://www.lemonde.fr/archives/article/1982/01/22/les-progres-de-l-annuaire-electronique_2900501_1819218.html.

7. "La télématique conviviale n'est plus une utopie," quoted in Salmona, "La Révolution du Vidéotex."

8. For a more detailed discussion of the natural language interface, see chapter 5.

9. Maurice Arvonny, "Un système informatique d'une grande complexité," *Le Monde*, December 28, 1983, accessed September 17, 2016, http://www.lemonde.fr/archives/article/1983/12/28/un-systeme-informatique-d-une-grande-complexite_2851921_1819218.html.

10. "L'Annuaire Électronique dès 1983," *Le Monde*, Deceber 9, 1982, accessed September 17, 2016, http://www.lemonde.fr/archives/article/1982/12/09/l-annuaire-electronique-des-1983_2905834_1819218.html.

11. Antonio Gonzalez and Emmanuelle Jouve, "Minitel: Histoire du Réseau Télématique Français," *Flux* 47, no. 1 (March 2002): 84–89; "L'Annuaire Électronique dès 1983."

12. Indeed, the use of telecomputing as an infrastructure for public culture was seldom known from the outset of a networking project. For example, participants in the ARPANET project were surprised to discover the utility of electronic mail. Janet Abbate, *Inventing the Internet.* (Cambridge, MA: MIT Press, 1999); Katie Hafner and Matthew Lyon, *Where Wizards Stay up Late: The Origins of the Internet* (New York: Simon and Schuster, 1996).

13. Éric Rohde, "Mode d'Emploi," *Le Monde*, September 5, 1984, accessed September 17, 2016, http://www.lemonde.fr/archives/article/1984/09/05/mode-d-emploi_3019896_1819218.html.

14. For more detailed data regarding the growth of third-party services on Minitel, see chapter 1.

15. The exact copy reads, "*7000 branché(e)s par jour.*" This is a play on the word *branché*, which can mean both an electric connection ("plugged in") and a cool or hip person ("plugged-in").

16. Hervé Kempf, "Le Minitel se Démasque," *Science et Vie Micro*, January 1985.

17. More than four years after its introduction, the Telic Minitel 1 continued to be featured on the cover of *Listel*.

18. To be precise, the Minitel 1B supported two display modes: *Télétel* mode supported the 40-column videotex standard specified by the CCETT and *téléinformatique* mode supported the 80-column, 7-bit ASCII standard used by time-sharing systems, microcomputers, and video terminals such as the DEC VT100. In addition, a "mixed" mode allowed the terminal to send and receive a subset of ASCII control characters while set to videotex mode. Except where noted, technical notes about the Minitel 1B are drawn from a specification pub-

lished by the DGT in November 1986. Direction générale des télécommunications, *Télétel, Minitel 1B: Spécifications techniques d'utilisation* (Paris: Ministère des Postes et des Télécommunications, 1986).

19. Arvonny, "Un système informatique d'une grande complexité."

20. France Telecom, "Minitel 1: Mode D'emploi, modèle TELIC," n.d.

21. In local mode, the microprocessor is running a standard "loop 3" local loop. See ITU Telecommunication Standardization Sector, *ITU-T Recommendation V.54: Data Communication Over the Telephone Network, Loop Test Devices for Modems* (Helsinki: International Telecommunication Union, 1988).

22. The Minitel 1 responded to the standard 1,300 Hz tone. ITU Telecommunication Standardization Sector, *ITU-T Recommendation V.25: Series V: Data Communication Over the Telephone Network, Interfaces and Voiceband Modems, Automatic Answering Equipment, and General Procedures for Automatic Calling Equipment on the General Switched Telephone Network Including Procedures for Disabling of Echo Control Devices for Both Manually and Automatically Established Calls* (Helsinki: International Telecommunication Union, 1996).

23. Hackers reprogramming the ROM have written demos indicating the capacity of Minitel to do other things. But the design of the terminal did not accommodate this type of intervention easily. See Jean-François del Nero. "Etude technique du Minitel," April 15, 2011, accessed September 17, 2016, http://hxc2001.free.fr/minitel/.

24. Direction générale des télécommunications, *Télétel, Minitel 1B*, 21.

25. Ibid., 46.

26. Ibid.

27. ITU Telecommunication Standardization Sector, *ITU-T Recommendation V.23: Data Communication Over the Telephone Network, 600/1200-Baud Modem Standardized for Use in the General Switched Telephone Network* (Helsinki: International Telecommunication Union, 1988).

28. *Baud* is a unit of measurement in data communication that describes the data transmission rate. One baud is equivalent to one bit per second, or in the case of more sophisticated equipment, one symbol per second where a *symbol* is defined as a single pulse or modulation of the carrier signal. In the case of Minitel, each character was made up of 10 bits so an ideal rate of 1,200 baud corresponded to approximately 120 characters per second.

29. Direction générale des télécommunications, *Télétel, Minitel 1B*, 51–52.

30. Ibid.

31. Martin Nisenholtz, "Graphics Artistry Online," *Byte*, July 1983, 104.

32. John Tydeman and Institute for the Future, *Teletext and Videotex in the United States: Market Potential, Technology, Public Policy Issues* (New York: McGraw-Hill, 1982).

33. The CCETT was created as a result of a 1972 merger between the research centers of the television's administration (*l'Office de radiodiffusion-télévision française*) and the telecommunications administration (*le Centre national d'études des télécommunications*).

34. Bernard Marti, *De Minitel à Internet: 30 ans de services en ligne* (Cesson-Sévigné: Armorhistel, 2011), 10.

35. The documentation for the Minitel 1B tends to use the more precise term *octet* rather than *byte*.

36. In téléinformatique mode, the display was divided into eighty columns and twenty-five rows, each of which was represented by a 12-bit word.

37. For an accessible discussion of the mechanics of the computer-controlled cathode-ray tube, see Nick Montfort and Ian Bogost, *Racing the Beam: The Atari Video Computer System* (Cambridge, MA: MIT Press, 2009).

38. *VT100 Series Technical Manual*, 2nd ed. (Maynard, MA: Digital Equipment Corporation, 1980), 100, accessed September 17, 2016, http://vt100.net/manx/details/ 1,2934. See also Marti, *De Minitel à Internet*, 11.

39. Marti, *De Minitel à Internet*, 12–14.

40. Benjamin Thierry, "De Tic-Tac au Minitel: la télématique grand public, une réussite française," in *Actes du colloque les ingénieurs des télécommunications dans la France contemporaine. Réseaux, innovation et territoires (XIXe-XXe siècles)*, ed. Pascal Griset (Vincennes: Institut de la gestion publique et du développement économique, 2013), 185–205.

41. Ibid.

42. Ministère des PTT, *Recommandations aux partenaires Télétel: Utilisation des touches de fonction du Minitel* (Paris: France Telecom, n.d.). For a more detailed discussion of the design principles and interface standards, see chapter 4.

43. "LECAM: Spécifications techniques d'utilisation," IBSI TBS, August 25, 1987, 10.

44. The LECAM allowed for programs to automatically "flip" the Minitel modem to achieve a faster asynchronous transmission rate.

45. Vincent Glad, "Minitel: comment les Dernières Nouvelles d'Alsace ont inventé l'Internet social," *Slate*, November 18, 2016, accessed September 17, 2016, http://www.slate.fr/story/46415/minitel-dna-internet-social; Isabelle Hanne, "«DNA»: en selle, Gretel," *Libération*, June 12, 2012, accessed September 17, 2016, http://www.liberation.fr/ecrans/2012/06/12/dna-en-selle-gretel_950059; Valérie Schafer and Benjamin G. Thierry, *Le Minitel: l'enfance numérique de la France* (Paris: Nuvis, 2012).

46. For a more detailed account of the emergence of real-time chat on Gretel, see chapter 5.

47. Thierry Bruhat and SPES/DGT, "Genèse. GRETEL: la messagerie interactive—Histoire d'un piratage," *Réseaux* 2, no. 6 (1984): 37–47, doi:10.3406/reso.1984. 1119; Glad, "Minitel."

48. See, in general, Rémi Després, "X.25 Virtual Circuits—Transpac in France—Pre-Internet Data Networking," *IEEE Communications Magazine* (November 2010); Thierry, "De Tic-Tac au Minitel."

49. See, in general, Valérie Schafer, "Évolution du nombre d'accès directs commerciaux à Transpac (1979–1985)," *Flux* 62, no. 4 (2005): 75–80.

50. Such a process was not so easy. In the words of Daniel Hannaby, a leading Minitel entrepreneur (see chapter 5), "It was a complicated process. It took a few months because we were not used at all to that because we were not in this business before. We just tried to get all this together. We went to see France Telecom and so they had to explain [to] us how it worked, so we went to buy these boxes to connect Transpac in a certain location in Paris that was the only reseller of these boxes. And well, it took a few months." Quoted in Julien Mailland and Marc Weber, "Oral History of Daniel Hannaby," Computer History Museum, March 20, 2015, reference number: X7439.2015, accessed September 17, 2016, http://

archive.computerhistory.org/resources/access/text/2015/09/102740083-05
-01-acc.pdf.

51. For a closer look at BBSs and early microcomputer networks, see Kevin Driscoll, "Hobbyist Inter-Networking and the Popular Internet Imaginary: Forgotten Histories of Networked Personal Computing, 1978–1998" (PhD diss., University of Southern California, 2014), accessed September 17, 2016, http://digitallibrary .usc.edu/cdm/compoundobject/collection/p15799coll3/id/444362/rec/2; Jason Scott, BBS: The Documentary, 2005, accessed September 17, 2016, http://archive.org/details/BBS.The.Documentary.

52. François Planque, "Stut One," Fplanque.net, 2013, accessed September 17, 2016, http://fplanque.net/about/stut-one; Christian Quest, Cristel, user manual, Paris, 1987. See Christian Quest, "Page Personnelle de Christian Quest," accessed November 2, 2016, http://www.cquest.org/cq/.

53. François Nicolas and Chorizo Kid, "En pratique: présentation et utilisation du serveur Minitel DEEP," Amiga News, March 1989, accessed September 17, 2016, http://obligement.free.fr/articles/serveur_minitel_deep.php.

54. Tydeman and Institute for the Future, Teletext and Videotex in the United States, 2; Marti, De Minitel à Internet, 11–12.

55. This narrative account is based on documentation published by the DGT as well as instructional material published in Listel. Direction générale des télécommunications, "Spécifications techniques d'utilisation du point d'accès Vidéotex."

56. For a more detailed discussion of the database of known and approved services, see chapter 3.

57. The standard PAVI was designed to communicate with Minitel terminal equipment at 1,200 baud. In 1993, a new "rapid" PAVI standard was approved to take advantage of the higher transmission rate modems included in "professional" Minitel terminals and commercially available for microcomputers. D. Caron, J. P. Martinière, and O. Normand, "Spécification technique du protocole de communication entre les équipments PAVI V27ter/V29—Terminal V23/V27ter/V29 vitesse rapide à 9600/4800 Bps," Cesson-Sévigné: Center commun d'études de télédiffusion et télécommunications (CCETT), April 2, 1993.

58. Arvonny, "Un système informatique d'une grande complexité."

59. For a more detailed discussion of the economics of Minitel as a multisided platform, see chapter 4.

Chapter 3

1. We refer to the French state as the State, with a capital S, throughout the manuscript to reflect the spelling of the French word for state: l'Etat. While the French language does not normally capitalize nouns unless they start a sentence, l'Etat is an exception, and the spelling reflects the traditional strong role of the State in French state–society relations.

2. See, in general, Eugen Weber, Peasants into Frenchmen: The Modernization of Rural France, 1870–1914 (Stanford, CA: Stanford University Press, 1976).

3. Peter McPhee, A Social History of France: 1789–1974, 2nd ed. (New York: Palgrave Macmillan, 2004), 8, 266.

4. See, in general, Etienne Balibar, "The Nation Form: History and Ideology," in *Race, Nation, Class: Ambiguous Identities*, by Etienne Balibar and Immanuel Wallerstein (London: Verso, 1991), 86–106; republished in Geoff Eley and Ronald Grigor Suny, eds., *Becoming National: A Reader* (New York: Oxford University Press, 1996), 132–149. See also Hervé Le Bras and Emmanuel Todd, *L'Invention de la France* (Paris: Librairie Générale Francaise, 1981), 9.

5. Ibid., 8, translated by author.

6. Balibar, "The Nation Form," 133.

7. James C. Scott, *Seeing Like a State: How Certain Schemes to Improve the Human Condition Have Failed* (New Haven, CT: Yale University Press, 1998), 72.

8. Ibid.

9. Alexandre Sanguinetti, quoted in *Le Figaro*, November 12, 1968, as quoted in ibid.

10. See, in general, Andrew Jack, *Sur la France: Vive la différence* (Paris: Odile Jacob, 1999); Scott, *Seeing Like a State*.

11. Christophe Charle, *Histoire sociale de la France au XIX siècle* (Paris: Seuil, 1991), 194.

12. Scott, *Seeing Like a State*.

13. Ibid., 75.

14. Ibid., 75–76.

15. Ibid., 75, quoting Weber, *Peasants*, 195. For a similar analysis, see also Jack, *Sur la France*, 49.

16. Scott, *Seeing Like a State*, 75. This hardwiring process of political traditions into communications networks is not specific to France. For example, Harmeet Sawhney argues that the USSR's "ideological bias was reflected in a telephone network which allowed for centre-to-periphery connectivity but did not provide direct linkages between regional centres." Harmeet S. Sawhney, "Circumventing the Centre: The Realities of Creating a Telecommunications Infrastructure in the USA," *Telecommunications Policy* 17, no. 7 (September–October 1993): 574–597.

17. Pierre E. Mounier-Kuhn, "Bull: A World-Wide Company Born in Europe," *IEEE Annals of the History of Computing* 11, no. 4 (1989): 279–297; Simon Nora and Alain Minc, *The Computerization of Society* (Cambridge, MA: MIT Press, 1981).

18. Catherine Bertho-Lavenir, "The Telephone in France, 1879–1979: National Characteristics and International Influences," in *The Development of Large Technical Systems*, ed. Renate Mayntz and Thomas Hugues (Boulder, CO: Westview Press, 1988), 169–170.

19. Marie Carpenter, *La bataille des télécoms: Vers une France numérique* (Paris: Economica, 2011), 40.

20. Valérie Schafer, "Évolution du nombre d'accès directs commerciaux à Transpac (1979–1985)," *Flux* 62, no. 4 (2005): 75–80, 34.

21. The gravity of this comparison may not be clear to US readers. Stuck behind the iron curtain, Czechoslovakia's centrally planned economy was considered slow moving and backward in contrast to its modern neighbors. For French citizens in the 1970s, a comparison with Czechoslovakia—particularly as regards the availability of new technology—would have been both shocking and deeply embarrassing.

22. Schafer, "Transpac," 34. Raynaud's performance remains one of the best-remembered skits in French comedy. For a closer discussion, see Philippe

Naszályi, "Allo New-York, je voudrais le 22 à Asnières," *La Revue des Sciences de Gestion* (April 2005): 214–215.

23. Naszályi (ibid.) refers to this as the "Atlantic submission" complex.

24. William L. Cats-Baril and Tawfik Jelassi, "The French Videotex System Minitel: A Successful Implementation of a National Information Technology Infrastructure," *MIS Quarterly* 18, no. 1 (March 1994): 2–3, Schafer, "Transpac," 38.

25. Carpenter, *La bataille*, 11–16; Marie Marchand, *The Minitel Saga: A French Success Story* (Paris: Larousse, 1988), 15–19.

26. Cats-Baril and Jelassi, "French Videotex System Minitel," 3.

27. Quoted in ibid.

28. Nora and Minc, *Computerization of Society*, 4, 1–2.

29. This echoes Herbert Schiller's warning that a "largely one-directional flow of information from core to periphery represents the reality of power. So, too, does the promotion of a single language—English ... [c]ultural-informational outputs represent much more than conventional units of personal-consumption goods: they are also embodiments of the ideological features of the world capitalist economy." Herbert I. Schiller, *Communication and Cultural Domination* (London: Routledge, 1976), 6.

30. Nora and Minc, *Computerization of Society*, 6–7.

31. Carpenter, *La bataille*, 535.

32. See, in general, ibid.; Benjamin Thierry, "De Tic-Tac au Minitel: la télématique grand public, une réussite française," in *Actes du colloque les ingénieurs des télécommunications dans la France contemporaine. Réseaux, innovation et territoires (XIXe–XXe siècles)*, edited by Pascal Griset, (Vincennes: Institut de la gestion publique et du développement économique, 2013), 185–205.

33. The notable exception is the phone book service. Since the analog phone book was maintained by the monopoly PTT operator, it made most sense to also have the PTT maintain the digital phone book itself, and host it on a PTT server. This was the only content service run by the PTT. Also note that the PTT did not have a monopoly over the phone book, and related services such as reverse lookup appeared on private servers.

34. On Prestel, see P. Troughton, "Prestel Operational Strategy," *Viewdata and Videotex, 1980–81: A Worldwide Report* (White Plains, NY: Knowledge Industry Publications, 1980), 51–62; K. E. Clarke and B. Fenn, "The UK Prestel Service: Technical Developments between March 1980 and March 1981," *Videotex 81* (Northwood Hills, Middlesex: Online Conferences, 1981), 147–162. On the German BTX, see H. Mantel, "The Seltext Center for the German Bildschirmtext Network," *Videotex 81* (Northwood Hills, Middlesex: Online Conferences, 1981), 179–188. On the Swiss network, see Peter A. Gfeller and Pierre E. Schmid, "Videotex Developments in Switzerland," *Videotex 81* (Northwood Hills, Middlesex: Online Conferences, 1981), 189–197.

35. For a more detailed discussion of decentralization in the architecture of Télétel, see chapter 4.

36. The Consultative Committee for International Telegraphy and Telephony, which is part of the ITU, standardized X.25 in 1974. X.25 was subsequently adopted by the International Organization for Standardization to become the protocol used in the first three layers of the Open System Interconnect reference model. For a more detailed discussion of this standardization process and its implications,

see Janet Abbate, *Inventing the Internet* (Cambridge, MA: MIT Press, 1999); Stuart L. Mathison, Lawrence G. Roberts, and Philip M. Walker, "The History of Telenet and the Commercialization of Packet Switching in the U.S.," *IEEE Communications Magazine* 50, no. 5 (May 2012): 28–45; Andrew L. Russell, "'Rough Consensus and Running Code' and the Internet-OSI Standards War," *IEEE Annals of the History of Computing* 28, no. 3 (2006): 48–61.

37. Other videotex networks of the period (i.e., Prestel) were more thoroughly centralized. For a closer comparison of these contemporary X.25 networks, see chapter 4.

38. Timothy Ramteke, *Networks* (Englewood Cliffs, NJ: Prentice Hall, 1994), 17.

39. Jean-Luc Beraudo De Pralormo, interview no. 1 with author, Cesson-Sévigné, June 25, 2012; Bernard Louvel, interview no. 1 with author, Cesson-Sévigné, June 25, 2012. See also France Telecom, in Jean-Yves Rincé, *Le Minitel* (Paris: Presses Universitaires de France, 1990), 122.

40. Louvel, interview no. 1. See also Carpenter, *La aataille*; Nora and Minc, *Computerization of Society*.

41. Minutes of the meeting of the Telematics Commission, February 18, 1981.

42. See, in general, Carpenter, *La bataille*; Nora and Minc, *Computerization of Society*.

43. Those computers were installed as micronetworks: six to eight terminals, usually Thomson MO5, used by students were connected to a microcomputer controlled by the teacher. See Jean-Pierre Archambault, "Une histoire de l'introduction des TIC dans le système éducatif français," *Médialog* 54 (2005): 42–45; Daniel Durandet, "Plan informatique: conférence de presse Fabius," *Soir 3*, France Régions 3, January 25, 1985, accessed April 14, 2013, http://www.ina.fr/video/CAC88029024/plan-informatique-conference-de-presse-fabius-video.html.

44. Carl Shapiro and Hal Varian, *Information Rules: A Strategic Guide to the Network Economy* (Boston: Harvard Business School Press, 1999), 21.

45. Even by 1995, the penetration of personal computers in France was still significantly behind that in the US. Consider the Technology Diffusion Index (TDI), which weights the diffusion of PCs based on the country's GDP (a score of 1 means that the adoption of PCs mirrors their GDP—lower numbers indicate that the diffusion is much lower than one would expect given the country's GDP). In 1995, France scored 0.053 compared to 0.577 for the US. Philip N. Howard, Laura Busch, and Spencer Cohen, ICT Diffusion and Distribution Dataset, 1990–2007, ICPSR23562-v1, Ann Arbor, MI: Inter-university Consortium for Political and Social Research [distributor], 2010-03-22, http://doi.org/10.3886/ICPSR23562.v1.

46. It was only after opposition from the press lobby that the DGT made the terminal available on the voluntary versus mandatory basis.

47. Carpenter, *La bataille*, 557.

48. Louvel, interview no. 1.

49. The restriction on Minitel advertising was the result of intense lobbying efforts by the newspaper industries. In a show of remarkable foresight, the entrenched players anticipated the threat that online services posed to traditional news media and attempted to kill Minitel before it reached mass adoption. Chapter 5 explores this conflict in greater depth.

50. "A 'killer app' usually refers to 'an application that is so compelling that it motivates people to purchase a computer to be able to use the application.'" Thomas J. Bergin, "The Origins of Word Processing Software for Personal Computers: 1976–1985," *IEEE Annals of the History of Computing* 28, no. 4 (2006): 47n54. Canonical examples include the VisiCalc spreadsheet for the Apple II series, Lotus 1-2-3 for the IBM PC, Space Invaders for the ATARI VCS, or Goldeneye 007 for the Nintendo 64. In the present context, we use the term *killer app* to characterize Kiosk because it was the key application that incited so many entrepreneurs to adopt the Minitel ecosystem as their platform for online content distribution.

51. For details on the role of the Kiosk system in the entrepreneurial "boom" in Minitel services, see chapter 5.

52. To be more precise, it was not possible to take advantage of either the billing or routing systems with direct links. Direct links were made between private servers over Transpac outside the Télétel platform, but they represented links between servers enclosed by large corporations or State administrators rather than public-facing Minitel services. By 1991, direct links between private servers made up 70 percent of all Transpac traffic. Schafer, "Transpac."

53. Unlike many Internet service providers today, the DGT did not inspect the contents of the data packets it monitored. This was another reason why direct circuits between servers were prohibited. If the gateways only saw a portion of the traffic between users and servers, the billing system might assess fees to the wrong parties, thereby undermining the trustworthiness and efficient nature of the entire system.

54. Utilisateurs de Tététel 3v, Association des Abonnés T3V, "TELETEL 3V: Le témoignage des utilisateurs," *Congrès de l'IDATE* (1982).

55. Ibid.

56. Carpenter, *La bataille*, 522.

57. The DGT did, however, embrace the chip card technology in another project: public pay phones. All French pay phones gradually became accessible only via a prepaid chip card one would buy from the PTT and then through chip credit cards. Carpenter, *La bataille*, 524. There is evidence that Gérard Théry, then head of the DGT, had embraced the technology on meeting Roland Moreno, its inventor, and internally pushed the DGT to find applications for the card. Ibid.; Gérard Théry, interview with author, Paris, June 27, 2012.

58. Scott, *Seeing Like a State*, 75.

59. Louvel, who at the time was a young engineer on Maury's team, confirms that the implementation was necessary in order to "enable the State to keep control [over the content of the network]." Louvel, however, insists on the benefits for the user and the fact that the "spirit of public service" moved the DGT. The implementation enabled the DGT to ensure quality control, such as by ensuring that crooks would not bill users to access empty shells. Louvel, interview no. 1.

60. Beraudo De Pralormo, interview no. 1.

61. Though the illegal nature of classified ads on the system was the result of efforts of the press industry lobby, which did not want its main source of revenue to be captured by online publishers.

62. Weber, *Peasants*, 194, citing an anonymous "historian of the center."

63. Gérard Théry, *Les autoroutes de l'information* (Paris: Documentation Française, 1994), 86.
64. For an in-depth look at the politics of payment systems, see Lana Swartz, "Tokens, Ledgers, and Rails: The Communication of Money" (PhD diss., University of Southern California, 2015).
65. Although in this case, the wannabe publisher could take the State to court.
66. The code of conduct, a contractual document entered into between the DGT and service providers, loosely mirrored the restrictions on speech content contained in the French Criminal Code. It enabled the DGT to cut service in the event it felt certain content was inappropriate, without needing to go through a judicial proceeding.
67. For more discussion of the process for approving new services, see chapter 4.
68. Pierre Huet, "Cadre juridique de l'audiotex en France et dans le monde," *Droit de l'Informatique et des Télécoms* 3 (1994): 57–62. Both the French administrative and judicial tribunals, however, validated the contractual mechanism. Conseil d'Etat, March 29, 1991 (Fr.); Cour d'Appel de Paris, October 13, 1992, Midratel.
69. Déclaration Universelle des Droits de l'Homme et du Citoyen (1789), articles 11, 5.
70. In 1945, Justice Robert H. Jackson remarked that the First Amendment was written expressly to prevent the state from taking up "a guardianship of the public mind." Thomas v. Collins, 323 U.S. 516, 545 (1945) (Jackson, J., concurring).
71. Julien Mailland, "Freedom of Speech, the Internet, and the Costs of Control: The French Example," *New York University Journal of International Law and Politics* 33 (2001): 1179–1234.
72. Syndicat national de la presse quotidienne régionale, *Contribution du SNPQR au rapport de la commission du suivi télématique: Les expériences et leur suivi* (October 18, 1982).
73. Sanguinetti, quoted in *Le Figaro*.
74. Sawhney, "Circumventing."
75. Déclaration Universelle des Droits de l'Homme et du Citoyen, 1789, article 11.
76. Quoted in Bernard Marti, *De Minitel à Internet: 30 ans de services en ligne*, (Cesson-Sévigné: Armorhistel, 2011), 30, 22, 23.
77. Both Maury and Michel Baujard, a former member of the Telematics Commission and former president of the National Syndicate of Telecommunications Media, insist that the background of key leaders of the Office de radiodiffusion-rélévision Française (the precursor agency to TDF) as former French colonies administrators played a crucial role in shaping their views of Minitel. Michel Baujard, interview no. 1 with author, Paris, June 29, 2012; Jean-Paul Maury, interview no. 1 with author, Paris, December 2011; Jean-Paul Maury, interview no. 2 with author, Paris, June 27, 2012.
78. Maury, interview no. 2.
79. Théry, interview. Théry (ibid.) also points out that in contrast to two-way information networks, today's digital television "does not produce any innovation."
80. Théry, interview. The conflict between the TFD and *Ouest France*, on the one hand, and the DGT, on the other hand, is well documented in Carpenter, *La bataille*; Marchand, *The Minitel Saga*; Marti, *De Minitel à Internet*; Valérie Schafer

and Benjamin G. Thierry, *Le Minitel: l'enfance numérique de la France* (Paris: Nuvis, 2014).

81. Maury, interview no. 1; Maury, interview no. 2.
82. Maury, interview no. 2; Théry, interview.
83. Maury, interview no. 1.
84. Baujard, interview no. 1.
85. Marti, *De Minitel à Internet*, 47.
86. In terms of intellectual property violation, "3615 Chirac," for example, a site that used the prime minister and Paris mayor's name, was sacked by the DGT. Maury, interview no. 1. On administrative technicalities, see Marti, *De Minitel à Internet*, 47. On the use of chat rooms by sex workers, see, for example, Cour des Comptes, *Rapport au président de la république*, June 28, 1989.
87. Daniel Hannaby, interview no. 1 with author, San Francisco, March 9, 2012.
88. Jean-Marc Manach, interview with author, Paris, June 29, 2012; Jean-Marc Manach, "J'ai été animatrice de Minitel rose," *OWNI*, June 28, 2012, accessed April 15, 2013, http://owni.fr/2012/06/28/jai-ete-animatrice-de-minitel-rose/.
89. Jacques Vistel, *Note à l'attention de M. Francois Xavier Gillier*, (Secrétariat d'Etat Auprès du Premier Ministre Chargé des Techniques de la Communication: Service Juridique and Technique de l'Information, March 26, 1985).
90. Ibid.
91. Confédération française démocratique du travail, *Note de la C.F.D.T. sur la Télématique Grand Public*, October 14, 1982, 9.
92. Utilisateurs de Tététel 3v, "TELETEL 3V," 10 (emphasis added).
93. Service d'Information et de Diffusion du Premier Ministre, *Le rôle du service d'information et de diffusion en matière d'information administrative par Vidéotex*, November 1983.
94. James Gillies and Robert Cailliau, *How the Web Was Born* (New York: Oxford University Press, 2000), 110.

Chapter 4

1. See, for example, Lyombe S. Eko, *New Media, Old Regimes: Case Studies in Comparative Communication Law and Policy* (Lanham, MD: Lexington Books, 2012), 235.
2. Ibid., 234.
3. A notable exception is Renate Mayntz and Volker Schneider, "The Dynamics of System Development in a Comparative Perspective: Interactive Videotex in Germany, France, and Britain," in *The Development of Large Technical Systems*, ed. Renate Mayntz and Thomas Hughes (Frankfurt am Main: Campus Verlag, 1988), 263–298.
4. Simon Nora and Alain Minc, *The Computerization of Society* (Cambridge, MA: MIT Press, 1981), 5–12.
5. Ibid., 6.
6. This architecture was later modified in the UK to also enable service providers to connect their own hosts to the platform. Mayntz and Schneider, "Dynamics of System Development," 271.
7. Ibid.

8. Gérard Théry, interview with author, Paris, June 27, 2012.

9. Mayntz and Schneider, "Dynamics of System Development," 271.

10. Paul E. Ceruzzi, *A History of Modern Computing* (Cambridge, MA: MIT Press, 1998).

11. Mayntz and Schneider, "Dynamics of System Development," 272.

12. On this topic, see, in general, Julien Mailland, "101 Online: American Minitel Network and Lessons from Its Failure," *IEEE Annals of the History of Computing* 38, no. 1 (January–March 2016): 6–22.

13. See, for example, Eko, *New Media*, 234.

14. Nora and Minc, *Computerization of Society*, 4.

15. "Minitel," Adminet, accessed September 20, 2016, http://www.adminet.com/minitel/videotex-international.html#AMERIQUE.

16. Francois Came, "Minitel: le 22 a Wichita Falls/3619 Siriel," *Libération*, March 3, 1995, accessed September 20, 2016, http://www.liberation.fr/ecrans/1995/03/03/minitel-le-22-a-wichita-falls-3619-siriel_128305.

17. Julien Mailland and Marc Weber, "Oral History of Daniel Hannaby," Computer History Museum, March 20, 2015, reference number: X7439.2015, accessed September 17, 2016, http://archive.computerhistory.org/resources/access/text/2015/09/102740083-05-01-acc.pdf.

18. Marie Marchand, *The Minitel Saga: A French Success Story* (Paris: Larousse, 1988), 124.

19. Pierre E. Mounier-Kuhn, "Bull: A World-Wide Company Born in Europe," *IEEE Annals of the History of Computing* 11, no. 4 (1989): 279.

20. Marchand, *Minitel Saga*, 124.

21. Martin Campbell-Kelly, *From Airline Reservations to Sonic the Hedgehog: A History of the Software Industry* (Cambridge, MA: MIT Press, 2003), 143–145.

22. Mailland and Weber, "Oral History of Daniel Hannaby."

23. "Taranis, tous azimuts," *Videotex* 57, February 1984.

24. Marchand, *Minitel Saga*, 125.

25. Ibid.

26. Ibid., 126, 143.

27. Ibid., 125, 126.

28. Mailland and Weber, "Oral History of Daniel Hannaby."

29. Marchand, *Minitel Saga*, 110. For more details about banking on Minitel, see chapter 5.

30. France Telecom, *TELETEL: Les fournisseurs de moyens 1* (Paris: Ministère des PTT, April 1986)

31. France Telecom, *TELETEL: Les fournisseurs de moyens* (Paris: France Telecom, April 1990).

32. Shawn M. Powers and Michael Jablonski, *The Real Cyberwar: The Political Economy of Internet Freedom* (Urbana: University of Illinois Press, 2015).

33. On the experiments, see, in general, Marchand, *Minitel Saga*, 52–60; Benjamin Thierry, "De Tic-Tac au Minitel: la télématique grand public, une réussite française," in *Actes du colloque les ingénieurs des télécommunications dans la France contemporaine. Réseaux, innovation et territoires (XIXe–XXe siècles)*, ed. Pascal Griset (Vincennes: Institut de la gestion publique et du développement économique, 2013), 185–205.

34. Marchand, *Minitel Saga*, 62. For a visual selection of various keyboard layouts tested by the DGT, see Bernard Marti, *De Minitel à Internet: 30 ans de services en ligne* (Cesson-Sévigné: Armorhistel, 2011), 27–28.

35. Marina Ponjaert, Pauline Georgiades, and Alain Magnier, *Communiquer par Télétel* (Paris: La Documentation française, 1983).

36. Ministère des PTT, *Formation télématique: Le CNFT votre partenaire*, flyer, n.d.

37. See, for example, "Laissez venir à moi les petits … fournisseurs Télétel!" *Industrie de l'Information*, July 16, 1984.

38. Marchand, *Minitel Saga*, 60, 124; Michel Landaret, "Minitel: La dernière séance 'Rendez-vous à jamais,'" *La Cantine*, roundtable, June 29, 2012, accessed September 20, 2016, http://www.youtube.com/watch?feature=player_embedded &v=KtXPTaSi8x8; Code Monétaire et Financier, Article L. 518–2.

39. Landaret, "Minitel."

40. On the information-industrial complex, see, in general, Powers and Jablonski, *The Real Cyberwar*, 52–73.

41. Quoted in ibid., 56.

42. Ibid., 59.

43. Quoted in ibid., 62, 57.

44. Eko, *New Media*, 235.

45. Ibid. Because different subfields in the literature use both *gated communities* and *walled gardens* to refer to the same thing, we will use both expressions interchangeably.

46. For a more detailed discussion of the comparison between the ecosystems of Minitel and Apple, see chapter 7.

47. For a discussion of *walled garden* and *gated community* as metaphors, see Payal Arora, *Leisure Commons: A Spatial History of Web 2.0* (New York: Routledge, 2014).

48. See, for example, Carolin Gerlitz and Anne Helmond, "The Like Economy: Social Buttons and the Data-Intensive Web," *New Media & Society* 15, no. 8 (December 1, 2013): 1348–1365, doi:10.1177/1461444812472322; Anne Helmond, "The Platformization of the Web: Making Web Data Platform Ready," *Social Media + Society* 1, no. 2 (July 1, 2015): 2056305115603080, doi:10.1177/2056305115603080; Ganaele Langlois, Fenwick McKelvey, Greg Elmer, and Kenneth Werbin, "Mapping Commercial Web 2.0 Worlds: Towards a New Critical Ontogenesis," *The Fibreculture Journal*, no. 14 (2009), http://fourteen.fibreculturejournal. org/fcj-095-mapping-commercial-web-2-0-worlds-towards-a-new-critical -ontogenesis/.

49. Robert Widing II and W. Wayne Talarzyk, "Videotex Project Reviews II," OCLC Online Computer Library Center Research Report #OCLC/OPR/RR-83/8, October 28, 1983, 20–21.

50. Ibid., 74–75.

51. See, in general, Yochai Benkler, "WikiLeaks and the PROTECT-IP Act: A New Public–Private Threat to the Internet Commons," *Daedalus, the Journal of the American Academy of Arts and Sciences* 140, no. 4 (Fall 2011): 154–164.

52. F. Froment-Meurice, "Principes généraux applicables au videotex: Premiers elements," Premier Ministre, Secrétariat Général du Gouvernment, June 30, 1980.

53. Minutes of the meeting of the Telematics Commission, February 18, 1981.

54. Pierre Huet, Letter to Telecommunications Minister M. Mexandeau, June 26, 1981.
55. Ibid.
56. The censorship system would eventually be declared deprived of legal basis by the courts. For an in-depth look at the censorship regime, see chapter 3.
57. Benkler, "WikiLeaks and the PROTECT-IP Act."
58. For a detailed look at the fringe cultures of Minitel, see chapter 6.
59. Marchand, *Minitel Saga*, 151.
60. Nora and Minc, *Computerization of Society*.
61. Gérard Théry, *Les autoroutes de l'information* (Paris: Documentation Française, 1994), 85–86.
62. Théry, interview.

Chapter 5

1. Howard Rheingold, *The Virtual Community: Homesteading on the Electronic Frontier* (Reading, MA: Addison-Wesley, 1993).
2. Ibid., 233.
3. André Lemos, "The Labyrinth of Minitel," in *Cultures of Internet: Virtual Spaces, Real Histories, Living Bodies*, ed. Rob Shields (Thousand Oaks, CA: Sage, 1996), 35.
4. Marie Marchand, *The Minitel Saga: A French Success Story* (Paris: Larousse, 1988); Valérie Schafer and Benjamin G. Thierry, *Le Minitel: L'enfance numérique de la France* (Paris: Nuvis, 2014), 96–100; Marie Carpenter, *La bataille des télécoms: Vers une France numérique* (Paris: Economica, 2011); Vincent Glad, "Minitel: comment les Dernières Nouvelles d'Alsace ont inventé l'Internet social," *Slate*, November 18, 2011, accessed September 17, 2016, http://www.slate.fr/story/46415/minitel-dna-internet-social.
5. Michel Landaret, "Minitel: La dernière séance 'Rendez-vous à jamais,'" *La Cantine*, roundtable, June 29, 2012, accessed September 20, 2016, http://www.youtube.com/watch?feature=player_embedded&v=KtXPTaSi8x8.
6. Ibid.
7. Michel Landaret, "Le père de la messagerie" (interview), *Minitel Magazine*, no. 14, April–May 1986, 22.
8. Landaret, "Minitel."
9. Ibid. See also Rheingold, *Virtual Community*, 228–229.
10. Julien Mailland and Marc Weber, "Oral History of Daniel Hannaby," Computer History Museum, March 20, 2015, reference number: X7439.2015, accessed September 17, 2016, http://archive.computerhistory.org/resources/access/text/2015/09/102740083-05-01-acc.pdf.
11. At 61.60 francs per hour, of which 38.50 are rebated to the service by the PTT.
12. "Minitel Maxi-Prix!" *Que Choisir*, no. 202, January 1985; "Minitel, Maxiprix," *Mieux Vivre*, June 1985. See also, for example, "Minitel: Gare à la Facture," *Le Nouvel Economiste*, December 24, 1984; "Minitel: gare à la note de téléphone," *La Marseillaise*, January 13, 1985; "Pour 60F de l'heure marivaudage de 5 à 7 sur Minitel," *France Soir*, July 16, 1985; "L'addition," *Le Point*, October 6, 1985; "Le Minitel, très pratique mais cher," *Femme Actuelle*, March 9–15, 1987; "Tarifs: c'est l'embrouille," *Teletel: Revue de Presse*, June–July 1985, undated press

clipping, Orange/DGCI; "Minitel en famille: 50F par jour," *Teletel: Revue de Presse*, June–July 1985, undated press clipping, Orange/DGCI.

13. *Listel* (Paris: Paul Cazenave, June 1986), 190, 228.

14. For a discussion of the dual role of Minitel in altering gender roles while also reinforcing a traditional, patriarchal model, see Josiane Jouët, "Le minitel rose: du flirt électronique ... et plus, si affinités," *Le Temps des médias* 2, no. 19 (2012), accessed September 21, 2016, https://www.cairn.info/revue-le-temps-des -medias-2012-2-p-221.htm.

15. *Listel*, 228.

16. Ibid., 16; Landaret, "Le père de la messagerie."

17. Rheingold, *Virtual Community*, 232–233.

18. Marchand, *Minitel Saga*, 103.

19. Mailland and Weber, "Oral History of Daniel Hannaby."

20. Jouët, "Le minitel rose."

21. For a further discussion of the blurring of on- and off-line community during the BBS period, see Kevin Driscoll, "Hobbyist Inter-Networking and the Popular Internet Imaginary: Forgotten Histories of Networked Personal Computing, 1978–1998" (PhD diss., University of Southern California, 2014), accessed September 17, 2016, http://digitallibrary.usc.edu/cdm/compoundobject/col-lection/p15799coll3/id/444362/rec/2.

22. Mailland and Weber, "Oral History of Daniel Hannaby."

23. For an overview of the key literature on online community and group communication on computer networks, see Nancy K. Baym, *Personal Connections in the Digital Age* (Cambridge, UK: Polity Press, 2010).

24. On the topic, see, in general, Jean-Marc Manach, "J'ai été animatrice de Minitel rose," *OWNI*, June 28, 2012, accessed April 15, 2013, http://owni.fr/2012/06/28/ jai-ete-animatrice-de-minitel-rose/; Schafer and Thierry, *Le Minitel*, 101; Rhein-gold, *Virtual Community*; TF1, "C'était un 1er juillet: Qui se cache derrière le Minitel rose?" news segment, circa 1988, accessed September 21, 2016, http://lci.tf1. fr/videos/2015/c-etait-un-1er-juillet-qui-se-cache-derriere-le-minitel-rose -8625789.html; "Marie-Laure menteuse par Minitel," *Le Journal du Dimanche*, March 10, 1986; "Téléanimation: SVP, Sophie ...," *Minitel Magazine*, March 1987, 29; "Les dessous de la messagerie," *Minitel Magazine*, no. 14, April–May 1986, 47–51; Michel Abadie, "'Koka' l'animateur de messagerie," *La Revue du Minitel*, no. 8, November–December 1986, 46–47 ; Mailland and Weber, "Oral History of Daniel Hannaby."

25. Manach, "J'ai été animatrice de Minitel rose."

26. Jouët, "Le minitel rose."

27. Mailland and Weber, "Oral History of Daniel Hannaby."

28. Manach, "J'ai été animatrice de Minitel rose."

29. TF1, "C'était un 1er juillet."

30. Schafer and Thierry, *Le Minitel*, 100, citing an internal report: Direction générale des télécommunications, "Rapport sur le service de communication par Minitel, 1985," Archives Historiques de France Télécom, box 97017/02; "Les messageries gagneuses de la telematique," *Libération*, August 30–31, 2015.

31. Schafer and Thierry, *Le Minitel*, 101. See also Mailland and Weber, "Oral History of Daniel Hannaby."

32. Consider Marchand, *Minitel Saga*, 103, discussing entrepreneur Cécile Alvergnat's efforts to promote her messagerie, Crac, in January 1986: "She leased billboard space in the Paris metro and put up posters for Minitel showing off the voluptuous Miss A.C.1, symbol of the Crac on-line electronic mail service … whose titilating come-on left no room for doubt about the nature of the service, which sounded truly 'rose.'"

33. "Le minitel rose n'a pas d'avenir, selon le ministre des PTT," Agence France-Presse, May 7, 1987.

34. For more discussion on the tense relationship between the print industries and the nascent Minitel, see chapters 3 and 6.

35. See, for example, *La Revue du Minitel*, no. 8, November–December 1986, 32.

36. Landaret, "Minitel."

37. See, for example, *La Revue du Minitel*, no. 8, November–December 1986, 62.

38. Mailland and Weber, "Oral History of Daniel Hannaby." User names were not an accurate way to count as any user could have as many *pseudos* (handles) as they wanted. This is also one of the reasons why the breakdowns of usage time by type of service we present in the book are estimates; the DGT was the only entity with accurate aggregated data, but it was busy minimizing the importance of Minitel rose for public relations reasons.

39. Julien Mailland, "Mythologies: The Minitel Kiosk Payment System," in *Paid: Tales of Dongles, Checks, and Other Money Stuff*, ed. Bill Maurer and Lana Swartz (Cambridge, MA: MIT Press, 2017).

40. See, for example, Scott Sayare, "On the Farms of France, the Death of a Pixelated Workhorse," *New York Times*, June 27, 2012, accessed September 22, 2016, http://www.nytimes.com/2012/06/28/world/europe/after-3-decades-in-france-minitels-days-are-numbered.html.

41. Many PC games of the same period featured a "boss key" that temporarily replaced the game screen with a fake spreadsheet or similar work-like display. For a sustained analysis of the affective dimensions of gaming in the workplace, see Aubrey Anable, "Casual Games, Time Management, and the Work of Affect," *Ada: A Journal of Gender, New Media, and Technology*, no. 2 (2013), doi:10.7264/N3ZW1HVD.

42. "L'accès Télétel sous haute surveillance," *Solutions Télématiques*, no. 15, 20.

43. Ibid., 20, 47; "Le Minitel excellent pour la vie de bureau: Le Minitel fait flipper les patrons," *Minitel Magazine*, no. 20, February 1987, 44.

44. "Le Minitel excellent pour la vie de bureau," 44. See also Manach, "J'ai été animatrice de Minitel rose."

45. Quoted in "Le Minitel excellent pour la vie de bureau," 44.

46. Quoted in ibid.

47. Ibid.

48. Landaret, "Minitel."

49. Mailland and Weber, "Oral History of Daniel Hannaby."

50. "Maya interdit le 'rose,'" *Science et Vie*, February 1987.

51. "Le Minitel excellent pour la vie de bureau," 43–44.

52. Jean-Paul Maury, interview no. 1 with author, Paris, December 2011.

53. "Un mouchard chez vous," *Que Choisir*, no. 202, January 1985. See also "Un mouchard dans chaque Minitel," *Le Figaro*, December 30, 1984; "Les PTT contre-attaquent: 'pas de mouchards dans les minitels,'" *Libération*, January 1, 1985.

54. Maury, interview no. 1.

55. Ibid.

56. Jim Stingl, "Carlin's Naughty Words Still Ring in Officer's Ears," *Milwaukee Journal Sentinel*, June 30, 2007, archived at https://web.archive.org/web/20070929124942/http://www.jsonline.com/story/index.aspx?id=626471, accessed November 29, 2016. Federal Communications Commission v. Pacifica Foundation, 438 U.S. 726 (1978), 751.

57. Landaret, "Le père de la messagerie."

58. See, for example, Pierre Jovanovic, "Le scandale de la prostitution d'adolescents sur Minitel," *Le Quotidien de Paris*, August 28, 1986.

59. "Cyberporn," *Time*, July 3, 1995, cover.

60. "Des associations familiales font le procès de l'Etats proxénète," *Le Monde*, July 16–17, 1989.

61. About fifteen services were shut down between 1989 and 1992. Schafer and Thierry, *Le Minitel*, 144. See also Bernard Marti, *De Minitel à Internet: 30 ans de services en ligne* (Cesson-Sévigné: Armorhistel, 2011).

62. See, for example, Jovanovic, "Le scandale de la prostitution d'adolescents sur Minitel"; Cour des Comptes, *Rapport au président de la république*, June 28, 1989.

63. See, for example, "Des associations familiales font le procès de l'Etats proxénète"; Denis Perier, *Le dossier noir du Minitel rose* (Paris: Albin Michel, 1988).

64. See, for example, Danièle Delaval, "Le nouveau code pénal et le renforcement de la protection morale des mineurs," *Solutions Télématiques*, no. 15 (July 1993).

65. Jovanovic, "Le scandale de la prostitution d'adolescents sur Minitel."

66. Lemos, "Labyrinth of Minitel," 40; Landaret, "Minitel."

67. Daniel Hannaby, interview with author, San Francisco, March 9, 2012; Mailland and Weber, "Oral History of Daniel Hannaby."

68. Marchand, *Minitel Saga*, 140.

69. Lemos, "Labyrinth of Minitel," 40.

70. Quoted in "Le minitel rose n'a pas d'avenir, selon le ministre des PTT."

71. Gérard Longuet, interviewed by *Libération*, cited in Miguel Mennig, *L'indispensable pour Minitel* (Paris: Marabout, 1987), 21.

72. Philippe Séguin, interviewed by Yves Mourousi, *La Revue du Minitel*, no. 11, June 1987, 13.

73. *Minitel Magazine*, no. 16, August–September 1986.

74. Francois de Valence, interviewed by J. Legros, *France Inter*, August 23, 1986. This echoed a previous statement by the PTT minister, who had declared that he did "not want the profits of the messageries to be such that they could invest so much in billboards, who are after all, the most chocking element of this affair." "Le minitel rose n'a pas d'avenir, selon le ministre des PTT."

75. Quoted in *Minitel Magazine*, no. 16, August–September 1986.

76. On export failures, see Julien Mailland, "101 Online: American Minitel Network and Lessons from Its Failure," *IEEE Annals of the History of Computing* 38, no. 1 (January–March 2016): 6–22.

77. Wolinski is sadly remembered today as one of the artists assassinated in the *Charlie Hebdo* terrorist attacks of January 2015.

78. The data in this section are sourced directly from France Telecom's official reports, including annual reports (*rapports annuels*), annual surveys (*baromètre*,

bilan et perspectives), and periodic newsletters (*La lettre de Télétel, La lettre de Télétel et d'Audiotel,* and *La lettre des Services en Ligne*), published between 1982 and 1997, and available at the France Telecom Archives (Orange/Direction de la Gestion et de la Conservation de l'Information) in Alfortville, France. The relevant boxes at Orange/Direction de la Gestion et de la Conservation de l'Information are as follows: 97030/1, 96030/2, 15078/01, 15078/02, 345, 347, 350, 353, 354, 355, 356, 357, and 358.

79. "The Greatest Defunct Web Sites and Dotcom Disasters," CNET, June 5, 2008, accessed September 22, 2016, http://web.archive.org/web/20080607211840/ http://crave.cnet.co.uk/0,39029477,49296926-6,00.htm.

80. Mennig, *L'indispensable pour Minitel,* 57–59. See also "Foie gras sur Minitel," *La Depeche du Midi,* February 20, 1987.

81. Mennig, *L'indispensable pour Minitel.*

82. *Minitel Magazine,* no. 16, August–September 1986, 35–38.

83. Jouët, "Le minitel rose."

84. "What Is SETI@home?" University of California at Berkeley, 2016, accessed September 22, 2016, http://setiathome.ssl.berkeley.edu/; *La Revue du Minitel,* no. 7, September–October 1986. See also "Débats," *Linx,* no. 17, 1987, "Le texte et l'ordinateur," sous la direction de Jacques Anis et Jean-Louis Lebrave, 71–75; Michael Dobbs, "Minitel Is New French Revolution," *Washington Post,* December 25, 1986, accessed September 22, 2016, https://www.washingtonpost.com/ archive/politics/1986/12/25/minitel-is-new-french-revolution/eeaf90f3 -90ca-4d60-bb46-fc4808fa2649/.

85. "SETI (Search for Extra Terrestrial Intelligence)," Station de Radio astronomie de Nançay, September 18, 2013, accessed September 23, 2016, http://www.obs- nancay.fr/SETI-Search-for-Extra-Terrestrial.html?lang=fr.

86. France Telecom, *La lettre de Télétel,* no. 22, Q3, 1991. See also Maurice Arvonny, "Un système informatique d'une grande complexité," *Le Monde,* December 28, 1983, accessed September 23, 2016, http://www.lemonde.fr/archives/article/ 1983/12/28/un-systeme-informatique-d-une-grande-complexite_2851921 _1819218.html.

87. "Ou sortons-nous ce soir? Et si vous posiez la question à Sophie?" *Le Quotidien de Paris,* February 15, 1984.

88. *Minitel Magazine,* no. 19, January–February 1987.

89. "Un fauteuil dans un fauteuil," *Le Point,* no. 750, February 2, 1987.

90. "La Fnac va proposer un service de billeterie de spectacle accessible dans les lieux publics," Agence France-Presse, January 30, 1987; "Du Minitel au spec- tacle," *Communication and Business,* no. 19, February 2, 1987; "Billetel: un plus pour Avignon," *Le Matin,* February 2, 1987.

91. Jaclyn Selby, "Anyone's Game: Economic and Policy Implications of the Internet of Things as a Market for Services," *Communications and Strategies* 87 (2012): 21–40.

92. "Domotique: La maison domestiquée," *Video* 7, March 1987, 104–110 ; Bernard Alter, "Le Minitel a-t-il un avenir ?" *Terminal,* no. 55, October–November 1991, 46; Philippe Dard, *Minitel et gestion de l'habitat: la domotique en questions* (Paris, Plan construction et architecture: 1991).

93. For more information on and a discussion of the vendor-neutral quality of Minitel design, see chapters 2 and 4.

94. See, in general, France Telecom, *La lettre de Teletel*; "Domotique: La maison domestiquée," 108.

95. For more details on the terminal's serial port, see chapter 2. For more information about Minitel BBSs, see chapter 6.

96. Direction générale des télécommunications, *Teletel: Repertoire des peripheriques pour le Minitel*, May 1989.

97. See, for example, "Home Banking Gets New Push," *Infoworld*, August 5, 1985; "Covidea to Add Information Service in New York," *Infoworld*, February 3, 1986; "Industry Giants Launch Second Videotex Wave," *Network World*, August 25, 1986; Jerome Aumente, *New Electronic Pathways: Videotex, Teletext, and Online Databases* (Newbury Park, CA: Sage, 1987), 44–74; Christopher H. Sterling, "Pioneering Risk: Lessons from the US Teletext/Videotex Failure," *IEEE Annals of the History of Computing* 28, no. 3 (July–September 2006), 41–47, doi:10.1109/MAHC.2006. 542006: 41–47; "Covidea Ends Endeavor in Commercial Videotex Mart," *Network World*, December 19, 1988.

98. David Marsh, "CCF Starts Home Banking Service," *Financial Times*, December 22, 1983; "65% des clients du CCF ont adopté le Minitel," *Le Quotidien de Paris*, no. 1577, December 13, 1984.

99. Patrick Arnoux, "Banque a domicile," *La Revue du Minitel*, February–March 1987.

100. France Telecom, *Minitel News*, no. 5, Q1, 1991, 10.

101. See, in general, Mailland, "101 Online."

102. Marchand, *Minitel Saga*, 105.

103. Vicent Jauvert, "Bourse: Le Minitel a la cote," *La Revue du Minitel*, no. 10, April–May 1987, 30.

104. See, in general, Conservatoire National des Arts et Métiers, *Carte à puce: Une histoire à rebonds* (Paris : CNAM, 2015).

105. Maury recalls that phone card advertising brought the DGT 100 million francs between 1990 and 1992. Maury, interview no. 1.

106. See, in general, Henry Jenkins, "Transmedia Storytelling and Entertainment: An Annotated Syllabus," *Continuum: Journal of Media and Cultural Studies* 24, no. 6 (2010): 943–958.

107. AB Production, *Premiers baisers: L'inconnu du Minitel* (Paris: ABH, 1995).

108. Liaison, *Minitel ... Miniquoi?* (Paris: Kangourou, 1987).

109. Les Inconnus, "C'est toi que je t'aime" (1991).

110. Noe Willer, "Sur Minitel" (Atoll Music, 1986); Marie-Paule Belle, "Mini-Minitel" (Carrere, 1987); Les Ignobles du Bordelais, "Minitel" (self-published, 1984).

111. Davy Mounier, *Minitel and Fulguropoint: Le monde avant Internet* (Paris: J'ai Lu, 2014).

Chapter 6

1. Wiebe E. Bijker, Thomas P. Hughes, and Trevor Pinch, eds., *The Social Construction of Technological Systems: New Directions in the Sociology and History of Technology* (Cambridge, MA: MIT Press, 1987).

2. Donald A. MacKenzie and Judy Wajcman, eds., *The Social Shaping of Technology: How the Refrigerator Got Its Hum* (Milton Keynes, UK: Open University Press,

1985). See also Carolyn Marvin, *When Old Technologies Were New: Thinking about Electric Communication in the Late Nineteenth Century* (New York: Oxford University Press, 1988).

3. Lisa Gitelman, *Always Already New: Media, History, and the Data of Culture* (Cambridge, MA: MIT Press, 2006).

4. Janet Abbate, "The Electrical Century: Inventing the Web," *Proceedings of the IEEE* 87, no. 11 (1999): 1999–2002, doi:10.1109/5.796364; Susan J. Douglas, *Inventing American Broadcasting, 1899–1922* (Baltimore: Johns Hopkins University Press, 1987); Claude S. Fischer, *America Calling: A Social History of the Telephone to 1940* (Berkeley: University of California Press, 1992); Kristen Haring, *Ham Radio's Technical Culture* (Cambridge, MA: MIT Press, 2008).

5. Marie Marchand, *The Minitel Saga: A French Success Story* (Paris: Larousse, 1988), 60.

6. One comment by Théry, the former DGT head, emphasizes the importance of the Kiosk in the overall ecosystem. In 1994, Théry, who had been commissioned by the State to pen a report on information superhighways, did not believe that the Internet would be viable, and under the leadership of the French State, called for the development of a distinct information highway, using "super-broadband" (fiber optics technology). The first chunk of the highway would be a Franco–German axis, something Théry had pushed for back in 1981, but that had failed for political reasons. In his report, Théry opined that the Internet could not successfully develop on the mass market because of its lack of a State-run, Kiosk-like billing system. Gérard Théry, *Les autoroutes de l'information* (Paris: Documentation Française, 1994), 86; Gérard Théry, interview with author, Paris, June 27, 2012.

7. Marchand, *Minitel Saga*, 105, referring to business experiments by pioneer Claude Kretzschmar, CEO of FUNITEL.

8. Daniel Hannaby, interview with author, San Francisco, March 9, 2012; Julien Mailland and Marc Weber, "Oral History of Daniel Hannaby," Computer History Museum, March 20, 2015, reference number: X7439.2015, accessed September 17, 2016, http://archive.computerhistory.org/resources/access/text/2015/09/102740083-05-01-acc.pdf.

9. Maury points to the Canadian/US videotex standard, North American Presentation Level Protocol Syntax, as one that accommodated visually pleasant ads, but also notes the much higher cost of the terminal. Jean-Paul Maury, interview no. 1 with author, Paris, December 2011.

10. Mailland and Weber, "Oral History of Daniel Hannaby."

11. James N. Butcher and Carolyn L. Williams, "Personality Assessment with the MMPI-2: Historical Roots, International Adaptations, and Current Challenges," *Applied Psychology: Health and Well-Being* 1, no. 1 (2009): 105–135.

12. Hannaby, interview; Mailland and Weber, "Oral History of Daniel Hannaby."

13. Such a requirement had actually been imposed by the DGT internally, outside any actual legal mandate, in order to appease the regional print-press lobby and its leader, Mr. Hutin. The service providers lobby would sue the DGT; eventually, the French Supreme Court would declare this requirement unconstitutional. The ruling did not occur until 1993, however—right before the platform would enter the negative feedback loop that lead to its demise. We discuss the lawsuit in greater detail later in this chapter.

14. Code Général des Impôts, Ann. III, articles 72 and 73 (Fr.).

15. "Les messageries, gagneuses de la télématique," *Libération*, August 30–31, 1986.

16. Albert du Roy, interview by Thierry Ardisson, *Double Jeu*, circa 1992, accessed September 25, 2016, http://player.ina.fr/player/embed/Io8158690/1/1bobd2o 3fbcd702f9bc9b10ac3d0fc21/460/259.

17. Hannaby, interview; Mailland and Weber, "Oral History of Daniel Hannaby." See also Marchand, *Minitel Saga*, 103, describing how the pink site Crac obtained a CP number when its founder, Céline Alvergnat, partnered up with Pierre Guinchat, publisher of *H* magazine, and used Guinchat's CP number to get Kiosk access.

18. Bernard Louis, interview by Thierry Ardisson, *Double Jeu*, January 25, 1992, accessed September 25, 2016,http://player.ina.fr/player/embed/Io8158690/1/ 1bobd2o3fbcd702f9bc9b10ac3d0fc21/460/259. The service providers' lobby is the Syndicat Professionnel des Médias de Télécommunications.

19. *Informations rigolotes et étranges*, no. 1, February 1986 (Editeur: H.D. Communication. Directeur de la publication: Hervé Delisle), reproduced in Vincent Glad, "Carte de presse: Pascale Clark aurait mieux fait de faire du minitel rose," *Libération: L'An 2000: Chroniques Numériques*, March 18, 2015, http://linkis. com/49f68.

20. Michel Baujard, interview no. 1 with author, Paris, June 29, 2012; Michel Baujard, telephone interview no. 2 with author, July 13, 2015.

21. Ibid.

22. Ibid.

23. Jean-Baptiste Ingold, interview with author, Paris, June 29, 2012.

24. Loi no. 63–1255, December 21, 1963, J.O., December 22, 1963, 11456.

25. See, in general, Planète Non Violence, "Objection de conscience," accessed April 14, 2013, http://www.planetenonviolence.org/Objection-de-conscience_ a132.html.

26. Ingold, interview.

27. Hannaby, interview no. 3.

28. Hannaby, interview no. 2; Hannaby, interview no. 3; Mailland and Weber, "Oral History of Daniel Hannaby."

29. Baujard, interview no. 2.

30. Théry, interview; Maury, interview no. 1; Jean-Paul Maury, interview no. 2 with author, Paris, June 27, 2012.

31. By then, however, 3615 SNCF had become a success, and was a high-value service for French denizens, who could now check schedules and book tickets. Marchand, *Minitel Saga*.

32. Bernard Marti, *De Minitel à Internet: 30 ans de services en ligne* (Cesson-Sévigné: Armorhistel, 2011), 46. Marti suggests that the SNCF itself created a ghost paper to obtain the short code. But because the ghost paper trick was commonplace by that point, Dondoux's and Maury's reactions suggest that there might have been more happening behind the scenes, and that a battle of ministries was likely taking place.

33. Maury, interview no. 1.

34. Ibid.

35. Julien Mailland, "Freedom of Speech, the Internet, and the Costs of Control: The French Example," *New York University Journal of International Law and Politics* 33 (2001): 1179–1234.

36. Maury, interview no. 1.

37. Ibid.

38. Orange executive, off-the-record interview with author, 2012.

39. Valérie Schafer, "Évolution du nombre d'accès directs commerciaux à Transpac (1979–1985)," *Flux* 62, no. 4 (2005) : 75–80.

40. Christian Quest, interview with author, Paris, June 29, 2012. On the delays in getting a Transpac line installed, see also Mailland and Weber, "Oral History of Daniel Hannaby."

41. Ordonnance du 1er décembre 1986, articles 1 et 2; Code de la Consommation, article L113–1; Loi no. 90–568 du 2 juillet 1990, article 2; Décret du 29 décembre 1990 relatif au cahier des charges de France Telecom et au Code des postes et télécommunications, articles 1 et 12. See also Marti, *De Minitel à Internet*, 47.

42. Maury, interview no. 1.

43. Marti, *De Minitel à Internet*, 47.

44. Ibid. See also a High Court case validating France Telecom's decision to turn off the faucet for a messagerie that had registered as a professional service in order to be able to charge 2.23 francs per minute over a 3618 short code, when it was only allowed to charge 1.23 francs per minute over the 3615: Cour de Cassation, November 21, 1990, Société RAPT (Fr).

45. Mailland and Weber, "Oral History of Daniel Hannaby."

46. Valérie Schafer and Benjamin G. Thierry, *Le Minitel: L'enfance numérique de la France* (Paris: Nuvis, 2012), 170 ; Josiane Jouët, "Le rapport a la technique," *Réseaux* 5, no. 1 (1987): 109–138.

47. Maury, interview no. 1. Hannaby also confirmed the practice, but pointed out that his company never used it. Mailland and Weber, "Oral History of Daniel Hannaby."

48. Maury, interview no. 1.

49. See, for example, Ministère des PTT, *Recommandations aux partenaires Télétel* (Paris: Ministère des PTT, 1986).

50. Note that not all imperfections were the result of scams. Amateurism was also often at stake. Schafer and Thierry, *Le Minitel*, 170; Jouët, "Le rapport a la technique," 138; Maury, interview no. 1: "the universities' servers kept overloading. … [T]he State didn't put enough money in it, as usual."

51. Merav Katz-Kimchi, "'Singing the Strong Light Works of [American] Engineers': Popular Histories of the Internet as Mythopoetic Literature," *Information & Culture* 50, no. 2 (May 1, 2015): 160–180, doi:10.7560/IC50202.

52. Schafer and Thierry, *Le Minitel*, 98, 96.

53. Consider the story of Virginie, a fifteen-year-old girl, on the time-delayed e-mail system offered over T3V: "What I'd like is to be able to communicate like this, right now, on the messagerie. … To be able to send a message and for the other[s] to be able to receive it like this, right now." Quoted in Schafer and Thierry, *Le Minitel*, 96, translation by author; note Virginie's naive tone, which is present in the original French version.

54. For a closer look at the effects of the phone book time limit, see Julien Mailland, "Mythologies: The Minitel Kiosk Payment System," in *Paid: Tales of Dongles,*

Checks, and Other Money Stuff, ed. Bill Maurer and Lana Swartz (Cambridge, MA: MIT Press, 2017).

55. For a passing mention of this story, but with no specifics, see Schafer and Thierry, *Le Minitel*, 176.

56. Maury, interview no. 1.

57. Ibid.

58. See, in general, Fabien Granjon and Asdrad Torres, "R@S: La nauissance d'un acteur majeur de 'l'Internet militant' Français," *Le Temps des Médias* 18, no. 1 (2012): 87–98.

59. Schafer and Thierry also point to uses of Télétel for "direct democracy." For instance, on the 3615 AGIR site, "a political personality responds for 3 days to the questions asked by users." Schafer and Thierry, *Le Minitel*, 113n147.

60. Jacques Anis, *Texte et ordinateur: l'écriture réinventée?* (Brussels: De Boeck and Larcier, 1998), 94.

61. Granjon and Torres, "R@S," 97n4.

62. There are references to these practices in the academic literature, but the content of the chat rooms itself was generally not archived.

63. On Minitel social engineering, consider Landaret's statement: "Because our system was set-up to study the way people use these services, we could perform social experiments. ... We found that we could feed a small piece of deliberately false information to one of [the users], and it spread throughout all the different groups, to as many as four thousand people within two days." Quoted in Howard Rheingold, *The Virtual Community: Homesteading on the Electronic Frontier* (Reading, PA: Addison-Wesley, 1993), 228.

64. Kevin Driscoll, "Social Media's Dial-Up Ancestor: The Bulletin Board System," *IEEE Spectrum*, November 2016, accessed November 2, 2016, http://spectrum.ieee .org/computing/networks/social-medias-dialup-ancestor-the-bulletin- board-system.

65. BBSs designed for personal computer users, similar to the United States' WELL, were "a technical minority in France" because of the wide availability of free Minitel terminals that included a modem. Rheingold, *Virtual Community*, 221. "It's no mystery why modem dial-up services for PC users in Paris did not grow explosively, when the government was handing out free terminals (with built-in modems) by the millions. Ibid., 225. For a case study of Calvacom, a French Apple-oriented BBS officially sponsored by Apple and the American University of Paris, see "Telematique and Messageries Roses: A Tale of Two Virtual Communities," in ibid., 220–240. On the history of RTC servers written from the standpoint of a sysop, see, in general, Godefroy Troude, *Pinky: histoire d'un micro-serveur*, February 9, 2006, accessed September 25, 2016, http://www. troude.com/pinky/index.html-ssi. Frédéric Cambus's sites (accessed September 25, 2016, www.goto10.fr; accessed September 25, 2016, www.minitel.org) also provide a rich repository of files and links related to RTC servers.

66. On the Apple Macintosh, see Christian Quest's CRISTEL software (on file with authors). On Oric Telestrat, see Troude, *Pinky*. On Amstrad CPC, see, for example, "Un serveur sur Amstrad," *CPC: La Revue de Utilizateurs d'Amstrad* 9 (March 1986): 64–65, testing Série Jagot and Leon, Minitel server software for Amstrad. The magazine editors created their own live micro-serveur as part of the review, and playfully hid the PSTN number of the server behind a code sequence that readers

were to enter into their machine to reveal the number: "10 PRINT CHR$ (57) CHR$ (57) CHR$ (45) CHR$ (53) CHR$ (55) CHR$ (45) CHR$ (57) CHR$ (48) CHR$ (45) CHR$ (51) CHR$ (55)." Ibid. On Amiga, see "Minitel Denise RTC Running on m68k-amigaos," accessed September 25, 2016, http://www.goto10.fr/minitel/amiga/madlertc.readme; for a discussion of both Amiga-based PSTN and Transpac servers, see also Philippe Janot, "Bidouille: créer un serveur Minitel 128 voies sur Amiga," *Amiga News*, November 1997, accessed September 25, 2016, http://obligement.free.fr/articles/serveur_minitel_128_voies_amiga.php. In terms of Atari ST, Francois Planque, a French hobbyist, developed it for his own use and then commercially sold Atari ST Minitel server software, named Stut. The software is now available free of charge under a GNU license; see François Planque, "Stut One," Fplanque.net, 2013, accessed September 17, 2016, http://fplanque.net/about/stut-one. See also Francois Planque, "Programmer un serveur Minitel (1)," *ST Magazine* 99 (November 1995), accessed September 25, 2016, http://www.fplanque.net/Blog/devblog/1995/07/01/programmer-un-serveur-minitel-1; Francois Planque, "Programmer un serveur Minitel (2): Dompter le Minitel!" *ST Magazine*, circa spring 1996, accessed September 25, 2016, http://www.fplanque.net/Articles/StutOne2Source/ProgrammerServeur Minitel2.html; Francois Planque, "STUT ONE 3—Le code source," *ST Magazine*, circa summer–fall 1996, accessed September 25, 2016, http://fplanque.net/Blog/devblog/1996/06/01/stut-one-3-le-code-source. See also Troude, *Pinky*. On IBM-compatible PCs, see "CyberNet Landes, parcours d'un sysop," December 14, 1996, accessed September 25, 2016, http://3430.free.fr/computing/servers/rtcrecit.htm.

67. Planque, "Stut One."
68. In contrast to the United States, French local calls placed over the PSTN were not free at the time.
69. Troude, *Pinky*.
70. Ibid.
71. The lack of serious indexing à la Internet Archive makes it impossible to pinpoint an accurate number. In a 1996 book chapter, André Lemos estimates that "there are more than fifty RTC servers in the Paris region." André Lemos, "The Labyrinth of Minitel," in *Cultures of Internet: Virtual Spaces, Real Histories, Living Bodies*, ed. Rob Shields (Thousand Oaks, CA: Sage, 1996), 42. A hobbyist text file directory from 1995 lists ninety in France and one in Monaco (http://3430.free.fr/computing/servers/rtc_list.htm); that particular text file, maintained by a SYSOP named XBIOS, aims to function as a sort of RTC domain name system. It starts with the following statement: "Thanks to SYSOPS from the various interested RTCs to make this file available for download on your respective RTC. Do not modify the file without contacting XBIOS. Please notify any change to me" (translation by authors). A hobbyist's directory posted as an html page in 2000 lists twenty-four (http://serveur 87thomson.free.fr/liens/rtc/rtc.htm).
72. Jean-Luc Beraudo De Pralormo, interview no. 1 with author, Cesson-Sévigné, June 25, 2012; Bernard Louvel, interview no. 1 with author, Cesson-Sévigné, June 25, 2012; Maury, interview no. 2; .Théry, interview.
73. Katie Hafner, *The Well: A Story of Love, Death, and Real Life in the Seminal Online Community* (New York: Carroll and Graf, 2001), 19.

74. Laurent Chemla recalls: "I lived the early days of Minitel, at the time where machines [Minitels] designed solely to offer banking services were used to access more or less pirate chat rooms [the PSTN servers]. I had the desire to communicate, to speak with strangers across the country while bypassing social and generational hurdles. That was before businesspeople turned Minitel into the national sex shop." Laurent Chemla, *Confessions d'un voleur: Internet, la liberté confisquée* (Paris: Éditions Denoël, 2002), 14–15, translation by author, accessed September 26, 2016, http://www.confessions-voleur.net/confessions.pdf. Chemla, who became the first French hacker to be prosecuted for hacking, went on to start Gandi, France's main Internet registrar, became a lobbyist with the Internet freedom group La Quadrature du Net, and was involved with such services as 3615 Internet (a Minitel service giving access to the Internet network) and altern.org, one of the first free hosting services in France. See also Lemos, "Labyrinth of Minitel," 42: "Normally, an adolescent *bricoleur* with an Amiga computer would create an alternative server. This new sysop (system operator) is thus visited by a relatively loyal public, who share common ideas and live the experience of being together, even at a distance. In a small, alternative *messagerie* the affinities between the members are more structuring of the interaction (some are more technical, other more ludic or leisure-oriented) and this allows us to speak of a true community, even if it is electronic and virtual [authors' note: notice the parallel with Rheingold's argument]. … In perceiving themselves as actual examples of and sites within cyberspace, some services give free access to newsgroups on Usenet (the alt. hierarchy for example). With the limited Minitel, one can even, for a small subscription fee, gain access to Internet to send and receive electronic mail or subscribe to a *lettre spécialisée*—a list server or mailing list. The logic of France Telecom was thus to promote the use of the Transpac network for the transmission of data and to limit the RTC to voice telecommunication. However, this has been turned upside down, as the effervescence of the alternative networks on RTC have redirected the use of the simple Minitel to their cheaper and more sociable or 'communitarian' services than those provided by the Kiosque system." As one might expect, a series of fanzines also connected this vibrant subcultures. See, for example, *Gigantex*, accessed September 26, 2016, http://3430.free.fr/computing/servers/gigantex/index.htm.

75. See, for example, Christian Quest, demo presented at "Minitel: La dernière séance 'Rendez-vous à jamais,'" *La Cantine*, June 29, 2012; Julien Mailland and Kevin Driscoll, "Minitel Terminal as Twitter Client" (demo presented at the Telecommunication Policy Research Conference, George Mason University School of Law, Arlington, VA, September 21, 2012); Renaud Février, "Des étudiants ont ressuscité le Minitel … et l'ont branché sur Internet!," *L'Obs*, October 27, 2016, accessed November 3, 2016, http://tempsreel.nouvelobs.com/l-histoire-du-soir/20161027.OBS0431/des-etudiants-ont-ressuscite-le-minitel-et-l-ont-branche-sur-internet.html; Graffiti Research Lab, *3615 Selfie* (undated), accessed November 3, 2016, http://graffitiresearchlab.fr/dl/3615selfie.pdf; Graffiti Research Lab, *DeMo (Dead Minitel Orchestra)*, performance, Espace Jean-Roger Caussimon - 6, rue des Alpes - 93290 Tremblay-en-France, October 12, 2016, accessed November 3, 2016, http://mjccaussimon.fr/?DeMo-Dead-Minitel-Orchestra.

Chapter 7

1. James Gillies and Robert Cailliau, *How the Web Was Born* (New York: Oxford University Press, 2000), 111.

2. See, in general, Jerome Aumente, *New Electronic Pathways: Videotex, Teletext, and Online Databases* (Newbury Park, CA: Sage, 1987); Julien Mailland, "101 Online: American Minitel Network and Lessons from Its Failure," *IEEE Annals of the History of Computing* 38, no. 1 (January–March 2016): 6–22.

3. See, for example, William L. Cats-Baril and Tawfik Jelassi, *The French Videotex System Minitel: An Example of the Critical Success Factors to Establish a National Information Technology Infrastructure* (Fontainebleau: INSEAD, 1992).

4. Julien Mailland and Marc Weber, "Oral History of Daniel Hannaby," Computer History Museum, March 20, 2015, reference number: X7439.2015, accessed September 17, 2016, http://archive.computerhistory.org/resources/access/text/2015/09/102740083-05-01-acc.pdf.; Jérémie Maire, "Encore 420.000 utilisateurs du Minitel pour sa dernière année d'exploitation," *Le Huffington Post*, June 29, 2012, accessed September 26, 2016, http://www.huffingtonpost.fr/2012/06/29/420000-utilisateurs-minitel-derniere-annee-exploitation_n_1636611.html.

5. "3615 Ulla, la fin d'un mythe," *01net*, July 10, 2012, accessed September 26, 2016, http://www.01net.com/actualites/3615-ulla-la-fin-dun-mythe-568601.html.

6. "Minitel: ses derniers fans se préparent à sa fin," *Nordéclair*, October 23, 2011, accessed September 26, 2016, http://www.nordeclair.fr/France-Monde/France/2011/10/23/minitel-ses-derniers-fans-se-preparent-a.shtml.

7. Maire, "Encore 420.000 utilisateurs du Minitel."

8. See, in general, Marc Weber and Julien Mailland, "Oral History of Georges Nahon," Computer History Museum, May 4, 2015, reference number: X7479.2015, accessed September 26, 2016, http://archive.computerhistory.org/resources/access/text/2016/04/102740081-05-01-acc.pdf.

9. See, in general, Mailland, "101 Online."

10. See, in general, Yochai Benkler, "WikiLeaks and the PROTECT-IP Act: A New Public–Private Threat to the Internet Commons," *Daedalus, the Journal of the American Academy of Arts and Sciences* 140, no. 4 (Fall 2011): 154–164.

11. Likewise, 101 Online, the "American Minitel," used a proprietary editing software environment. Mailland, "101 Online."

12. See, for example, Lyombe S. Eko, *New Media, Old Regimes: Case Studies in Comparative Communication Law and Policy* (Lanham, MD: Lexington Books, 2012), 235.

13. Mailland and Weber, "Oral History of Daniel Hannaby."

14. Quoted in Shawn M. Powers and Michael Jablonski, *The Real Cyberwar: The Political Economy of Internet Freedom* (Urbana: University of Illinois Press, 2015), 57.

15. Susannah Fox and Lee Rainie, "The Web at 25 in the U.S.," Pew Research Center, February 27, 2014, accessed September 26, 2016, http://www.pewinternet.org/2014/02/27/the-web-at-25-in-the-u-s/.

16. "In my view, the world we are entering is not a world of perpetual freedom; or more precisely, the world we are entering is not a world where freedom is assured. Cyberspace has the potential to be the most fully, and extensively,

regulated space that we have ever known—anywhere, at any time in our history. It has the potential to be the antithesis of a space of freedom. And unless we understand this potential, unless we see how this might be, we are likely to sleep through this transition from freedom into control. For that, in my view, is the transition we are seeing just now." Lawrence Lessig, "The Laws of Cyberspace" (paper presented at the Taiwan Net '98 Conference, Taipei, March 1998).

17. Under Major League Baseball's policy, "all live games on MLB.TV and available through MLB.com At Bat are subject to local blackouts. Such live games will be blacked out in each applicable Club's home television territory, regardless of whether that Club is playing at home or away. If a game is blacked out in an area, it is not available for live game viewing.... MLB.com live game blackouts are determined in part by IP address. MLB.com At Bat live game blackouts are determined using one or more reference points, such as GPS and software within your mobile device." "Blackouts FAQ," MLB.com, accessed October 31, 2016, http://mlb.mlb.com/mlb/help/faq_blackout.jsp.

•

Bibliography

Text

Abadie, Michel. "'Koka' l'animateur de messagerie." *La Revue du Minitel*, no. 8, November–December 1986, 46–47.

Abbate, Janet. "The Electrical Century: Inventing the Web." *Proceedings of the IEEE* 87, no. 11 (1999): 1999–2002, doi:10.1109/5.796364.

Abbate, Janet. *Inventing the Internet.* Cambridge, MA: MIT Press, 1999.

Alter, Bernard. "Le Minitel a-t-il un avenir ?" *Terminal*, no. 55, October–November 1991, 46.

Anable, Aubrey. "Casual Games, Time Management, and the Work of Affect." *Ada: A Journal of Gender, New Media, and Technology*, no. 2 (2013). doi:10.7264/N3ZW1HVD.

Anis, Jacques. *Texte et ordinateur: l'écriture réinventée?* Brussels: De Boeck and Larcier, 1998.

Ankerson, Megan Sapnar. "Writing Web Histories with an Eye on the Analog Past." *New Media and Society* 14, no. 3 (May 1, 2012): 384–400, doi:10.1177/1461444811414834.

Antenne 2. "Election présidentielle 1981: Mitterrand élu." Paris, May 10, 1981, accessed September 18, 2016, http://www.ina.fr/video/I00002041.

Archambault, Jean-Pierre. "Une histoire de l'introduction des TIC dans le système éducatif français." *Médialog* 54 (2005): 42–45.

Armstrong, Mark. "Competition in Two-Sided Markets." *The RAND Journal of Economics* 37, no. 3 (September 1, 2006): 668–691, doi:10.1111/j.1756-2171.2006.tb00037.x.

Arnoux, Patrick. "Banque a domicile." *La Revue du Minitel*, February–March 1987.

Arora, Payal. *Leisure Commons: A Spatial History of Web 2.0.* New York: Routledge, 2014.

Arvonny, Maurice. "Un système informatique d'une grande complexité." *Le Monde*, December 28, 1983, accessed September 23, 2016, http://www.lemonde.fr/archives/article/1983/12/28/un-systeme-informatique-d-une-grande-complexite_2851921_1819218.html.

Aumente, Jerome. *New Electronic Pathways: Videotex, Teletext, and Online Databases.* Newbury Park, CA: Sage, 1987.

Balibar, Etienne. "The Nation Form: History and Ideology." In *Race, Nation, Class: Ambiguous Identities*, by Balibar, Etienne, and Wallerstein, Immanuel, 86–106. London: Verso, 1991.

Bartle, Richard A. "Archaeology versus Anthropology: What Can Truly Be Preserved?" In *Gaming Environments and Virtual Worlds*, edited by Janet Delve and David Anderson, 92–97. London: Facet Publishing, 2013.

Baym, Nancy K. *Personal Connections in the Digital Age.* Cambridge, UK: Polity Press, 2010.

Benkler, Yochai. "WikiLeaks and the PROTECT-IP Act: A New Public–Private -Threat to the Internet Commons." *Daedalus, the Journal of the American Academy of Arts and Sciences* 140, no. 4 (Fall 2011): 154–164.

Bergin, Thomas J. "The Origins of Word Processing Software for Personal Computers: 1976–1985." *IEEE Annals of the History of Computing* 28, no. 4 (2006): 32–47.

Bertho-Lavenir, Catherine. "The Telephone in France, 1879–1979: National Characteristics and International Influences." In *The Development of Large Technical Systems*, edited by Renate Mayntz and Thomas Hugues, 169–170. Boulder, CO: Westview Press, 1988.

Bijker, Wiebe E., Thomas P. Hughes, and Trevor Pinch, eds. *The Social Construction of Technological Systems: New Directions in the Sociology and History of Technology.* Cambridge, MA: MIT Press, 1987.

"Billetel: un plus pour Avignon." *Le Matin*, February 2, 1987.

Black, Michael L. "Narrative and Spatial Form in Digital Media: A Platform Study of the SCUMM Engine and Ron Gilbert's The Secret of Monkey Island." *Games and Culture*, April 12, 2012, doi:10.1177/1555412012440317.

"Blackouts FAQ." MLB.com, accessed April 15, 2013, http://mlb.mlb.com/mlb/help/faq_blackout.jsp.

Bogost, Ian, and Nick Montfort. "New Media as Material Constraint: An Introduction to Platform Studies." In *Electronic Techtonics: Thinking at the Interface* (Durham, NC: First International HASTAC Conference, Duke University, 2007), 176–192.

Bowker, Geoffrey C., and Susan Leigh Star. *Sorting Things Out: Classification and Its Consequences.* Cambridge, MA: MIT Press, 1999.

Bronson, Po. *The Nudist on the Late Shift.* New York: Random House, 1999.

Bruhat, Thierry, and SPES/DGT. "Genèse. GRETEL: la messagerie interactive—Histoire d'un piratage." *Réseaux* 2, no. 6 (1984): 37–47, doi:10.3406/reso.1984.1119.

Bucher, Taina. "A Technicity of Attention: How Software 'Makes Sense.'" *Culture Machine* 13 (2012), accessed September 15, 2016, http://www.culturemachine.net/index.php/cm/article/view/470.

Bucher, Taina. "Want to Be on the Top? Algorithmic Power and the Threat of Invisibility on Facebook." *New Media and Society* 14, no. 7 (November 1, 2012): 1164–1180, doi:10.1177/1461444812440159.

Burrington, Ingrid. *Networks of New York: An Illustrated Field Guide to Urban Internet Infrastructure.* New York: Melville House Books, 2016.

Burrington, Ingrid. "Seeing Networks in New York City." 2014, accessed September 14, 2016, http://seeingnetworks.in/nyc/.

Butcher, James N., and Carolyn L. Williams. "Personality Assessment with the MMPI-2: Historical Roots, International Adaptations, and Current Challenges." *Applied Psychology: Health and Well-Being* 1, no. 1 (2009): 105–135.

Caillaud, Bernard, and Bruno Jullien. "Chicken and Egg: Competing Matchmakers." Scholarly paper, Social Science Research Network, Rochester, NY, July 1, 2001, accessed September 15, 2016, http://papers.ssrn.com/abstract=278562.

Caillaud, Bernard, and Bruno Jullien. "Chicken and Egg: Competition among Intermediation Service Providers." *RAND Journal of Economics* 34, no. 2 (2003): 309–328, doi:10.2307/1593720.

Came, François. "Minitel: le 22 a Wichita Falls/3619 Siriel." *Libération*, March 3, 1995, accessed September 20, 2016, http://www.liberation.fr/ecrans/1995/03/03/minitel-le-22-a-wichita-falls-3619-siriel_128305.

Campbell-Kelly, Martin. *From Airline Reservations to Sonic the Hedgehog: A History of the Software Industry*. Cambridge, MA: MIT Press, 2003.

Caron, D., J. P. Martinière, and O. Normand. "Spécification technique du protocole de communication entre les équipments PAVI V27ter/V29—Terminal V23/V27ter/V29 vitesse rapide à 9600/4800 Bps." Cesson-Sévigné: Center commun d'études de télédiffusion et télécommunications (CCETT), April 2, 1993.

Carpenter, Marie. *La bataille des télécoms: Vers une France numérique*. Paris: Economica, 2011.

Cats-Baril, William L., and Tawfik Jelassi. *The French Videotex System Minitel: An Example of the Critical Success Factors to Establish a National Information Technology Infrastructure*. Fontainebleau: INSEAD, 1992.

Cats-Baril, William L., and Tawfik Jelassi. "The French Videotex System Minitel: A Successful Implementation of a National Information Technology Infrastructure." *MIS Quarterly* 18, no. 1 (March 1994): 2–3.

Ceruzzi, Paul E. *A History of Modern Computing*. Cambridge, MA: MIT Press, 1998.

Ceruzzi, Paul E. *Internet Alley: High Technology in Tysons Corner, 1945–2005*. Cambridge, MA: MIT Press, 2008.

Ceruzzi, Paul E. "Not Quite Machu Picchu, but Close." IT History Society Blog, September 23, 2008.

Charle, Christophe. *Histoire sociale de la France au XIX siècle*. Paris: Seuil, 1991.

Chemla, Laurent. *Confessions d'un voleur: Internet, la liberté confisquée*. Paris: Éditions Denoël, 2002, accessed September 26, 2016, http://www.confessions-voleur.net/confessions.pdf.

Clarke, K. E., and N. Fenn. "The UK Prestel Service: Technical Developments between March 1980 and March 1981." In *Videotex 81*, 147–162. Northwood Hills, Middlesex: Online Conferences, 1981.

Commission Supérieure de la Télématique. Meeting minutes, February 18, 1981.

Confédération française démocratique du travail. *Note de la C.F.D.T. sur la Télématique Grand Public*. October 14, 1982.

Consalvo, Mia. *Cheating Gaining Advantage in Videogames*. Cambridge, MA: MIT Press, 2007.

Conservatoire National des Arts et Métiers, *Carte à puce: Une histoire à rebonds*. Paris: CNAM, 2015.

Cour des Comptes. *Rapport au président de la république*. June 28, 1989.

"Covidea Ends Endeavor in Commercial Videotex Mart," *Network World*, December 19, 1988.

"Covidea to Add Information Service in New York." *Infoworld*, February 3, 1986.

Cusumano, Michael. "Technology Strategy and Management: The Evolution of Platform Thinking." *Communications of the ACM* 53, no. 1 (January 2010): 32–34, doi:10.1145/1629175.1629189.

"CyberNet Landes, parcours d'un sysop."December14,1996,accessedSeptember25,2 016,http://3430.free.fr/computing/servers/rtcrecit.htm.

"Cyberporn." *Time*, July 3, 1995, cover.

Dard, Philippe. *Minitel et gestion de l'habitat: la domotique en questions*. Paris, Plan construction et architecture, 1991.

de Valence, Francois. Interviewed by J. Legros, *France Inter*, August 23, 1986.

"Débats." *Linx*, no. 17, 1987. "Le texte et l'ordinateur." Sous la direction de Jacques Anis et Jean-Louis Lebrave, 71–75.

Del Nero, Jean-François. "Etude technique du Minitel." April 15, 2011, accessed September 17, 2016, http://hxc2001.free.fr/minitel/.

Delaval, Danièle. "Le nouveau code pénal et le renforcement de la protection morale des mineurs." *Solutions Télématiques*, no. 15, July 1993.

Delve, Janet, and David Anderson, eds. *Gaming Environments and Virtual Worlds*. Vol. 3, *The Preservation of Complex Objects*. London: Facet Publishing, 2013.

"Des associations familiales font le procès de l'Etats proxénète." *Le Monde*, July 16–17, 1989.

Després, Rémi. "X.25 Virtual Circuits—Transpac in France—Pre-Internet Data Networking." *IEEE Communications Magazine* (November 2010).

Direction Générale des Télécommunications. *La Lettre de Télétel*, no. 16, Q1, 1989.

Direction Générale des Télécommunications. *Rapport sur le service de communication par Minitel, 1985*. Archives Historiques de France Telécom, box 97017/02.

Direction Générale des Télécommunications. *Recommandations aux Partenaires Télétel*. Paris, France: Ministère des Postes et des Télécommunications, 1986.

Direction Générale des Télécommunications. *Réseau Minitel, Spécifications techniques d'utilisation*. Paris: Ministère des Postes et des Télécommunications, n.d.

Direction Générale des Télécommunications. *Spécifications techniques d'utilisation du point d'accès Vidéotex*. Paris: Ministère des Postes et des Télécommunications, 1987.

Direction Générale des Télécommunications. *Spécifications vidéotex de visualisation et de codage*. Paris, France: Ministère des Postes et des Télécommunications, circa 1980.

Direction Générale des Télécommunications. *Télétel, Minitel 1B: Spécifications Techniques d'Utilisation*. Paris: Ministère des Postes et des Télécommunications, 1986.

Direction Générale des Télécommunications. *Teletel: Repertoire des peripheriques pour le Minitel*. May 1989.

Dobbs, Michael. "Minitel Is New French Revolution." *Washington Post*, December 25, 1986, accessed September 22, 2016, https://www.washingtonpost.com/archive/politics/1986/12/25/minitel-is-new-french-revolution/eeaf90f3-90ca-4d60-bb46-fc4808fa2649/.

"Domotique: La maison domestiquée." *Vidéo 7*, March 1987, 104–110.

Douglas, Susan J. *Inventing American Broadcasting, 1899–1922*. Baltimore: Johns Hopkins University Press, 1987.

Driscoll, Kevin. "Hobbyist Inter-Networking and the Popular Internet Imaginary: Forgotten Histories of Networked Personal Computing, 1978–1998." PhD diss., University of Southern California, 2014, accessed September 17, 2016, http://digitallibrary.usc.edu/cdm/compoundobject/collection/p15799coll3/id/444362/rec/2.

Driscoll, Kevin. "Social Media's Dial-Up Ancestor: The Bulletin Board System." *IEEE Spectrum*, November 2016, accessed November 2, 2016, http://spectrum.ieee.org/computing/networks/social-medias-dialup-ancestor-the-bulletin-board-system.

"Du Minitel au spectacle." *Communication and Business*, no. 19, February 2, 1987.

du Roy, Albert. Interview by Thierry Ardisson. *Double Jeu*, circa 1992, accessed September 25, 2016, http://player.ina.fr/player/embed/I08158690/1/1bobd203fbc d702f9bc9b10ac3d0fc21/460/259.

Durandet, Daniel. "Plan informatique: conférence de presse Fabius." *Soir 3*, France Régions 3, January 25, 1985, accessed April 14, 2013, http://www.ina.fr/video/CAC88029024/plan-informatique-conference-de-presse-fabius-video.html.

Edwards, Paul N. *The Closed World Computers and the Politics of Discourse in Cold War America*. Cambridge, MA: MIT Press, 1997.

Eko, Lyombe S. *New Media, Old Regimes: Case Studies in Comparative Communication Law and Policy*. Lanham, MD: Lexington Books, 2012.

Eley, Geoff , and Ronald Grigor Suny, eds. *Becoming National: A Reader*. New York: Oxford University Press, 1996.

Espace des sciences, "France Télécom et la Bretagne," accessed September 14, 2016, http://www.espace-sciences.org/archives/science/17865.html.

Février, Renaud. "Des étudiants ont ressuscité le Minitel … et l'ont branché sur Internet!" *L'Obs*, October 27, 2016, accessed November 3, 2016, http://tempsreel.nouvelobs.com/l-histoire-du-soir/20161027.OBS0431/des-etudiants-ont-ressuscite-le-minitel-et-l-ont-branche-sur-internet.html.

Fischer, Claude S. *America Calling: A Social History of the Telephone to 1940*. Berkeley: University of California Press, 1992.

"Foie gras sur Minitel." *La Dépêche du Midi*, February 20, 1987.

Fox, Susannah, and Lee Rainie. "The Web at 25 in the U.S." Pew Research Center, February 27, 2014, accessed September 26, 2016, http://www.pewinternet.org/2014/02/27/the-web-at-25-in-the-u-s/.

France Telecom. *La lettre de Télétel*, no. 22, Q3, 1991.

France Telecom. *Minitel News*, no. 5, Q1, 1991, 10.

France Telecom. *Minitel 1: Mode d'emploi, modèle TELIC*. Paris: France Telecom, n.d.

France Telecom. *Minitel 12: Spécifications techniques d'utilisation*. Paris: France Telecom, 1990.

France Telecom. *TELETEL: Les fournisseurs de moyens 1*. Paris: Ministère des PTT, April 1986.

France Telecom. *TELETEL: Les fournisseurs de moyens*. Paris: France Telecom, April 1990.

Froment-Meurice, F. "Principes généraux applicables au videotex: Premiers eléments." Premier Ministre, Secrétariat Général du Gouvernment, June 30, 1980.

Gehl, Robert W. "FCJ-190 Building a Better Twitter: A Study of the Twitter Alternatives GNU Social, Quitter, Rstat.us, and Twister." *Fibreculture Journal* 26 (December 22, 2015): 60–86, doi:10.15307/fcj.26.190.2015.

Gehl, Robert W. *Reverse Engineering Social Media: Software, Culture, and Political Economy in New Media Capitalism*. Philadelphia: Temple University Press, 2014.

Gerlitz, Carolin, and Anne Helmond. "The Like Economy: Social Buttons and the Data-Intensive Web." *New Media & Society* 15, no. 8 (December 1, 2013): 1348–1365, doi:10.1177/1461444812472322.

Gfeller, Peter A., and Pierre E. Schmid. "Videotex Developments in Switzerland." In *Videotex 81*, 189–197. Northwood Hills, Middlesex: Online Conferences, 1981.

Gibson, William. *Burning Chrome*. New York: Arbor House, 1982.

Gigantex, accessed September 26, 2016, http://3430.free.fr/computing/servers/gigantex/index.htm.

Gilbert, Richard J., and Michael L. Katz. "An Economist's Guide to U.S. v. Microsoft." *Journal of Economic Perspectives* 15, no. 2 (2001): 25–44.

Gillespie, Tarleton. "The Politics of 'Platforms.'" *New Media and Society* 12, no. 3 (May 1, 2010): 347–364, doi:10.1177/1461444809342738.

Gillies, James, and Robert Cailliau. *How the Web Was Born*. New York: Oxford University Press, 2000.

Gitelman, Lisa. *Always Already New: Media, History, and the Data of Culture*. Cambridge, MA: MIT Press, 2006.

Glad, Vincent. "Minitel: comment les Dernières Nouvelles d'Alsace ont inventé l'Internet social." *Slate*, November 18, 2011, accessed September 17, 2016, http://www.slate.fr/story/46415/minitel-dna-internet-social.

Gonzalez, Antonio, and Emmanuelle Jouve. "Minitel, Histoire du Réseau Télématique Français." *Flux* 47, no. 1 (March 2002): 84–89.

Graffiti Research Lab. *3615 Selfie*. Undated, accessed November 3, 2016, http://graffitiresearchlab.fr/dl/3615selfie.pdf.

Graffiti Research Lab. *DeMo (Dead Minitel Orchestra)*. Performance, Espace Jean-Roger Caussimon - 6, rue des Alpes - 93290 Tremblay-en-France, October 12, 2016, accessed November 3, 2016, http://mjccaussimon.fr/?DeMo-Dead -Minitel-Orchestra.

Granjon, Fabien, and Asdrad Torres. "R@S: La nauissance d'un acteur majeur de 'l'Internet militant' Français." *Le Temps des Médias* 18, no. 1 (2012): 87–98.

"The Greatest Defunct Web Sites and Dotcom Disasters." CNET, June 5, 2008, accessed September 22, 2016, http://web.archive.org/web/20080607211840/http://crave.cnet.co.uk/0,39029477,49296926-6,00.htm.

Hafner, Katie. *The Well: A Story of Love, Death, and Real Life in the Seminal Online Community*. New York: Carroll and Graf, 2001.

Hafner, Katie, and Matthew Lyon. *Where Wizards Stay up Late: The Origins of the Internet*. New York: Simon and Schuster, 1996.

Hands, Joss. "Introduction: Politics, Power, and 'Platformativity.'" *Culture Machine* 14 (2013): 1–9.

Hanne, Isabelle. "«DNA»: en selle, Gretel." *Libération*, June 12, 2012, accessed September 17, 2016, http://www.liberation.fr/ecrans/2012/06/12/dna-en-selle -gretel_950059.

Haring, Kristen. *Ham Radio's Technical Culture*. Cambridge, MA: MIT Press, 2008.

Helmond, Anne. "The Platformization of the Web: Making Web Data Platform Ready." *Social Media + Society* 1, no. 2 (July 1, 2015): 2056305115603080, doi:10.1177/2056305115603080.

"Home Banking Gets New Push." *Infoworld*, August 5, 1985.

Howard, Philip N., Laura Busch, and Spencer Cohen. ICT Diffusion and Distribution Dataset, 1990–2007. ICPSR23562-v1. Ann Arbor, MI: Inter-university Consortium for Political and Social Research [distributor], 2010-03-22. http://doi. org/10.3886/ICPSR23562.v1.

Huet, Pierre. "Cadre juridique de l'audiotex en France et dans le monde." *Droit de l'Informatique et des Télécoms* 3 (1994): 57–62.

Huet, Pierre. Letter to Telecommunications Minister M. Mexandeau, June 26, 1981.

"Industry Giants Launch Second Videotex Wave." *Network World*, August 25, 1986.

Informations rigolotes et étranges, no.1, February 1986. Edited by H. D. Communication. Directed by Hervé Delisle. Reproduced in Vincent Glad. "Carte de presse: Pascale Clark aurait mieux fait de faire du minitel rose." *Libération : L'An 2000: Chroniques Numériques*, March 18, 2015, accessed November 3, 2016, http:// an-2000.blogs.liberation.fr/2015/03/18/pascale-clark-aurait-mieux-fait -detre-hotesse-de-minitel-rose/.

Intelmatique. *Télétel Videotex*. February 1982.

ITU Telecommunication Standardization Sector. *ITU-T Recommendation V.23: Data Communication Over the Telephone Network, 600/1200-Baud Modem Standardized for Use in the General Switched Telephone Network.* Helsinki: International Telecommunication Union, 1988.

ITU Telecommunication Standardization Sector. *ITU-T Recommendation V.25: Series V: Data Communication Over the Telephone Network, Interfaces and Voiceband Modems, Automatic Answering Equipment, and General Procedures for Automatic Calling Equipment on the General Switched Telephone Network Including Procedures for Disabling of Echo Control Devices for Both Manually and Automatically Established Calls.* Helsinki: International Telecommunication Union, 1996.

ITU Telecommunication Standardization Sector. *ITU-T Recommendation V.54: Data Communication Over the Telephone Network, Loop Test Devices for Modems.* Helsinki: International Telecommunication Union, 1988.

Jack, Andrew. *Sur la France: Vive la différence.* Paris: Odile Jacob, 1999.

Janot, Philippe. "Bidouille: créer un serveur Minitel 128 voies sur Amiga." *Amiga News*, November 1997, accessed September 25, 2016, http://obligement.free.fr/ articles/serveur_minitel_128_voies_amiga.php.

Jauvert, Vincent. "Bourse: Le Minitel a la cote." *La Revue du Minitel*, no. 10, April–May 1987, 30.

Jenkins, Henry. "Transmedia Storytelling and Entertainment: An Annotated Syllabus." *Continuum: Journal of Media and Cultural Studies* 24, no. 6 (2010): 943–958.

Jouët, Josiane. "Le minitel rose: du flirt électronique ... et plus, si affinités." *Le Temps des médias* 2, no. 19 (2012, accessed September 21, 2016, https://www.cairn. info/revue-le-temps-des-medias-2012-2-p-221.htm.

Jouët, Josiane. "Le rapport a la technique." *Réseaux* 5, no. 1 (1987): 109–138.

Jovanovic, Pierre. "Le scandale de la prostitution d'adolescents sur Minitel." *Le Quotidien de Paris*, August 28, 1986.

Katz-Kimchi, Merav. "'Singing the Strong Light Works of [American] Engineers': Popular Histories of the Internet as Mythopoetic Literature." *Information & Culture* 50, no. 2 (May 1, 2015): 160–180. doi:10.7560/IC50202.

Kempf, Hervé. "Le Minitel se Démasque." *Science et Vie Micro*, January 1985.

"La Fnac va proposer un service de billeterie de spectacle accessible dans les lieux publics." *Agence France-Presse*, January 30, 1987.

La Revue du Minitel, no. 2, September–October 1985.

La Revue du Minitel, no. 7, September–October 1986.

La Revue du Minitel, no. 8, November–December 1986.

La Revue du Minitel, no. 11, June 1987.

"L'accès Télétel sous haute surveillance." *Solutions Télématiques*, no. 15, 20.

"Laissez venir à moi les petits … fournisseurs Télétel!" *Industrie de l'Information*, July 16, 1984.

Landaret, Michel. "Le père de la messagerie" (interview). *Minitel Magazine*, no.14, April–May 1986, 22.

Landaret, Michel. "Minitel: La dernière séance 'Rendez-vous à jamais.'" *La Cantine*, roundtable, June 29, 2012, accessed September 20, 2016, http://www.youtube.com/watch?feature=player_embedded&v=KtXPTaSi8x8.

Langlois, Ganaele, and Greg Elmer. "The Research Politics of Social Media Platforms." *Culture Machine* 14 (2013): 1–9.

Langlois, Ganaele, Fenwick McKelvey, and Zachary Devereaux, "Networked Publics: The Double Articulation of Code and Politics on Facebook," *Canadian Journal of Communication* 34, no. 3 (2009), accessed September 16, 2016, http://www.cjc-online.ca/index.php/journal/article/view/2114.

Langlois, Ganaele, Fenwick McKelvey, Greg Elmer, and Kenneth Werbin. "Mapping Commercial Web 2.0 Worlds: Towards a New Critical Ontogenesis." *The Fibreculture Journal*, no. 14 (2009). http://fourteen.fibreculturejournal.org/fcj-095-mapping-commercial-web-2-0-worlds-towards-a-new-critical-ontogenesis/.

"L'addition." *Le Point*, October 6, 1985.

"L'Annuaire Électronique dès 1983." *Le Monde*, December 9, 1982, accessed September 17, 2016, http://www.lemonde.fr/archives/article/1982/12/09/l-annuaire-electronique-des-1983_2905834_1819218.html.

Le Bras, Hervé, and Emmanuel Todd. *L'Invention de la France*. Paris: Librairie Générale Francaise, 1981.

"Le Minitel excellent pour la vie de bureau: Le Minitel fait flipper les patrons." *Minitel Magazine*, no. 20, February 1987.

"Le Minitel, très pratique mais cher." *Femme Actuelle*, March 9–15, 1987.

"Le minitel rose n'a pas d'avenir, selon le ministre des PTT." Agence France-Presse, May 7, 1987.

Leloup, Damien. "Aux Etats-Unis, le 'modèle Minitel' surprend toujours." *Le Monde*, June 19, 2012, accessed September 14, 2016, http://www.lemonde.fr/technologies/article/2012/06/29/aux-etats-unis-le-modele-minitel-surprend-toujours_1726833_651865.html.

"LECAM: Spécifications techniques d'utilisation." IBSI TBS, August 25, 1987.

Lemos, André. "The Labyrinth of Minitel." In *Cultures of Internet: Virtual Spaces, Real Histories, Living Bodies*, edited by Rob Shields, 33–48. Thousand Oaks, CA: Sage, 1996.

"Les dessous de la messagerie." *Minitel Magazine*, no. 14, April–May 1986, 47–51.

"Les messageries, gagneuses de la télématique." *Libération*, August 30–31, 1986.

"Les Progrès de l'Annuaire Électronique." *Le Monde*, January 22, 1982, accessed September 17, 2016, http://www.lemonde.fr/archives/article/1982/01/22/les-progres-de-l-annuaire-electronique_2900501_1819218.html.

"Les PTT contre-attaquent: 'pas de mouchards dans les minitels.'" *Libération*, January 1, 1985.

Lessig, Lawrence. "The Laws of Cyberspace." Paper presented at the Taiwan Net '98 Conference, Taipei, March 1998.

Listel. Paris: Paul Cazenave, June 1986.

Listel: Annuaire des services Télétel. Vol. 5. Paris: Les Editions Télématiques de France, 1987.

Louis, Bernard. Interview by Thierry Ardisson. *Double Jeu,* January 25, 1992, accessed September 25, 2016, http://player.ina.fr/player/embed/I08158690/1/1b0bd203 fbcd702f9bc9b10ac3d0fc21/460/259.

Lowood, Henry, Devin Monnens, Zach Vowell, Judd Ethan Ruggill, Ken S. McAllister, and Andrew Armstrong. "Before It's Too Late: A Digital Game Preservation White Paper." *American Journal of Play* 2, no. 2 (October 1, 2009): 139–166.

MacKenzie, Donald A., and Judy Wajcman, eds. *The Social Shaping of Technology: How the Refrigerator Got Its Hum.* Milton Keynes, UK: Open University Press, 1985.

Mailland, Julien. "Freedom of Speech, the Internet, and the Costs of Control: The French Example." *New York University Journal of International Law and Politics* 33 (2001): 1179–1234.

Mailland, Julien. "Mythologies: The Minitel Kiosk Payment System." In *Paid: Tales of Dongles, Checks, and Other Money Stuff,* edited by Bill Maurer and Lana Swartz. Cambridge, MA: MIT Press, 2017.

Mailland, Julien. "101 Online: American Minitel Network and Lessons from Its Failure." *IEEE Annals of the History of Computing* 38, no. 1 (January–March 2016): 6–22.

Mailland, Julien, and Kevin Driscoll. "Minitel Terminal as a Twitter Client." Demo presented at the Telecommunications Policy Research Conference, George Mason University School of Law, Arlington, VA, September 21, 2012.

Mailland, Julien, and Marc Weber. "Oral History of Daniel Hannaby." Computer History Museum, March 20, 2015, reference number: X7439.2015, accessed September 17, 2016, http://archive.computerhistory.org/resources/access/text/2015/09/102740083-05-01-acc.pdf.

Maher, Jimmy. *The Future Was Here: The Commodore Amiga.* Cambridge, MA: MIT Press, 2012.

Maire, Jérémie. "Encore 420.000 utilisateurs du Minitel pour sa dernière année d'exploitation." *Le Huffington Post,* June 29, 2012, accessed September 26, 2016, http://www.huffingtonpost.fr/2012/06/29/420000-utilisateurs-minitel-derniere-annee-exploitation_n_1636611.html.

Manach, Jean-Marc. "J'ai été animatrice de Minitel rose." *OWNI,* June 28, 2012, accessed April 15, 2013, http://owni.fr/2012/06/28/jai-ete-animatrice-de-minitel-rose/.

Mantel, H. "The Seltext Center for the German Bildschirmtext Network." In *Videotex 81,* 179–188. Northwood Hills, Middlesex: Online Conferences, 1981.

Marchand, Marie. *The Minitel Saga: A French Success Story.* Paris: Larousse, 1988.

"Marie-Laure menteuse par Minitel." *Le Journal du Dimanche,* March 10, 1986.

Marsh, David. "CCF Starts Home Banking Service." *Financial Times,* December 22, 1983.

Marti, Bernard. *De Minitel à Internet: 30 ans de services en ligne.* Cesson-Sévigné: Armorhistel, 2011.

Marvin, Carolyn. *When Old Technologies Were New: Thinking about Electric Communication in the Late Nineteenth Century.* New York: Oxford University Press, 1988.

Mathison, Stuart L., Lawrence G. Roberts, and Philip M. Walker. "The History of Telenet and the Commercialization of Packet Switching in the U.S." *IEEE Communications Magazine* 50, no. 5 (May 2012): 28–45.

"Maya interdit le 'rose.'" *Science et Vie*, February 1987.

Mayntz, Renate, and Volker Schneider. "The Dynamics of System Development in a Comparative Perspective: Interactive Videotex in Germany, France, and Britain." In *The Development of Large Technical Systems*, edited by Renate Mayntz and Thomas Hughes, 263–298. Frankfurt am Main: Campus Verlag, 1988.

McDonough, Jerome P., Robert Olendorf, Matthew Kirschenbaum, Kari Kraus, Doug Reside, Rachel Donahue, Andrew Phelps, Christopher Egert, Henry Lowood, and Susan Rojo. "Preserving Virtual Worlds Final Report," August 31, 2010, accessed September 15, 2016, https://www.ideals.illinois.edu/handle/2142/17097.

McPhee, Peter. *A Social History of France: 1789–1974*. 2nd ed. New York: Palgrave Macmillan, 2004.

Mennig, Miguel. *L'indispensable pour Minitel*. Paris: Marabout, 1987.

Metz, Cade. "Say *Bonjour* to the Internet's Long-Lost French Uncle." *Wired*, January 3, 2013, accessed September 14, 2016, http://www.wired.com/2013/01/louis_pouzin_internet_hall/.

Ministère des PTT. "Formation télématique: Le CNFT votre partenaire." Flyer, n.d.

Ministère des PTT. *Recommandations aux partenaires Télétel*. Paris: Ministère des PTT, 1986.

Ministère des PTT. *Recommandations aux partenaires Télétel: Utilisation des touches de fonction du Minitel*. Paris: France Telecom, n.d.

"Minitel." Adminet, accessed September 20, 2016, http://www.adminet.com/minitel/videotex-international.html#AMERIQUE.

"Minitel Denise RTC Running on m68k-amigaos." Accessed September 25, 2016, http://www.goto10.fr/minitel/amiga/madlertc.readme.

"Minitel en famille: 50F par jour." *Teletel: Revue de Presse*, June–July 1985. Undated press clipping, Orange/DGCI.

"Minitel: Gare à la Facture." *Le Nouvel Economiste*, December 24, 1984.

"Minitel: gare à la note de téléphone." *La Marseillaise*, January 13, 1985.

Minitel Magazine, no. 16, August–September 1986.

Minitel Magazine, no. 19, January–February 1987.

"Minitel, Maxiprix." *Mieux Vivre*, June 1985.

"Minitel Maxi-Prix!" *Que Choisir*, no. 202, January 1985.

"Minitel: ses derniers fans se préparent à sa fin." *Nordéclair*, October 23, 2011, accessed September 26, 2016, http://www.nordeclair.fr/France-Monde/France/2011/10/23/minitel-ses-derniers-fans-se-preparent-a.shtml.

Montfort, Nick, and Ian Bogost. *Racing the Beam: The Atari Video Computer System*. Cambridge, MA: MIT Press, 2009.

Montfort, Nick, and Mia Consalvo. "The Dreamcast, Console of the Avant-Garde." *Loading...* 6, no. 9 (January 2, 2012), accessed September 16, 2016, http://journals.sfu.ca/loading/index.php/loading/article/view/104.

Mounier, Davy. *Minitel and Fulguropoint: Le monde avant Internet*. Paris: J'ai Lu, 2014.

Mounier-Kuhn, Pierre E. "Bull: A World-Wide Company Born in Europe." *IEEE Annals of the History of Computing* 11, no. 4 (1989): 279–297.

Naszályi, Philippe. "Allo New-York, je voudrais le 22 à Asnières." *La Revue des Sciences de Gestion* (April 2005): 214–215.

Nicolas, François, and Chorizo Kid. "En pratique: présentation et utilisation du serveur Minitel DEEP." *Amiga News*, March 1989, accessed September 17, 2016, http://obligement.free.fr/articles/serveur_minitel_deep.php.

Nisenholtz, Martin. "Graphics Artistry Online." *Byte*, July 1983.

Noam, Eli. "Why the Internet Will Be Regulated." *Educom Review* 32, no. 5 (September–October 1997), accessed September 15, 2016, http://net.educause.edu/apps/er/review/reviewArticles/32512.html.

Nora, Simon, and Alain Minc. *The Computerization of Society*. Cambridge, MA: MIT Press, 1981.

"Ou sortons-nous ce soir? Et si vous posiez la question à Sophie?" *Le Quotidien de Paris*, February 15, 1984.

Parker, Geoffrey, and Marshall van Alstyne. "Information Complements, Substitutes, and Strategic Product Design." Scholarly paper, Social Science Research Network, Rochester, NY, November 8, 2000, accessed September 15, 2016, http://papers.ssrn.com/abstract=249585.

Perier, Denis. *Le dossier noir du Minitel rose*. Paris: Albin Michel, 1988.

Planète Non Violence. "Objection de conscience." Accessed April 14, 2013, http://www.planetenonviolence.org/Objection-de-conscience_a132.html.

Planque, François. "Programmer un serveur Minitel (1)." *ST Magazine* 99, November 1995, accessed September 25, 2016, http://www.fplanque.net/Blog/devblog/1995/07/01/programmer-un-serveur-minitel-1.

Planque, François. "Programmer un serveur Minitel (2): Dompter le Minitel!" *ST Magazine*, circa spring 1996, accessed September 25, 2016, http://www.fplanque.net/Articles/StutOne2Source/ProgrammerServeurMinitel2.html.

Planque, François. "Stut One." Fplanque.net, 2013, accessed September 17, 2016, http://fplanque.net/about/stut-one.

Planque, François. "STUT ONE 3—Le code source." *ST Magazine*, circa summer–fall 1996, accessed September 25, 2016, http://fplanque.net/Blog/devblog/1996/06/01/stut-one-3-le-code-source.

Ponjaert, Marina, Pauline Georgiades, and Alain Magnier. *Communiquer par Télétel*. Paris: La Documentation française, 1983.

Porte, Xavier de La. "Fred Turner: Google, Uber et l'idéologie de la Silicon Valley en treize mots." *L'Obs avec Rue 89*, December 21, 2014, accessed September 15, 2016, http://rue89.nouvelobs.com/2014/12/21/fred-turner-google-uber-lideologie-silicon-valley-treize-mots-256671.

"Pour 60F de l'heure marivaudage de 5 à 7 sur Minitel." *France Soir*, July 16, 1985.

Powers, Shawn M., and Michael Jablonski. *The Real Cyberwar: The Political Economy of Internet Freedom*. Urbana: University of Illinois Press, 2015.

Premiers baisers: L'inconnu du Minitel. Paris: ABH, 1995.

Quest, Christian. *Cristel*. User manual. Paris, 1985.

Quest, Christian. Demo presented at "Minitel: La dernière séance 'Rendez-vous à jamais.'" *La Cantine*, June 29, 2012.

Quest, Christian. "Page Personnelle de Christian Quest," accessed November 2, 2016, http://www.cquest.org/cq/.

Ramteke, Timothy. *Networks*. Englewood Cliffs, NJ: Prentice Hall, 1994.

Rheingold, Howard. *The Virtual Community: Homesteading on the Electronic Frontier*. Reading, MA: Addison-Wesley, 1993.

Rincé, Jean-Yves. *Le Minitel*. Paris: Presses Universitaires de France, 1990.

Rochet, Jean-Charles, and Jean Tirole. "Platform Competition in Two-Sided Markets." *Journal of the European Economic Association* 1, no. 4 (2003): 990–1029.

Rochet, Jean-Charles, and Jean Tirole. "Two-Sided Markets: A Progress Report." *RAND Journal of Economics* 37, no. 3 (September 1, 2006): 645–667, doi:10.1111/j.1756-2171.2006.tb00036.x.

Rohde, Éric. "Mode d'Emploi." *Le Monde*, September 5, 1984, accessed September 17, 2016 http://www.lemonde.fr/archives/article/1984/09/05/mode-d-emploi_3019896_1819218.html.

Russell, Andrew L. "'Rough Consensus and Running Code' and the Internet-OSI Standards War." *IEEE Annals of the History of Computing* 28, no. 3 (2006): 48–61.

Russell, Andrew L., and Valérie Schafer. "In the Shadow of ARPANET and Internet: Louis Pouzin and the Cyclades Network in the 1970s." *Technology and Culture* 55, no. 4 (2014): 880–907.

Rysman, Marc. "The Economics of Two-Sided Markets." *The Journal of Economic Perspectives* 23, no. 3 (2009): 125–143.

Salmona, Jean. "La Révolution du Vidéotex." *Le Monde*, March 10, 1979, accessed September 17, 2016, http://www.lemonde.fr/archives/article/1979/03/10/la-revolution-du-videotex_2769676_1819218.html.

Sayare, Scott. "On the Farms of France, the Death of a Pixelated Workhorse." *New York Times*, June 27, 2012, accessed September 22, 2016, http://www.nytimes.com/2012/06/28/world/europe/after-3-decades-in-france-minitels-days-are-numbered.html.

Sawhney, Harmeet S. "Circumventing the Centre: The Realities of Creating a Telecommunications Infrastructure in the USA." *Telecommunications Policy* 17, no. 7 (September–October 1993): 574–597.

Schafer, Valérie. "Évolution du nombre d'accès directs commerciaux à Transpac (1979–1985)." *Flux* 62, no. 4 (2005): 75–80.

Schafer, Valérie, and Benjamin G. Thierry. *Le Minitel: L'enfance numérique de la France*. Paris: Nuvis, 2012.

Schiller, Herbert I. *Communication and Cultural Domination*. London: Routledge, 1976.

Schmalensee, Richard. Testimony. United States v. Microsoft, January 13, 1999.

Scott, James C. *Seeing Like a State: How Certain Schemes to Improve the Human Condition Have Failed*. New Haven, CT: Yale University Press, 1998.

Scott, Jason. *BBS: The Documentary*, 2005, accessed September 17, 2016, http://archive.org/details/BBS.The.Documentary.

Séguin, Philippe. Interviewed by Yves Mourousi, *La Revue du Minitel*, no. 11, June 1987, 13.

Selby, Jaclyn. "Anyone's Game: Economic and Policy Implications of the Internet of Things as a Market for Services." *Communications and Strategies* 87 (2012): 21–40.

Service d'Information et de Diffusion du Premier Ministre. *Le rôle du service d'information et de diffusion en matière d'information administrative par Vidéotex*. November 1983.

"SETI (Search for Extra Terrestrial Intelligence)." Station de Radio astronomie de Nançay, September 18, 2013, accessed September 23, 2016, http://www.obs-nancay.fr/SETI-Search-for-Extra-Terrestrial.html?lang=fr.

Shapiro, Carl, and Hal Varian. *Information Rules: A Strategic Guide to the Network Economy*. Boston: Harvard Business School Press, 1999.

Siapera, Eugenia. "Platform Infomediation and Journalism." *Culture Machine* 14 (2013): 1–28.

"65% des clients du CCF ont adopté le Minitel." *Le Quotidien de Paris*, no. 1577, December 13, 1984.

Sterling, Christopher H. "Pioneering Risk: Lessons from the US Teletext/Videotex Failure." *IEEE Annals of the History of Computing* 28, no. 3 (July–September 2006), 41–47, doi:10.1109/MAHC.2006.54.

Stingl, Jim. "Carlin's Naughty Words Still Ring in Officer's Ears." *Milwaukee Journal Sentinel*, June 30, 2007. Archived at https://web.archive.org/web/20070929124942/http://www.jsonline.com/story/index.aspx?id=626471, accessed November 29, 2016.

Swartz, Lana. "Tokens, Ledgers, and Rails: The Communication of Money." PhD diss., University of Southern California, 2015.

Syndicat national de la presse quotidienne régionale. *Contribution du SNPQR au rapport de la commission du suivi télématique: Les expériences et leur suivi.* October 18, 1982.

"Taranis, tous azimuts." *Videotex* 57, February 1984.

"Tarifs: c'est l'embrouille." *Teletel: Revue de Presse*, June–July 1985. Undated press clipping, Orange/DGCI.

"Téléanimation: SVP, Sophie …" *Minitel Magazine*, March 1987, 29.

TF1. "C'était un 1er juillet: Qui se cache derrière le Minitel rose?" News segment, circa 1988, accessed September 21, 2016, http://lci.tf1.fr/videos/2015/c-etait-un-1er-juillet-qui-se-cache-derriere-le-minitel-rose-8625789.html.

Théry, Gérard. *Les autoroutes de l'information.* Paris: Documentation Française, 1994.

Thierry, Benjamin. "De Tic-Tac au Minitel: la télématique grand public, une réussite française." In *Actes du colloque les ingénieurs des télécommunications dans la France contemporaine. Réseaux, innovation et territoires (XIXe–XXe siècles)*, edited by Pascal Griset, 185–205. Vincennes: Institut de la gestion publique et du développement économique, 2013.

"3615 Ulla, la fin d'un mythe." *01net*, July 10, 2012, accessed September 26, 2016, http://www.01net.com/actualites/3615-ulla-la-fin-dun-mythe-568601.html.

Troude, Godefroy. *Pinky: histoire d'un micro-serveur.* February 9, 2006, accessed September 25, 2016, http://www.troude.com/pinky/index.html-ssi.

Troughton, P. "Prestel Operational Strategy." In *Viewdata and Videotex, 1980–81: A Worldwide Report*, 51–62. White Plains, NY: Knowledge Industry Publications, 1980.

Turner, Fred. *From Counterculture to Cyberculture: Stewart Brand, the Whole Earth Network, and the Rise of Digital Utopianism.* Chicago: University of Chicago Press, 2006.

Tydeman, John, and Institute for the Future. *Teletext and Videotex in the United States: Market Potential, Technology, Public Policy Issues.* New York: McGraw-Hill, 1982.

Tymes, LaRoy W. "Routing and Flow Control in Tymnet." *IEEE Transactions on Communications*, 29:4 (April 1981).

"Un Annuaire Téléphonique 'Électronique' en 1981." *Le Monde*, March 2, 1979, accessed September 17, 2016, http://www.lemonde.fr/archives/article/1979/03/02/un-annuaire-telephonique-electronique-en-1981_2767824_1819218.html.

"Un fauteuil dans un fauteuil." *Le Point*, no. 750, February 2, 1987.

"Un mouchard chez vous." *Que Choisir*, no. 202, January 1985.

"Un mouchard dans chaque Minitel." *Le Figaro*, December 30, 1984.

"Un serveur sur Amstrad." *CPC: La Revue de Utilisateurs d'Amstrad* 9 (March 1986): 64–65.

United States District Court for the District of Columbia. "Transcript of Trial before the Honorable Thomas P. Jackson, United States District Judge," January 13, 1999, 81–82, accessed September 15, 2016, https://cyber.law.harvard.edu/msdoj/transcripts/0113b.doc.

Utilisateurs de Tététel 3v, Association des Abonnés T3V. "TELETEL 3V: Le témoignage des utilisateurs." *Congrès de l'IDATE* (1982).

Vallée, Jacques. *The Heart of the Internet: An Insider's View of the Origin and Promise of the On-Line Revolution*. Charlottesville, VA: Hampton Roads Publishing, 2003.

Vistel, Jacques. *Note à l'attention de M. Francois Xavier Gillier*. Secrétariat d'Etat Auprès du Premier Ministre Chargé des Techniques de la Communication: Service Juridique et Technique de l'Information, March 26, 1985.

VT100 Series Technical Manual. 2nd ed. Maynard, MA: Digital Equipment Corporation, 1980.

Weber, Eugen. *Peasants into Frenchmen: The Modernization of Rural France, 1870–1914*. Stanford, CA: Stanford University Press, 1976.

Weber, Marc, and Julien Mailland. "Oral History of Georges Nahon." Computer History Museum, May 4, 2015, reference number: X7479.2015, accessed September 26, 2016, http://archive.computerhistory.org/resources/access/text/2016/04/102740081-05-01-acc.pdf.

"What Is SETI@home?" University of California at Berkeley, 2016, accessed September 22, 2016, http://setiathome.ssl.berkeley.edu/.

Widing, Robert, II, and W. Wayne Talarzyk. "Videotex Project Reviews II." OCLC Online Computer Library Center Research Report #OCLC/OPR/RR-83/8, October 28, 1983.

Audio/Video

Belle, Marie-Paule. "Mini-Minitel." Carrere, 1987.

"(HZ) France Minitel," AP Archive, June 27, 2012, accessed September 14, 2016, http://www.aparchive.com/metadata/youtube/a9ef10495e306b24603507a56cf2d99d.

Les Ignobles du Bordelais. "Minitel." Self-published, 1984.

Les Inconnus. "C'est toi que je t'aime." 1991.

Liaison. *Minitel ... Miniquoi?* Paris: Kangourou, 1987.

Willer, Noe. "Sur Minitel." Atoll Music, 1986.

Interviews

Michel Baujard, interview no. 1 with author, Paris, June 29, 2012.

Michel Baujard, telephone interview no. 2 with author, July 13, 2015.

Jean-Luc Beraudo De Pralormo, interview no. 1 with author, Cesson-Sévigné, June 25, 2012.

Jean-Luc Beraudo De Pralormo, interview no. 2 with author, Cesson-Sévigné, June 30, 2012.

Laurent Chemla, interview with author, Paris, June 29, 2012.

John Coate, interview with author, Boonville, California, March 10, 2012.

Daniel Hannaby, interview no. 1 with authors, San Francisco, March 9, 2012.

Daniel Hannaby, interview no. 2 with author, San Francisco, December 15, 2014.

Daniel Hannaby, interview no. 3 with author, Mountain View, March 20, 2015.

Jean-Baptiste Ingold, interview with author, Paris, June 29, 2012.
Michel Landaret, interview with author, Paris, June 29, 2012.
Bernard Louvel, interview no. 1 with author, Cesson-Sévigné, June 25, 2012.
Bernard Louvel, interview no. 2 with author, Cesson-Sévigné, June 30, 2012.
Allan Lundell, interview with authors, Santa Cruz, California, March 8, 2012.
Jean-Marc Manach, interview with author, Paris, June 29, 2012.
Bernard Marti, interview with author, Cesson-Sévigné, June 30, 2012.
Jean-Paul Maury, e-mail to author, July 3, 2012.
Jean-Paul Maury, interview no. 1 with author, Paris, December 2011.
Jean-Paul Maury, interview no. 2 with author, Paris, June 27, 2012.
Georges Nahon, interview with author, San Francisco, October 5, 2012.
Orange executive, off-the-record interview with author, 2012.
Dusty Parks, interview with authors, Richmond, California, March 11, 2012.
Jean-Eudes Queffélec, interview with author, San Francisco, October 5, 2012.
Christian Quest, interview with author, Paris, June 29, 2012.
Gérard Théry, interview with author, Paris, June 27, 2012.
LaRoy Tymes, interview with author, Monument, Colorado, July 24, 2013.

French Laws

Code de la Consommation, article. L113–1.
Code Général des Impôts, Ann. III, articles 72 and 73.
Code Monétaire et Financier, Article L. 518–2.
Déclaration Universelle des Droits de l'Homme et du Citoyen, 1789.
Décret du 29 décembre 1990 relatif au cahier des charges de France Telecom et au
    Code des postes et télécommunications, articles 1 et 12.
Loi no. 63–1255, December 21, 1963, J.O., December 22, 1963, 11456.
Loi no. 90–568 du 2 juillet 1990, article 2.
Ordonnance du 1er décembre 1986, articles 1 et 2.

Court Decisions (in Chronological Order)

Thomas v. Collins, 323 U.S. 516, 545 (1945) (US).
Federal Communications Commission v. Pacifica Foundation, 438 U.S. 726 (1978)
    (US).
Cour de Cassation, November 21, 1990, Société RAPT (Fr.).
Conseil d'Etat, March 29, 1991 (Fr.).
Cour d'Appel de Paris, October 13, 1992, Midratel (Fr.).
Cons. const., DC. No. 96–378, July 23, 1996, J.O., July 27, 1996, 11400 (Fr.).

Index

Matra, 3, 30, 152
Maury, Jean-Paul, 20, 37, 65–66, 99,
110, 137, 141, 142
Maya, 112. *See also* Censorship; Minitel
rose; Minitel terminal
Mayntz, Renate, 76
McDonnell-Douglas, 80
McPhee, Peter, 50
Médecins de nuit, 23
Media industries, 5, 63–66, 89–90,
109, 133–135, 137. *See also* Lobbying;
Ouest-France
Mélenchon, Jean-Luc, 138. *See also*
Tontonmania
Memory card. *See* Smart card
Messageboard. *See* Messageries
Messageries, 2, 13, 18, 19, 24, 30,
42, 44, 86, 87, 91, 96–98, 127,
151. *See also* 3615; Gretel;
Masquerade; Minitel rose; Online
community
business model, 99, 124, 131
censorship, 67–68
invention of, 98, 141
moderation of (*see* Animatrices)
pseudonymity, 101–107
slang, 120–121
sociality, 101–107
MGS, 121
Microcomputer, 80, 107, 144–146. *See
also* Micro-serveurs
interface to Minitel terminal, 32
as Minitel client, 78, 153
as Minitel server, 42–43
software, 34–35
Micropayment. *See* Payment
Micro-serveurs, 42–43, 46, 138, 144–
146. *See also* Bulletin-board system;
Microcomputer; Pinky
Microsoft, 15–16, 121
MS-DOS, 145
Military-industrial complex, 2–3, 91

Military service, 135–136
Minc, Alain. See *Computerization of
Society, The*
Minicomputer, 42, 46, 55, 81
Mini-Minitel, 127
Ministries, 51, 68, 136
Finance, 51, 144
Foreign Affairs, 111
Health, 132
Information and communications, 65,
66, 68, 136
Interior, 66, 114
National Education, 69, 144
Post, Telegraph and Telephone (*see*
France Telecom)
Prime Ministry, 62, 68, 70, 90, 92,
138–139
Social affairs, 115
Minitel. *See also* France Telecom; Kiosk;
Minitel terminal; PAVI; Télétel
argument in favor of, 54–55
colloquial meaning, 8–9
death of, 154
diffusion, 9–11, 29, 129
failure, 150 (*see also* Walled gardens)
generativity, 47, 149, 153
misconceptions, 14–15, 88, 91
preservation, 18–20
statistics, 9–13, 99, 116–119, 124
success, 14, 60–61, 70, 80, 85, 97,
150–155
"wake," 1, 3, 5–6
Minitel (song), 127
*Minitel and Fulguropoint: Le monde avant
Internet*, 127
Minitelistes, 13, 30, 103, 106, 119
Minitel Magazine, 20, 29, 101, 105, 112,
115–117
Minitelmaster, 110
Minitel … Miniquoi?, 127. *See also*
Liaison
Minitel.org, 20

Printed in the United States
by Baker & Taylor Publisher Services